The Mission

Frederick Marryat

Complete & Unabridged

Tutis Digital Publishing Private Limited

First Published in 1845 as *The Mission*.

This edition published by
Tutis Digital Publishing Pvt Ltd,
2008.

All rights reserved. No part of this publication may be reproduced, stored in a retrieval system, or transmitted in any form without the prior written permission of Tutis Digital Publishing Private Limited.

This book is sold subject to the condition that it shall not, by way of trade or otherwise, be lent, resold, hired out or otherwise circulated without the publisher's prior consent in any form of binding or cover other than that in which it is published and without a similar condition including this condition being imposed on the subsequent purchaser.

CHAPTER I

The Expedition

It was in the autumn of the year 1828, that an elderly and infirm gentleman was slowly pacing up and down in a large dining-room. He had apparently finished his dinner, although it was not yet five o'clock, and the descending sun shone bright and warm through the windows, which were level with the ground, and from which there was a view of a spacious park, highly ornamented with old timber. He held a newspaper in one hand, and had the other behind his back, as if for support, for he was bent forward, and looked very feeble and emaciated.

After pacing for some time, he sat down in an easy chair and remained in deep thought, holding the newspaper in both his hands.

This old gentleman's name was Sir Charles Wilmot. He had in early life gone out to India as a writer, and after remaining there for a few years, during which he had amassed a handsome fortune, was advised to leave the country for a time on account of his health. He returned to England on furlough, and had not been there more than six months when the death, without issue, of his eldest brother, Sir Henry Wilmot, put him in possession of the entailed estates and of the baronetcy.

This decided him not to return to India for his wife and three daughters, whom he had left out there, but to write, desiring them to return home by the first ship. The reply which he received was most painful; his wife and two of his daughters had been carried off by the cholera, which had been very fatal during the previous rainy season. His remaining daughter was about to sail, in obedience to his wishes, in the *Grosvenor* East-Indiaman, under the care of Colonel and Mrs. James, who were near connections.

This was a heavy blow with which it pleased God to visit him in his prosperity, and was almost a total wreck of all his hopes and anticipations. But he was a good man and a religious one, and he bowed in humility to the dispensation, submitting with resignation to his loss, and still thankful to Heaven that it had graciously spared one of the objects of his affections to console him, and to watch his declining years.

Sir Charles Wilmot took possession of the family mansion and estate in Berkshire, in which he was still residing at the time our history commences. By degrees he became more resigned, and waited with anxiety for the return of his only daughter, who now seemed more dear to him than ever. He employed himself in making preparations for her reception, fitting up her apartments in the Oriental style which she had been accustomed to, and devising every little improvement and invention which he thought would give pleasure to a child of ten years old.

But it pleased Heaven that Sir Charles should be more severely chastised; the *Grosvenor's* time of arrival had elapsed, and still she was not reported in the Channel; week after week of anxiety and suspense passed slowly away, and the East-India ship did not make her appearance. It was supposed that she had been captured by the enemy, but still no tidings of her capture were received. At length, however, this state of anxiety and doubt was put an end to by the dreadful intelligence that the ship had been wrecked on the east coast of Africa, and that nearly the whole of the crew and passengers had perished. Two men belonging to her had been brought home by a Danish East-Indiaman, and shortly after the first intelligence, these men arrived in London, and gave a more particular detail of what had occurred.

Sir Charles, in a state of feverish anxiety, as soon as he heard of their arrival, hastened up to town to question these men; and the result of his interrogatories fully convinced him that he was now quite bereaved and childless. This was the last blow and the most severe; it was long before he could resign himself to the unsearchable dispensations of Providence; but time and religion had at last overcome all his repining feelings, – all disposition to question the goodness or wisdom of his Heavenly Father, and he was enabled to say, with sincerity, "Not my will, but

Thine be done."

But although Sir Charles was thus left childless, as years passed away, he at last found that he had those near to him for whom he felt an interest, and one in particular who promised to deserve all his regard. This was his grand-nephew, Alexander Wilmot, who was the legal heir to the title and entailed property, – the son of a deceased nephew, who had fallen during the Peninsular war.

On this boy Sir Charles had lavished those affections which it pleased Heaven that he should not bestow upon his own issue, and Alexander Wilmot had gradually become as dear to him as if he had been his own child. Still the loss of his wife and children was ever in his memory, and as time passed on, painful feelings of hope and doubt were occasionally raised in Sir Charles's mind, from the occasional assertions of travelers, that all those did not perish who were supposed so to do when the *Grosvenor* was wrecked, and that, from the reports of the natives, some of them and of their descendants were still alive. It was a paragraph in the newspaper, containing a renewal of these assertions, which had attracted the attention of Sir Charles, and which had put him in the state of agitation and uneasiness in which we have described him at the opening of this chapter.

We left him in deep and painful thought, with the newspaper in his hands. His reveries were interrupted by the entrance of Alexander Wilmot, who resided with him, being now twenty-two years of age, and having just finished his college education. Alexander Wilmot was a tall, handsome young man, very powerful in frame, and very partial to all athletic exercises; he was the best rower and the best cricketer at Oxford, very fond of horses and hunting, and an excellent shot; in character and disposition he was generous and amiable, frank in his manner, and obliging to his inferiors. Every one liked Alexander Wilmot, and he certainly deserved to be liked, for he never injured or spoke ill of any body. Perhaps his most prominent fault was obstinacy; but this was more shown in an obstinate courage and perseverance to conquer what appeared almost impossible, and at the greatest risk to himself; he was of that disposition that he would hardly get out of the way of a mad bull if it crossed his path, but risk his life probably, and to no purpose; but there is no perfection in this world, and it was still less to be expected in a young man of only twenty-two years of age.

"Well, uncle, I've conquered him," said Alexander, as he came into the room, very much heated with exercise.

"Conquered whom, my boy?" replied Sir Charles.

"The colt; I've backed him, and he is now as gentle as a lamb; but he fought hard for two hours at least."

"Why should you run such risk, Alexander, when the horsebreaker would have broke him just as well?"

"But not so soon, uncle."

"I did not know that you were in such want of a horse as to require such hurry; I thought you had plenty in the stable."

"So I have, uncle, thanks to you, more than I can use; but I like the pleasure –

the excitement."

"There you state the truth, my dear Alexander; when you have lived as long as I have, you will find more pleasure in quiet and repose," replied Sir Charles, with a heavy sigh.

"Something has disturbed you, my dear uncle," said Alexander, going up to Sir Charles and taking his hand; "what is it, sir?"

"You are right, Alexander; something has unsettled me, has called up painful feelings and reminiscences; it is that paragraph in the newspaper."

Alexander was now as subdued almost as his uncle; he took a chair and quietly read the paragraph.

"Do you think there is any foundation for this, my dear sir?" said he, after he had read it.

"It is impossible to say, my dear boy; it may be so, it has often been asserted before. The French traveler Le Vaillant states that he received the same information, but was prevented from ascertaining the truth; other travelers have subsequently given similar accounts. You may easily credit the painful anxiety which is raised in my mind when I read such a statement as this. I think I see my poor Elizabeth, the wife or slave to some wild savage; her children, merciful Heaven! my grandchildren, growing up as the brutes of the field, in ignorance and idolatry. It is torture, my dear Alexander – absolute torture, and requires long prayer and meditation to restore my mind to its usual tone, and to enable me to bow to the dispensations of the Divine will."

"Although I have long been acquainted with the general statement, my dear uncle, respecting the loss of the ship, I have never yet heard any such details as would warrant this apprehension of yours. It is generally supposed that all perished, perished indeed most miserably, except the few men who made their way to the Cape, and returned to England."

"Such was the supposition, my dear boy, but subsequent reports have to a certain degree contradicted it, and there is reason to believe that all did not perish who were accounted as dead. If you have nothing particularly to engage you at this moment, I will enter into a detail of what did occur, and of the proofs that the fate of a large portion, among which that of your aunt Elizabeth, was never ascertained."

"If it will not be too painful to you, my dear uncle, I will most gladly hear it."

"I will not dwell longer upon it than is necessary, Alexander; believe me, the subject is distressing, but I wish you to know it also, and then to give me your opinion. You are of course aware that it was on the coast of Caffraria, to the southward of Port Natal, that the *Grosvenor* was wrecked. She soon divided and went to pieces, but by a sudden — I know not that I can say a *fortunate* — change of wind, yet such was the will of Heaven, — the whole of the crew and passengers (with the exception of sixteen who had previously attempted to gain the shore by a hawser, and one man who was left on board in a state of intoxication) were all safely landed, even to the little children who were coming home in the vessel; among whom was my poor Elizabeth."

Alexander made no observation when Sir Charles paused for a while: the latter then continued: –

"By the time that they had all gained the shore, the day was far spent; the natives, who were of the Caffre race, and who had been busy in obtaining all the iron that they could from the mainmast, which had drifted on shore, left the beach at dark. The wretched sufferers lighted fires, and having collected some casks of beef and flour, and some live stock, they remained on the rocks during that night. The next morning the captain proposed that they should make their way to Cape Town, the Dutch settlement, to which they all unanimously consented; certainly a most wild proposition, and showing very little judgment."

"Could they have done otherwise, my dear uncle?"

"Most certainly; they knew that they were in a country of lawless savages, who had already come down and taken by force every thing that they could lay their hands upon. The Captain calculated that they would reach Cape Town in sixteen or seventeen days. How far his calculation was correct, is proved by the fact that those who did reach it at last were one hundred and seventeen days on their journey. But even admitting that the distance could have been performed in the time stated by the captain, the very idea of attempting to force their way through a country inhabited by savage people, with such a number of helpless women and children, and without any arms for their defense, was indeed an act of folly and madness, as it eventually proved."

"What then should have been their plan?"

"Observe, Alexander, the ship was wrecked not a cable's length from the shore, firmly fixed upon a reef of rocks upon which she had been thrown; the water was smooth, and there was no difficulty in their communication. The savages, content with plundering whatever was washed on shore, had to the time of their quitting the rocks left them uninjured. They might have gone on board again, have procured arms to defend themselves and the means of fortifying their position against any attempt of the savages, who had no other weapons but assaguays or spears, and then might have obtained the provisions and other articles necessary for their support. Armed as they might have been, and numerous as they were, for there were one hundred and fifty souls on board at the time of the wreck, they might have protected themselves until they had built boats or small vessels out of the timber of the wreck; for all their carpenters and blacksmiths were safely landed on shore with them. By taking this course they might have coasted along shore, and have arrived without difficulty at the Cape."

"Most certainly, sir, it would have been the most judicious plan."

"The captain must have been very deficient in judgment to have acted as he did. He had every thing to his hand – the means – the men to build the boats, provisions, arms, sails and cordage, and yet he threw all these chances away, and attempted to do what was impossible."

"He was not one of those who were saved, I believe, sir?"

"No, he is one of those who have not been heard of; but to proceed: The first day of their march from the site of the wreck ought to have been a warning to them to turn back. The savages robbed them of every thing and threw stones at them. A Dutchman of the name of Trout, who had fled to the Caffre country for some murder he had committed in the colony, fell in with them and told them the attempt was impracticable, from the number of savage nations, the width of the rivers, the desert countries without water, and the number of wild beasts which they would encounter; but still they were not persuaded, and went on to their destruction. They were not five miles from the wreck at the time, and might have returned to it before night."

"May it not fairly be supposed that after such a dreadful shipwreck any thing was considered preferable by the major portion of them, especially the passengers, to re-embarking?"

"It may be so; but still it was a feeling that was to be surmounted, and would have been, had they been counseled by a judicious leader; for he might fairly have pointed out to them, – without re embarkation, how are you to arrive in England?"

"Very true, uncle. Pray continue."

"From the accounts given by the seamen who returned, before they had traveled a week they were attacked by a large party of natives, to whose blows and ill-treatment as they passed along they had hitherto submitted; but as in this instance the natives appeared determined to massacre them, they resisted as well as they could, and, being nearly one hundred men in force, succeeded in driving them off, not without receiving many severe wounds. After a few days' more traveling, their provisions were all expended, and the seamen began to murmur, and resolved to take care of themselves, and not to be encumbered with women and children. The consequence was, that forty-three of the number separated from the rest, leaving the captain and all the male and female passengers and children (my dear Elizabeth among them), to get on as they could."

"How cruel!"

"Yes! but self-preservation is the first law of nature, and I fear it is in vain to expect that persons not under the influence of religious principles will risk their lives, or submit to much self-denial, for the sake of alleviating the miseries of others. The reason given for this separation was, that it was impossible to procure food for so large a number, and that they would be more likely to obtain sustenance when divided. The party who thus proceeded in advance encountered the most terrible difficulties; they coasted along the seashore because they had no other food than the shell-fish found on the rocks; they had continually to cross rivers from a mile to two miles wide; they were kept from their slumbers by the wild beasts which prowled around them, and at length they endured so much from want of water, that their sufferings were extreme. They again subdivided and separated, wandering they hardly knew where, exposed to a burning sun, without clothing and without food. One by one they sat down and were left behind to die, or to be devoured by the wild beasts before they were dead. At last they were reduced to such extremity, that they proposed to cast lots for one to be killed to support the others; they turned back on their route, that they might find the dead bodies of their companions for food. Finally, out of the whole crew, three or four, purblind and staggering from exhaustion, craving for death, arrived at the borders of the colony, where they were kindly received and gradually recovered."

"You now speak of the first party who separated from the captain and the passengers, do you not, uncle?"

"Yes."

"And what became of the captain's party?"

"No tidings were heard of them; their fate was unknown; it was long supposed that they had all perished; for if the sufferings of the seamen, inured to toil and danger, had been so great, what chance was there for helpless women and children? But after some years, there was a report that they had been saved, and were living with the savages. Le Vaillant first mentioned it, and then it died away and was not credited; but since that, the reports of various travelers appear to give confirmation to what Le Vaillant asserted. The paragraph you have now read in the newspaper has again renewed the assertion, and the parties from whom it proceeds are by all accounts worthy of credence. You may imagine, my dear boy, what a pang it gives me when I read these reports, – when I reflect that my poor girl, who was with that party, may at this moment be alive, may have returned to a state of barbarism, – the seeds of faith long dead in her bosom, – now changed to a wild, untutored savage, knowing no God."

"But, my dear uncle, allowing that my aunt is alive, she was not so young at the time of the wreck as to forget entirely what she had been taught."

"That is possible; but then her condition

must be still more painful, or rather I should say must have been, for probably she is dead long before this, or if not dead, she must be a woman advanced in life; indeed, as you may observe in the account given by the traveler in the paragraph you have read, it speaks only of the *descendants* of those who were lost in the *Grosvenor*. The idea of my grandchildren having returned to a state of barbarism is painful enough; I wish it were possible that I could discover the truth, for it is the uncertainty which so much distresses me. I have but a few years to live, Alexander; I am a very old man, as you know, and may be summoned to-morrow or to-night, for we know not what a day may bring forth. If I were only certain that my child had died, miserable as her death must have been, it would be happiness, to the idea that she was one of those whose descendants they speak of. If you knew how for the last thirty years this has preyed upon my mind, you would comprehend my anxiety on this account; but God's will be done. Do not let me detain you longer, Alexander; I should prefer being alone."

Alexander, at this intimation, took the proffered hand of his grand-uncle in a reverential and feeling manner, and, without saying any more, quitted the room.

CHAPTER II

The conversation which he had had with his grand-uncle made a very forcible impression upon Alexander Wilmot; it occasioned him to pass a very sleepless night, and he remained till nearly four o'clock turning it over in his mind. The loss of the *Grosvenor* Indiaman had occurred long before he was born; he was acquainted with the outline of what had taken place, and had been told, when a child, that a relation of his family had perished; but although the narrative had, at the time, made some impression upon his young mind, he had seldom, if ever, heard it spoken of since, and may have been said to have almost forgotten it. He was therefore not a little surprised when he found how great an influence it had upon his grand-uncle, who had never mentioned it to him before; indeed it had escaped Alexander's memory that it was his grand-uncle's only surviving daughter who had been lost in the vessel.

Alexander Wilmot was warmly attached to the old gentleman; indeed he would have been very ungrateful if he had not been, for it was impossible that any one could have been treated with more kindness and liberality than he was by Sir Charles. It was but the week before, that he had expressed a wish to travel on the continent, and Sir Charles had immediately given his consent that he should remain abroad, if he pleased, for two years. When he approved, however, of Alexander's plans, he had made a remark as to his own age and infirmity, and the probable chance that they might not meet again in this world; and this remark of his grand-uncle left such an impression upon Alexander, that he almost repented having made the request, and had been ever since in a state of indecision as to whether he should avail himself of his grand-uncle's kindness and disregard of self shown toward him in thus having granted his permission.

The conversation with Sir Charles had brought up a new idea in his mind; he had witnessed the anxiety and longing which his good old relation had shown about the fate of his daughter; he had heard from his own lips how long the ignorance of her fate had preyed upon his mind, and that to be satisfied on this point was the one thing wanting to enable the old man to die happy, – to permit him to say with sincerity, "Lord, now lettest Thou thy servant depart in peace." Why, then, should he not go to discover the truth? It would not, perhaps, occupy him so long as the two years of traveling on the continent, which had been consented to by his grand-uncle, and, instead of traveling for his own pleasure, he might be the means of satisfying the mind and quieting the anxiety of one who had been so kind to him. Indeed, he should actually prefer a journey into the interior of Africa to a mere sojourn of some time on the continent; the very peril and danger, the anticipation of distress and hardship, were pleasing to his high and courageous mind, and before he fell asleep Alexander had made up his mind that he would propose the expedition, and if he could obtain his uncle's permission would proceed upon it forthwith. Having come to this resolution, he fell fast asleep and dreamed away, till eight o'clock in the morning, that he was hunting elephants and having hand-to-hand conflicts with every variety of beast with which he had peopled Africa in his fancy. When he was called up in the morning, he found his determination of the night before rather strengthened than otherwise, and accordingly, after breakfast was over, he opened the subject.

"My dear sir," said he to Sir Charles, "you were kind enough to give me your permission to travel on the continent for two years."

"I did do so, Alexander; it is natural at your age that you should wish to see the world, and you have my full permission. When do you think of starting?"

"That depends upon circumstances, sir, and I must be altogether guided by you; to tell you the truth, I do not think that one sees much of the world by following in the beaten track made by so many of our countrymen."

"There I agree with you; in the present high state of civilization there will be found little or no difference in the manners and customs of people; in the courts, none; very little in the best society, in which you will of course mix; and not so very much as people may imagine among the mass of population; but the scenery of the countries and the remains of ancient times are still interesting, and will afford pleasure; it must be your own reflections and comments upon what you see which must make it profitable; most people, however, travel from the love of change added to the love of excitement."

"I grant it, sir, and I do not mean to say but that I should receive much pleasure from a continental tour; perhaps I may add that I should derive more profit if I were to delay it till I am a little older and a little wiser; do you not think so?"

"I certainly do, Alexander. What then? do you propose remaining in England for the present? – if so, I am sure it is on my account, and I am very grateful to you for your sacrifice."

"If you wish it, sir, I will undoubtedly remain in England; at all events, if I do not go elsewhere. I have abandoned my continental tour for the present; but I have another proposal to make, which I hope will meet with your approbation."

"Why, my dear Alexander, on what expedition would you now proceed? Do you wish to visit the United States or South America?"

"No, sir; I wish to make a voyage of still more interest – I wish to go to Africa, – that is, to embark for the Cape of Good Hope, and from thence proceed to the northward, to ascertain, if possible, what now is a source of sad disquiet to you, the actual fate of those who were wrecked in the *Grosvenor*, and have not since been heard of with any degree of certainty."

Sir Charles was for a time silent. He pressed his hands to his forehead; at last he removed them, and said, – "I can not, much as I wish it, no, – I can not consent, my dear boy; the danger will be too great. You must not risk your life. It is very kind of you – very kind; but no, it must not be."

"Indeed, sir, I think, on reflection, you will alter your mind. As for danger – what danger can there be when missionaries are permitted to form their stations, and reside uninjured among the very savages who were so hostile when the *Grosvenor* was lost? The country, which was then a desert, is now inhabited by Europeans, within 200 miles of the very spot where the *Grosvenor* was wrecked. The continual emigration since the Cape has fallen under British government, and the zeal of those who have braved all dangers to make known the Word of God to the heathen and idolater, have in forty years made such an alteration, that I see no more danger in the mission which I propose than I do in a visit to Naples; and as for time, I have every reason to expect that I shall be back sooner than in the two years which you have proposed for my stay on the continent."

"But if some accident were to happen to you, I should never forgive myself for having given my consent, and the few days that are left to me would be rendered miserable."

"My dear sir, we are in the hands of God; and (short-sighted as we are) in running away from danger, as often run into it.

What we call an accident, the fall of a brick or a stone, the upsetting of a vehicle, any thing trivial or seemingly improbable, may summon us away when we least expect it: 'In the midst of life we are in death,' and that death I may meet by staying in this country, which I might have avoided by going on this expedition. Difficulties may arise, and some danger there may be, I admit; but when prepared to encounter both, we are more safe than when, in fancied security, we are taken unawares. Do not, I entreat you, sir, refuse me this favor; I have considered well, and shall be most unhappy if I am not permitted to obtain the information for you which you have so much at heart. Let my travels be of some advantage to you as well as to myself. Do not refuse, I entreat you."

"You are a good boy, Alexander, and your kindness makes me still more unwilling to part with you. I hardly know what to say. Let us drop the subject for the present; we will talk of it to-morrow or next day. I must have time for reflection."

Alexander Wilmot did not fail to renew

his entreaties on the following day, but could not gain Sir Charles's consent. He was not, however, discouraged. He had taken from the library all the works he could find relative to Southern Africa, and continually enforcing his arguments by quotations from various authors, all tending to prove that he might travel through the country without much risk, if he took proper precautions, his grand-uncle's objections grew daily more feeble, and at last Sir Charles gave his unwilling consent. In the meantime, the books which Alexander had read had produced a great effect upon him. When he first proposed the mission, it was more from a feeling of gratitude toward his old relative than any other, but now he was most anxious to go on his own account. The narratives of combats with wild beasts, the quantity and variety of game to be found, and the continual excitement which would be kept up, inflamed his imagination and his love of field sports, and he earnestly requested to be permitted to depart immediately, pointing out to Sir Charles that the sooner he went away, the sooner he would be back again. This last argument was not without its weight, and Alexander was allowed to make every preparation for his journey. Inquiries were made, and a passage secured on board of a free-trader, which was to touch at the Cape, and in six weeks from the time that the subject had been brought up, Alexander Wilmot took leave of his grand-uncle.

"May God bless you, sir, and keep you well till my return," said Alexander, pressing his hand.

"May the Lord protect you, my dear boy, and allow you to return and close my eyes," replied Sir Charles, with much emotion.

Before night Alexander Wilmot was in London, from thence he hastened down to Portsmouth to embark. The next day, the *Surprise* weighed anchor and ran through the Needles, and before the night closed in was well down the Channel, standing before the wind, with studding sails below and aloft.

CHAPTER III

A melancholy feeling clouded the features of Alexander Wilmot as, on the following morning, the vessel, under a heavy press of sail, was fast leaving the shores of his native country. He remained on the poop of the vessel with his eyes fixed upon the land, which every moment became more indistinct. His thoughts may easily be imagined. Shall I ever see that land again? Shall I ever return, or shall my bones remain in Africa, perhaps not even buried, but bleaching in the desert? And if I do return, shall I find my old relation still alive, or called away, loaded as he is with years, to the silent tomb? We are in the hands of a gracious God. His will be done.

Alexander turned away, as the land had at last become no longer visible, and found a young man of about his own age standing close to him, and apparently as much lost in reverie as he had been. As in turning round Alexander brushed against him, he thought it right to apologize for the unintentional act, and this occasioned a conversation.

"I believe, sir," said the other party, who was a tall, spare, slight-built man, with a dark complexion, "that we were both indulging in similar thoughts as we took leave of our native shores. Every Englishman does the same, and indeed every true lover of his country, let the country be what it will. We find the feeling as strong in the savage as in the enlightened; it is universal. Indeed, we may fairly say that it extends lower – down to the brute species, from their love of localities."

"Very true, sir," replied Alexander; "but with brutes, as you say, it is merely the love of locality; with men, I trust, the feeling is more generous and noble."

"So it ought to be, or else why are we so much more nobly endowed? This is not your first voyage, I presume?" continued the stranger.

"Indeed, it is," said Alexander; "I never was out of England, or on board of a vessel, before yesterday."

"I should have imagined otherwise,"

remarked his companion: "the other passengers are all suffering from sea-sickness, while you and I only are on the deck. I presumed, therefore, that you had been afloat before."

"I did feel very giddy yesterday evening," observed Alexander, "but this morning I have no unpleasant sensation whatever. I believe that some people do not suffer at sea."

"A very few; but it appears that you are one of those most fortunate, for by experience I know how painful and distressing the sickness is for some time. Breakfast will soon be ready; do you think that you can eat any?"

"Yes, a little – not much; a cup of tea or coffee," replied Alexander; "but I can not say that I have my usual appetite. What bird is that which skims along the water?"

"It is the *procellarius*, as we naturalists call it, but in English, the stormy petrel; its presence denotes rough weather coming on."

"Then I wish it had not made its

appearance," said Alexander, laughing; "for with rough weather, there will of course be more motion in the vessel, and I feel the motion too much already."

"I think if you eat your breakfast (although without appetite), and keep on deck, you may get over any further indisposition," replied the stranger.

"Have we many passengers on board?"

"No; nine or ten, which is considered a small number, at least by the captain, who was complaining of his ill-luck. They are mostly females and children. There is a Cape gentleman who has long resided in the colony, and is now returning there. I have had some conversation with him, and he appears a very intelligent person. But here is the steward coming aft, to let us know that breakfast is ready."

The person who had thus conversed with Alexander Wilmot was a Mr. Swinton, who, as he had accidentally observed, was a naturalist; he was a person of some independent property, whose ardor for science had induced him to engage in no profession, being perfectly satisfied with his income, which was sufficient for his wants and to enable him to follow up his favorite study. He was now on his passage to the Cape of Good Hope, with no other object than to examine the natural productions of that country, and to prosecute his researches in science there, to a greater extent than had hitherto been practicable.

Before they had arrived at Madeira, at which island the ship remained three days to take in wine and fresh provisions, a great intimacy had been established between Alexander and Mr. Swinton, although as yet neither knew the cause of the other's voyage to the Cape; they were both too delicate to make the inquiry, and waited till the other should of his own accord impart his reasons.

We have mentioned that there were other passengers, one of whom was a gentleman who resided in Cape Town, and who held a lucrative situation under the government. He was an elderly gentleman, of about sixty years of age, of a very benign and prepossessing appearance; and it so happened that

Alexander found out, on looking over his letters of introduction when at anchor at Madeira, that he possessed one to this gentleman. This of course he presented at once, although they were already on intimate terms; and this introduction made Mr. Fairburn (for such was his name) take an immediate interest in his welfare, and also warranted his putting the question, as to what were Alexander's views and intentions in visiting the Cape: for Mr. Fairburn knew from the letter that he was heir to Sir Charles Wilmot, and therefore that he was not likely to be going out as a speculator or emigrant.

It hardly need be said that Alexander made no hesitation in confiding to one who could so materially assist him in the object of his voyage.

The other passengers were three young ladies bound to their friends in India, and a lady returning with her two marriageable daughters to rejoin her husband, who was a colonel in the Bengal army. They were all pleasant people, the young ladies very lively, and on the whole the cabin of the *Surprise* contained a very agreeable party; and soon after they left Madeira, they had fine weather, smooth water, and every thing that could make a voyage endurable.

The awnings were spread, chairs brought up, and the major portion of the day was spent upon the quarter-deck and poop of the vessel, which for many days had been running down before the trade-winds, intending to make Rio, and there lay in a supply of fresh provisions for the remainder of her voyage.

One morning, as Alexander and Mr. Fairburn were sitting together, Alexander observed –

"You have passed many years at the Cape, Mr. Fairburn, have you not?"

"Yes; I was taken prisoner when returning from India, and remained a year in Cape Town during the time that it was in the hands of the Dutch; I was about to be sent home as a prisoner to Holland, and was embarked on board one of the vessels in Saldanha Bay, when they were attacked by the English. Afterward, when the English captured the Cape, from my long residence in, and knowledge of, the country, I was offered a situation, which I accepted: the colony was restored to the Dutch, and I came home. On its second capture I was again appointed, and have been there almost ever since."

"Then you are well acquainted with the history of the colony?"

"I am, certainly, and if you wish it, shall be happy to give you a short account of it."

"It will give me the greatest pleasure, for I must acknowledge that I know but little, and *that* I have gleaned from the travels which I have run through very hastily."

"I think it was in the year 1652 that the Dutch decided upon making a settlement at the Cape. The aborigines, or natives, who inhabited that part of the country about Cape Town, were the Hottentots, a mild, inoffensive people, living wholly upon the produce of their cattle; they were not agriculturists, but possessed large herds of cattle, sheep and goats, which ranged the extensive pastures of the country. The history of the founding of one colony is, I fear, the history of most, if not all – commencing in doing all that is possible to obtain the goodwill of the people until a firm footing has been obtained in the land, and then treating them with barbarity and injustice.

"The Hottentots, won over by kindness and presents, thought it of little consequence that strangers should possess a small portion of their extensive territory, and willingly consented that the settlement should be made. They, for the first time in their lives, tasted what proved the cause of their ruin and subsequent slavery – tobacco and strong liquors. These two poisons, offered gratuitously, till the poor Hottentots had acquired a passion for them, then became an object of barter – a pipe of tobacco or a glass of brandy was the price of an ox; and thus daily were the colonists becoming enriched, and the Hottentots poor.

"The colony rapidly increased, until it was so strong, that the governor made no ceremony of seizing upon such land as the government wished to retain or to give away; and the Hottentots soon discovered that not only their cattle, but the means of feeding them, were taken from them. Eventually, they were stripped of every thing except their passion for tobacco and spirits, which they could not get rid of. Unwilling to leave the land of their forefathers, and seeing no other way of procuring the means of intoxication which they coveted, they sold themselves and their services to the white colonists, content to take care of those herds which had once been their own, and to lead them out to pasture on the very lands which had once been their birthright."

"Did they then become slaves?" inquired Alexander.

"No; although much worse treated, they never were slaves, and I wish to point that out; but they became a sort of feudal property of the Dutch, compelled to hire themselves out, and to work for them upon nominal wages, which they seldom or never received, and liable to every species of harsh treatment and cruelty, for which they could obtain no redress. Yet still they were not bought and sold as were the slaves which were subsequently introduced into the colony from the east coast of Africa and Madagascar. The position of the slave was, in my opinion, infinitely superior, merely from the self-interest of the owner, who would not kill or risk the life of a creature for whom he had paid two or three hundred rix-dollars; whereas, the Dutch boors, or planters, thought little of the life of a Hottentot. If the cattle were to be watched where lions were plentiful, it was not a slave who had charge of them, but a Hottentot, as he had cost nothing, and the planter could procure another. In short, the life of a Hottentot was considered as of no value, and there is no denying that they were shot by their masters or employers upon the most trifling offense."

"How dreadful! but did the Dutch government suffer this?"

"They could not well help it, and therefore were compelled to wink at it; the criminals were beyond its reach. But now I will proceed to give you some further insight, by describing the Dutch boors, or planters, who usurped and stood in the shoes of the poor Hottentots.

"The Dutch government seized upon all the land belonging to the Hottentots, and gave it away in grants to their own countrymen, who now became herdsmen, and possessed of a large quantity of cattle; they also cultivated the ground to a certain extent round about their habitations. As the colony increased, so did the demand for land, until the whole of the country that was worth having was disposed of as far as to the country of the Caffres, a fine, warlike race, of whom we will speak hereafter. It must not, however, be supposed that the whole of the Hottentot tribes became serfs to the soil. Some few drove away their cattle to the northward, out of reach of the Dutch, to the borders of the Caffre land; others, deprived of their property, left the plains, and took to the mountains, living by the chase and by plunder. This portion were termed boshmen, or bushmen, and have still retained that appellation: living in extreme destitution, sleeping in caves, constantly in a state of starvation, they soon dwindled down to a very diminutive race, and have continued so ever since.

"The Dutch boors, or planters, who lived in the interior, and far away from Cape Town, had many enemies to contend with: they had the various beasts of the forest, from the lion to the jackal, which devastated their flocks and herds, and also these bushmen, who lived upon plunder. Continually in danger, they were never without their muskets in their hands, and they and their descendants became an athletic, powerful, and bulky race, courageous, and skilled in the use of fire-arms, but at the same time cruel and avaricious to the highest degree. The absolute power they possessed over the slaves and Hottentots demoralized them, and made them tyrannical and blood-thirsty. At too great a distance from the seat of government for its power to reach them, they defied it and knew no law but their own imperious wills, acknowledging no authority, – guilty of every crime openly, and careless of detection."

"I certainly have read of great cruelty on the part of these Dutch boors, but I had no idea of the extent to which it was carried."

"The origin was in that greatest of all curses, slavery; nothing demoralizes so much. These boors had been brought up with the idea that a Hottentot, a bushman, or a Caffre were but as the mere brutes of the field, and they have treated them as such. They would be startled at the idea of murdering a white man, but they will execute wholesale slaughter among these poor natives, and think they have committed no crime. But the ladies are coming up, and we shall be interrupted, so I will not task your patience any more to-day. I shall therefore conclude what I may term part the first of my little history of the Cape colony."

CHAPTER IV

Alexander Wilmot was too much pleased with Mr. Swinton not to cultivate his acquaintance, and they soon became very intimate. The conversation often turned upon Mr. Swinton's favorite study, that of natural history.

"I confess myself wholly ignorant of the subject," observed Alexander one day, "though I feel that it must be interesting to those who study it; indeed, when I have walked through the museums, I have often wished that I had some one near who could explain to me what I wished to know and was puzzled about. But it appears to me that the study of natural history is such an immense undertaking if you comprehend all its branches. Let me see, – there is botany, mineralogy, and geology – these are included, are they not?"

"Most certainly," replied Mr. Swinton, laughing; "and perhaps the three most interesting branches. Then you have zoology, or the study of animals, ornithology for birds, entomology for insects, conchology for shells, ichthyology for fishes; all very hard names, and enough to frighten a young beginner. But I can assure you, a knowledge of these subjects, to an extent sufficient to create interest and afford continual amusement, is very easily acquired."

"'The proper study of mankind is man,' says the poet," – observed Alexander, smiling.

"Poets deal in fiction, Mr. Wilmot," replied Mr. Swinton; "to study man is only to study his inconsistencies and his aberrations from the right path, which the free-will permitted to him induces him to follow; but in the study of nature, you witness the directing power of the Almighty, who guides with an unerring hand, and who has so wonderfully apportioned out to all animals the means of their providing for themselves. Not only the external, but the inward structure of animals, shows such variety and ingenuity to surmount all difficulties, and to afford them all the enjoyment their nature is capable of, that after every examination you rise with increased astonishment and admiration at the condescension and goodness of the Master Hand, thus to calculate and provide for the necessities of the smallest insect; and you are compelled to exclaim with the Psalmist, 'O God, how manifold are thy works; in wisdom hast Thou made them all!'"

"You certainly do put the study in a new and most pleasurable light," replied Alexander.

"The more you search into nature, the more wonderful do you find her secrets, and, by the aid of chemistry, we are continually making new discoveries. Observe, Mr. Wilmot," said Swinton, picking up a straw which had been blown by the wind on the quarter-deck, "do you consider that there is any analogy between this straw and the flint in the lock of that gun?"

"Certainly, I should imagine them as opposite particles of nature as well might be."

"Such is not the case. This piece of wheat-straw contains more than sixty per cent. of silica or flint in its composition; so that, although a vegetable, it is nearly two-thirds composed of the hardest mineral substance we know of. You would scarcely believe that the fibers of the root of this plant were capable of dissolving, feeding upon, and digesting such a hard substance; but so it is."

"It is very wonderful."

"It is, but it is not a solitary instance; the phosphate of lime, which is the chief component part of the bones of animals, is equally sought by plants, dissolved in the same manner, and taken into their bodies; barley and oats have about thirty per cent. of it in their composition, and most woods and plants have more or less."

"I am less surprised at that than I am with the flint, which appears almost incomprehensible."

"Nothing is impossible with God; there is a rush in Holland which contains much more silex than the wheat-straw, and it is employed by the Dutch to polish wood and brass, on that very account. We know but little yet, but we do know that mineral substances are found in the composition of most living animals, if not all; indeed, the coloring-matter of the blood is an oxide and phosphate of iron."

"I can now understand why you are so enthusiastic in the science, Mr. Swinton, and I regret much that the short time which will be occupied in the remainder of our voyage will not enable me to profit as I should wish by your conversation; for when we arrive at the Cape, I fear our pursuits will lead us different ways."

"I presume they will, for I am about to penetrate as far as possible into the interior of the country," replied Mr. Swinton, "which of course is not your intention."

"Indeed, but it is," replied Alexander; "I am about to do the same, although perhaps not in the same direction. May I ask your intended route, if not too inquisitive?"

"Not at all; I can hardly say myself. I shall be guided by the protection I may fall in with. Africa is a wide field for science, and I can hardly go any where without being well rewarded for my journey; and I will say, that should it meet both our views, I should be very glad if we were to travel in company."

Mr. Fairburn, who had come on deck, had been standing close to them at the latter portion of the conversation, and made the observation –

"I think it would be a very good plan if Mr. Swinton would venture to go where you are bound, Mr. Wilmot, but you can talk of that another day, when you have been longer together. There is nothing that requires more deliberation than the choice of a traveling companion; any serious imperfection of temper may make a journey very miserable. Now, Wilmot, if you are tired of natural history, and wish to change it for the painful history of human nature, I am ready to continue my observations."

"With great pleasure, sir."

"I hope you have no objection to my reaping the benefit also?" said Mr. Swinton.

"Oh, most certainly not," replied Mr. Fairburn, "although I fear you will not gain much information, as you have been at the Cape before. In a former conversation with Mr. Wilmot I have pointed out the manner in which the Cape was first settled, and how the settlers had gradually reduced the original possessors of the land to a state of serfdom; I will now continue.

"The Dutch boors, as they increased their wealth in cattle, required more pasture, and were now occupying the whole of the land south of the Caffre country: the Caffres are wild, courageous savages, whose wealth consists chiefly in cattle, but in some points they may be considered superior to the Hottentots.

"The weapon of the Hottentot may be said to be the bow and arrow, but the Caffre scorns this warfare, or indeed any treachery; his weapons are his assaguay, or spear, and his shield; he fights openly and bravely. The Caffres also cultivate their land to a certain extent, and are more cleanly and civilized. The boors on the Caffre frontier were often plundered by the bushmen, and perhaps occasionally by some few of the Caffres who were in a lawless state on the frontier; but if any complaint was made to the Caffre chiefs, every redress in their power was given: this, however, did not suit the Dutch boors.

"They had entered the Caffre country, and had perceived that the Caffres possessed large herds of cattle, and their avarice pointed out to them how much easier it would be to grow rich by taking the cattle of the Caffres than by rearing them themselves. If the bushmen stole a few head of cattle, complaints were immediately forwarded to Cape Town, and permission asked to raise a force, and recover them from the Caffres.

"The force raised was termed a *Commando*, and was composed of all the Dutch boors and their servants, well armed and mounted; these would make an incursion into the Caffre territory, and because a few head of cattle had been stolen by parties unknown, they would pour down upon the Caffres, who had but their assaguays to oppose to destructive fire-arms, set the kraals or villages in flames, murder indiscriminately man, woman, and child, and carry off, by way of indemnification for some trifling loss, perhaps some twenty thousand head of cattle belonging to the Caffres.

"The Caffres, naturally indignant at such outrage and robbery, made attacks upon the boors to recover the cattle, but with this difference between the Christian boor and the untutored savage: the boors murdered women and children wantonly, the Caffres never harmed them, and did not even kill men, if they could obtain possession of their property without bloodshed."

"But how could the Dutch government permit such atrocities?"

"The representations made to the government were believed, and the order was given in consequence. It is true that afterward the government attempted to put a stop to these horrors, but the boors were beyond their control; and in one instance in which the home government had insisted that punishment should be inflicted for some more than common outrage on the part of the boors, the Cape governor returned for answer, that he could not venture to do as they wished, as the system was so extensive and so common, that all the principal people in the colony were implicated, and would have to be punished.

"Such was therefore the condition of the colony at the time that it fell into the possession of the English – the Hottentots serfs to the land, and treated as the beasts of the field; the slave-trader supplying slaves; and continual war carried on between the boors and the Caffres."

"I trust that our government soon put an end to such barbarous iniquities."

"That was not so easy; the frontier boors rose in arms against the English government, and the Hottentots, who had been so long patient, now fled and joined the Caffres. These people made a combined attack upon the frontier boors, burned their houses to the ground, carried off the cattle, and possessed themselves of their arms and ammunition. The boors rallied in great force; another combat took place, in which the Hottentots and Caffres were victorious, killing the leader of the boors, and pursuing them with great slaughter, till they were stopped by the advance of the English troops. But I can not dwell long upon this period of the Cape history; these wars continued until the natives, throwing themselves upon the protection of the English, were induced to lay down their arms, and the Hottentots to return to their former masters. The colony was then given up to the Dutch, and remained with them until the year 1806, when it was finally annexed to the British empire. The Dutch had not learned wisdom from what had occurred; they treated the Hottentots worse than before, maiming them and even murdering them in their resentment, and appeared to defy the British government; but a change was soon to take place."

"Not before it was necessary, at all events," said Alexander.

"It was by the missionaries chiefly that this change was brought about; they had penetrated into the interior, and saw with their own eyes the system of cruelty and rapine that was carried on; they wrote home accounts, which were credited, and which produced a great alteration. To the astonishment and indignation of the boors, law was introduced where it had always been set at defiance; they were told that the life of a Hottentot was as important in the eye of God, and in the eye of the law, as that of a Dutch boor, and that the government would hold it as such. Thus was the first blow struck; but another and a heavier was soon to fall upon those who had so long sported with the lives of their fellow-creatures. The press was called to the aid of the Hottentot, and a work published by a missionary roused the attention of the public at home to their situation. Their cause was pleaded in the House of Commons, and the Hottentot was emancipated forever."

"Thank God!" exclaimed Alexander; "my blood has been boiling at the description which you have been giving. Now, when I hear that the poor Hottentot is a free man, it will cool down again."

"Perhaps it will be as well to leave off just now, Mr. Wilmot," said Mr. Fairburn; "we will renew our conversation to-morrow, if wind and weather permit, as the seamen say."

CHAPTER V

The next day the ship was off Rio, and immediately sent her boats for provisions and supplies; the passengers did not land, as the captain stated that he would not stay an hour longer than was necessary, and on the second evening after their arrival they again made sail for the Cape.

The gulls were flying in numbers astern of the ship, darting down and seizing every thing edible which was thrown overboard, and the conversation turned upon aquatic birds.

"What difference is there in the feathers of aquatic birds and others?" inquired Alexander; "a hen, or any land bird, if it falls into the water, is drowned as soon as its feathers are saturated with the water."

"There is, I believe, no difference in the feathers of the birds," replied Mr. Swinton; "but all aquatic birds are provided with a small reservoir, containing oil, with which they anoint their feathers, which renders them water-proof. If you will watch a duck pluming and dressing itself, you will find it continually turns its bill round to the end of its back, just above the insertion of the tail; it is to procure this oil, which, as it dresses its feathers that they may carefully overlap each other, it smears upon them so as to render them impenetrable to the water; but this requires frequent renewal, or the duck would be drowned as well as the hen."

"How long can a sea-bird remain at sea?"

"I should think not very long, although it has been supposed otherwise; but we do not know so much of the habits of these birds as of others."

"Can they remain long under water?"

"The greater portion of them can not; ducks and that class, for instance. Divers can remain some time; but the birds that remain the longest under water are the semi-aquatic, whose feet are only half-webbed. I have watched the common English water-hen for many minutes walking along at the bottom of a stream, apparently as much in its element as if on shore, pecking and feeding as it walked."

"You say that aquatic birds can not remain long at sea, – where do they go to?"

"They resort to the uninhabited islands over the globe, rocks that always remain above water, and the unfrequented shores of Africa and elsewhere; there they congregate to breed and bring up their young. I have seen twenty or thirty acres of land completely covered with these birds or their nests, wedged together as close as they could sit. Every year they resort to the same spot, which has probably been their domicile for centuries, – I might say since the creation. They make no nests, but merely scrape so as to form a shallow hole to deposit their eggs. The consequence of their always resorting to the same spot is that, from the voidings of the birds and the remains of fish brought to feed the young, a deposit is made over the whole surface, a fraction of an inch every year, which by degrees increases until it is sometimes twenty or thirty feet deep, if not more, and the lower portion becomes almost as hard as rock. The deposit is termed guano, and has, from time immemorial, been used by the Peruvians and Chilians as manure for the land; it is very powerful, as it contains most of the essential salts, such as ammonia, phosphates, etc., which are required for agriculture. Within these last few years samples have been brought to England, and as the quantities must be inexhaustible, when they are sought for and found, no doubt it may one day become a valuable article of our carrying trade. Here comes Mr. Fairburn; I hope he intends to continue his notices of the Cape settlement."

"They have interested me very much, I must confess; he appears well acquainted with the colony."

"He has had the advantage of a long residence, and during that time an insight into all the public documents: this you may be certain of, that he knows more than he will tell."

As soon as Mr. Fairburn joined them, Alexander requested him to continue his narrative, which he did as follows.

"You must not suppose, Mr. Wilmot, that because the English had now possession of the colony, every thing went right; governors who are appointed to the control of a colony require to be there some time before they can see with their own eyes; they must, from their want of information, fall into the hands of some interested party or another, who will sway their councils. Thus it was at the Cape.

"It is true that much good had already been done by the abolition of slavery and the emancipation of the Hottentot; but this was effected, not by the colonial government, but by the representations of the missionaries and an influential and benevolent party at home. The prejudices against the Hottentots, and particularly the Caffres, still existed, and were imbibed by the colonial authorities. Commandoes, or, as they should be more properly termed, marauding parties, were still sent out, and the Caffre was continually oppressed, and, in defiance of the government orders, little justice could be obtained for the Hottentot, although his situation was somewhat improved.

"I will give one instance to show how the rights of the Hottentots were respected by the Cape authorities in 1810, – previous to the emancipation, it is true, but still at a time when the position of the Hottentots and their sufferings had been strenuously pressed upon the colonial authorities by the government at home.

"When the conduct of the Dutch boors had roused the Caffres and Hottentots to war, there were three brothers by the name of Stuurman, Hottentots, who were the leaders. Peace was at length restored, which was chiefly effected by the exertions of these men, who retired peaceably with their own kraal to Algoa Bay; and the government, being then Dutch, appointed Stuurman as captain of the kraal. This independent horde of Hottentots gave great offense to the Dutch boors, – the more so as the three brothers had been the leaders of the Hottentots in the former insurrection. For seven years they could find no complaint to make against them, until at last two of his Hottentots, who had engaged to serve a boor for a certain time, went back to the kraal at the expiration of the term, against the wish of the boor, who would have detained them; the boor went and demanded them back, but Stuurman refused to give them up; upon which, although justice was clearly on the side of the Hottentots, an armed force was dispatched to the kraal. Stuurman still refused to surrender the men, and the armed men retired, for they knew the courage of the Hottentots, and were afraid to attack them.

"By treachery they gained possession of Stuurman and one of his brothers (the other having been killed hunting the buffalo), and sent them to Cape Town, from whence, against all justice, they were sent as prisoners to Robin Island, where malefactors are confined. They made their escape, and returned to Caffreland. Three years afterward, Stuurman, anxious to see his family, returned to the colony without permission. He was discovered and apprehended, and sent as a convict to New South Wales; for the government was at that time English.

"Such was the fate of the first Hottentot who stood up for the rights of his countrymen, and such was the conduct of the English colonial government; so you will observe, Mr. Wilmot, that although the strides of cruelty and oppression are most rapid, the return to even-handed justice is equally slow. Eventually the gross injustice to this man was acknowledged, for an order from the home government was procured for his liberation and return; but it was too late, – Stuurman had died a convict.

"I have mentioned this circumstance, as it will prepare you for a similar act of injustice to the Caffres. When the colony was in possession of the Dutch there was a space of about thirty thousand square miles between the colonial boundary (that is, the land formerly possessed by the Hottentots) and the Great Fish River. This extent of thirty thousand square miles belonged to the Caffres, and was the site of continual skirmishing and marauding between the Dutch boors and the Caffres.

"In 1811 it was resolved by the colonial government that the Caffres should be driven from this territory, and confined to the other side of the Great Fish River. This was an act of injustice and great hardship, and was proceeded in with extreme cruelty, the Caffres being obliged to leave all their crops, and turned out with great and unnecessary slaughter.

"It may be proper, however, to state the causes which led to this Caffre war with the English. At this time the colonial governor had entered into negotiations with a Caffre chief of the name of Gaika. He was a chief of a portion of the Caffres, but not the principal chief, and although the English treated with him as such, the Caffres would not acknowledge his authority. This is a very frequent error committed in our intercourse with savage nations, who are as pertinacious of their rights as the monarchs of Europe. The error on our part was soon discovered, but the government was too proud to acknowledge it.

"It so happened that the other Caffre chiefs formed a powerful confederacy against Gaika, who, trusting to the support of the English, had treated them with great arrogance. They fought and conquered him, carrying off, as usual, his cattle. As this was a war between the Caffres, and confined to their own land, we certainly had no business to interfere; but the colonial government thought otherwise, and an expedition was prepared.

"The Caffres sent forward messengers declaring their wish to remain at peace with the English, but refusing to submit to Gaika, who was only a secondary chief, and whom they had conquered. No regard was paid to this remonstrance; the English troops were sent forward, the Caffres attacked in their hamlets, slaughtered or driven into the woods, 23,000 head of cattle taken from them, of which 9,000 were given to Gaika, and the rest distributed to the Dutch boors, or sold to defray part of the expenses of the expedition.

"Deprived of their means of subsistence by the capture of their cattle, the Caffres were rendered furious reckless, and no sooner had the expedition returned, than they commenced hostilities. They poured into the frontier districts, captured several detached military forts, drove the Dutch boors from the Zurweld, or neutral territory, and killed a great many of our soldiers and of the Dutch boors. All the country was overrun as far as the vicinity of Algoa Bay, and nothing could at first check their progress."

"Why, it really does not appear that the colonial government, when in our hands, was more considerate than when it was held by the Dutch," replied Alexander.

"Not much, I fear," said Mr. Fairburn.

"The councils of the Caffre chiefs were at that time much influenced by a most remarkable personage of the name of Mokanna. In the colony he was usually known by the sobriquet of 'Links,' or the left-handed. He was not a chief, but had by his superior intellect obtained great power. He gave himself out to be a prophet, and certainly showed quite as much skill as ever did Mahommed or any other false prophet. He had often visited Cape Town, and had made himself

The Mission

master of all that he could acquire of European knowledge.

"This man, by his influence, his superior eloquence, and his pretended revelations from heaven, was now looked up to by the whole Caffre nation; and he promised the chiefs, if they would implicitly obey his orders, he would lead them to victory, and that he would drive the English into the ocean. He resolved upon the bold measure of making an attack upon Graham's Town, and marched an army of between nine and ten thousand men to the forest bordering on the Great Fish River.

"According to the custom of the Caffres, who never use surprise or ambush on great occasions, they sent a message to the commandant of Graham's Town, stating that they would breakfast with him the next morning. The commandant, who had supposed the message to be a mere bravado, was very ill prepared when on the following morning he perceived, to his great astonishment, the whole force of the Caffres on the heights above the town.

"Had the Caffres advanced in the night, there is no doubt but that they would have had possession of the place, and that with the greatest ease. There were about 350 regular troops and a small force of Hottentots in Graham's Town, and fortunately a few field-pieces. The Caffres rushed to the assault, and for some time were not to be checked; they went up to the very muzzles of the field-pieces, and broke their spears off short, to decide the battle by a hand-to-hand conflict.

"At this critical moment, the field-pieces opened their fire of grape and canister, and the front ranks of the Caffres were mowed down like grass. After several rallyings under Mokanna, the Caffres gave way and fled. About 1400 of the bravest remained on the field of battle, and as many more perished from their wounds before they could regain their country. Mokanna, after using every exertion, accompanied the Caffre army in their flight."

"It certainly was a bold attempt on the part of the Caffres, and showed Mokanna to be a great man even in the failure."

"It was so unprecedented an attempt, that the colonial government were dreadfully alarmed, and turned out their whole force of militia as well as of regular troops. The Caffre country was again overrun, the inhabitants destroyed, without distinction of age or sex, their hamlets fired, cattle driven away, and when they fled to the thickets, they were bombarded with shells and Congreve rockets. Mokanna and the principal chiefs were denounced as outlaws, and the inhabitants threatened with utter extermination if they did not deliver them up dead or alive. Although driven to despair, and perishing from want, not a single Caffre was to be found who would earn the high reward offered for the surrender of the chiefs."

"The more I hear of them, the more I admire the Caffres," observed Alexander Wilmot; "and I may add – but never mind, pray go on."

"I think I could supply the words which you have checked, Mr. Wilmot, but I will proceed, or dinner will be announced before I have finished this portion of my history."

"The course adopted by Mokanna under these circumstances was such as will raise him much higher in your estimation. As he found that his countrymen were to be massacred until he and the other chiefs were delivered up, dead or alive, he resolved to surrender himself as a hostage for his country. He sent a message to say that he would do so, and the next day, with a calm magnanimity that would have done honor to a Roman patriot, he came, unattended, to the English camp. His words were 'People say that I have occasioned this war: let me see if my delivering myself up will restore peace to my country.' The commanding officer, to whom he surrendered himself, immediately forwarded him as a prisoner to the colony."

"What became of him?"

"Of that hereafter; but I wish here to give you the substance of a speech made by one of Mokanna's head men, who came after Mokanna's surrender into the English camp. I am told that the imperfect notes taken of it afford but a very faint idea of its eloquence; at all events, the speech gives a very correct view of the treatment which the Caffres received from our hands.

"'This war,' said he, 'British chiefs, is an unjust one, for you are trying to extirpate a people whom you have forced to take up arms. When our fathers and the fathers of the boors first settled on the Zurweld, they dwelt together in peace. Their flocks grazed the same hills, their herdsmen smoked out of the same pipe; they were brothers until the herds of the Amakosa (Caffres) increased so much as to make the hearts of the Dutch boors sore. What those covetous men could not get from our fathers for old buttons, they took by force. Our fathers were men; they loved their cattle; their wives and children lived upon milk; they fought for their property; they began to hate the colonists, who coveted their all, and aimed at their destruction.

"'Now their kraals and our fathers' kraals were separate. The boors made commandoes for our fathers; our fathers drove them out of the Zurweld, and we dwelt there because we had conquered it; there we married wives; there our children were born; the white men hated us, but could not drive us away; when there was war, we plundered you; when there was peace, some of our bad people stole; but our chiefs forbade it.

"'We lived in peace; some bad people stole, perhaps; but the nation was quiet; Gaika stole; his chiefs stole; you sent him copper; you sent him beads; you sent him horses, on which he rode to steal more; to *us* you only sent *commandoes*. We quarreled with Gaika about grass; – no business of yours; you send a commando; you take our last cow; you leave only a few calves, which die for want, and so do our children; you give half the spoil to Gaika; half you kept yourselves.

"'Without milk; our corn destroyed; we saw our wives and children perish; we followed, therefore, the tracks of our cattle into the colony; we plundered, and we fought for our lives; we found you weak, and we destroyed your soldiers; we saw that we were strong, and we attacked your headquarters, and if we had succeeded, our right was good, for

The Mission

you began the war; we failed, and you are here.

"We wish for peace; we wish to rest in our huts; we wish to get milk for our children; our wives wish to till the land; but your troops cover the plains, and swarm in the thickets, where they can not distinguish the men from the women, and shoot *all*. You wish us to submit to Gaika; that man's face is fair to you, but his heart is false; leave him to himself; make peace with us: let him fight for himself; and we shall not call upon you for help; set Mokanna at liberty, and all our chiefs will make peace with you at any time you fix; but if you still make war, you may indeed kill the last man of us, but Gaika shall not rule over the followers of those who think him a woman.'

"If eloquence consists (as it does not in the English House of Commons) in saying much in few words, I know no speech more comprehensive of the facts and arguments of a case than the above. I am sorry to say it had no effect in altering the destination of Mokanna, or of obtaining any relief for his countrymen, who were still called upon to deliver up the other chiefs *outlawed* by the government."

"I before remarked the absurdity of that expression," said Mr. Swinton; "we outlaw a member of our own society and belonging to our own country; but to *outlaw* the chiefs of another country is something too absurd; I fear the English language is not much studied at the Cape."

"At all events, every attempt made to obtain possession of these *outlawed* chiefs was unavailing. After plundering the country of all that could be found in it, leaving devastation and misery behind, the expedition returned without obtaining their object, but with the satisfaction of knowing that by taking away 30,000 more cattle, they left thousands of women and children to die of starvation. But I must leave off now. The results of the war, and the fate of Mokanna, shall be the subject of another meeting."

"We are much obliged to you, Mr. Fairburn, for the interesting narrative you have given us. It is, however, to be hoped that you will have no more such painful errors and injustice to dwell upon."

"As I before observed, Mr. Wilmot, it requires time for prejudice and falsehood to be overthrown; and until they are mastered, it can not be expected that justice can be administered. The colonial government had to contend with the whole white population of the colony who rose up in arms against them, considering, from long habit, that any interference with their assumed despotism over the natives was an infringement of their rights.

"You must also recollect how weak was the power of the colonial government for a long time, and how impossible it was to exert that power over such an extensive country; and to give you some idea of this, I will state what was the reply of some of the Dutch boors to the traveler La Vaillant, when the latter expressed his opinion that the government should interfere with an armed force to put an end to their cruelty and oppression.

"'Are you aware,' said they, 'what would be the result of such an attempt? – Assembling all in an instant, we would massacre half of the soldiers, salt their flesh, and send it back by those we might spare, with threats to do the same thing to those who should be bold enough to appear among us afterward.' It is not an easy task for any government to deal with such a set of people, Mr. Wilmot."

"I grant it," replied Alexander; "and the conviction makes me more anxious to know what has been since done."

CHAPTER VI

The following morning the wind was very slight, and before noon it fell calm. Two sharks of a large size came under the stern of the vessel, and the sailors were soon very busy trying to hook one of them; but they refused the bait, which was a piece of salt pork, and after an hour they quitted the vessel and disappeared, much to the disappointment of both passengers and ship's company, the former wishing very much to see the sharks caught, and the latter very anxious to cut them up and fry them for their suppers.

"I thought that sharks always took the bait," observed Alexander.

"Not always, as you have now seen," replied Mr. Swinton; "all depends upon whether they are hungry or not. In some harbors where there are plenty of fish, I have seen sharks in hundreds, which not only refused any bait, but would not attempt to seize a man if he was in the water; but I am surprised at these Atlantic sharks refusing the bait, I must confess, for they are generally very ravenous, as are, indeed, all the sharks which are found in the ocean."

"I can tell you, sir, why they refused the bait," said the boatswain of the vessel, who was standing by; "it's because we are now on the track of the Brazilian slavers, and they have been well fed lately, depend upon it."

"I should not be surprised if you were correct in your idea," replied Mr. Swinton.

"There are many varieties of sharks, are there not?" inquired Wilmot.

"Yes, a great many; the fiercest, however, and the largest kind is the one which has just left us, and is termed the white shark; it ranges the whole Atlantic Ocean, but is seldom found far to the northward, as it prefers the tropics: it is, however, to be seen in the Mediterranean, in the Gulf of Lyons, and is there remarkably fierce. In the English Channel you find the blue shark, which is seldom dangerous; there is also a very large-sized but harmless shark found in the north seas, which the whalers frequent. Then there is the spotted or tiger-shark, which is very savage, although it does not grow to a large size; the hammer-headed shark, so called from the peculiar formation of its head; and the ground shark, perhaps the most dangerous of all, as it lies at the bottom and rises under you without giving you notice of its approach. I believe I have now mentioned the principal varieties."

"If a man was to fall overboard and a shark was nigh, what would be the best plan to act upon – that is, if there would be any chance of escape from such a brute?"

"The best plan, and I have seen it acted upon with success, is, if you can swim well, to throw yourself on your back and splash as much as you can with your feet, and halloo as loud as you can. A shark is a cowardly animal, and noise will drive it away.

"When I went out two or three years ago, I had a Newfoundland dog, which was accustomed to leap into the water from almost any height. I was very partial to him, and you may imagine my annoyance when, one day, as we were becalmed along the Western Islands, and a large shark came up alongside, the dog, at once perceiving it, plunged off the taffrail to seize it, swimming toward the shark, and barking as loud as he could. I fully expected that the monster would have dispatched him in a moment; but to my surprise the shark was frightened and swam away, followed by the dog, until the boat that was lowered down picked him up."

"I don't think the shark could have been very hungry."

"Probably not; at all events I should not have liked to have been in Neptune's place. I think the most peculiar plan of escaping from sharks is that pursued by the Cingalese divers, and often with success."

"Tell me, if you please."

"The divers who go down for the pearl oysters off Ceylon generally drop from a boat, and descend in ten or twelve fathoms of water before they come to the bed of pearl oysters, which is upon a bank of mud: it often happens that when they are down, the sharks make for them, and I hardly need say that these poor fellows are constantly on the watch, looking in every direction while they are filling their baskets. If they perceive a shark making for them, their only chance is to stir up the mud on the bank as fast as they can, which prevents the animal from distinguishing them, and under the cover of the clouded water they regain the surface; nevertheless, it does not always answer, and many are taken off every year."

"A lady, proud of her pearl necklace, little thinks how many poor fellows may have been torn to pieces to obtain for her such an ornament."

"Very true; and when we consider how many pearl-fisheries may have taken place, and how many divers may have been destroyed, before a string of fine pearls can be obtained, we might almost say that every pearl on the necklace has cost the life of a human creature."

"How are the pearls disposed of, and who are the proprietors?"

"The government are the proprietors of the fishery, I believe; but whether they farm it out yearly, or not, I can not tell; but this I know, that as the pearl oysters are taken, they are landed unopened and packed upon the beach in squares of a certain dimension. When the fishing is over for the season, these square lots of pearl oysters are put up to auction, and sold to the highest bidder, of course 'contents unknown;' so that it becomes a species of lottery; the purchaser may not find a single pearl in his lot, or he may find two or three, which will realize twenty times the price which he has paid for his lot."

"It is, then, a lottery from beginning to end; the poor divers' lottery is shark or no shark; the purchasers', pearls or no pearls. But Mr. Fairburn is coming up the ladder, and I am anxious to know what was the fate of Mokanna."

Mr. Fairburn, who had come on deck on purpose to continue the narrative, took his seat by his two fellow passengers and went on as follows: –

"I stated that Mokanna had been forwarded to the Cape. You must have perceived that his only crime was that of fighting for his native land against civilized invaders; but this was a deep crime in the eyes of the colonial government; he was immediately thrown into the common gaol, and finally was condemned to be imprisoned for life on Robben Island, a place appropriated for the detention of convicted felons and other malefactors, who there work in irons at the slate-quarries."

"May I ask, where is Robben Island?"

"It is an island a few miles from the mainland, close to Table Bay, upon which the Cape Town is built.

"Mokanna remained there about a year, when, having made his intentions known to some Caffres who were confined there with him, he contrived out of the iron hoops of the casks to make some weapons like cutlasses, with which he armed his followers, rose upon the guard and overpowered them; he then seized the boat, and with his Caffres made for the mainland. Unfortunately, in attempting to disembark upon the rocks of the mainland, the boat was upset in the surf, which was very violent; Mokanna clung some time to a rock, but at last was washed off, and thus perished the unfortunate leader of the Caffres."

"Poor fellow," said Alexander; "he deserved a better fate and a more generous enemy; but did the war continue?"

"No; it ended in a manner every way worthy of that in which it was begun. You recollect that the war was commenced to support Gaika, our selected chief of the Caffres, against the real chiefs. The Caffres had before been compelled to give up their territories on our side of the Fish River; the colonial government now insisted upon their retiring still further, that is, beyond the Keisi and Chumi rivers, by which 3,000 more square miles were added to the colonial territory. This was exacted, in order that there might be a neutral ground to separate the Caffres and the Dutch boors, and put an end to further robberies on either side. The strangest part of the story is, that this territory was not taken away from the Caffre chiefs, against whom we had made war, but from Gaika, our ally, to support whom we had entered into the war."

"Well, it was even-handed – not justice, but injustice, at all events."

"Exactly so; and so thought Gaika, for when speaking of the protection he received from the colonial government, he said, 'But when I look upon the large extent of fine country which has been taken from me, I am compelled to say, that, although protected, I am *rather oppressed* by my *protectors*.'"

"Unjust as was the mode of obtaining the neutral ground, I must say that it appears to me to have been a good policy to put one between the parties."

"I grant it; but what was the conduct of the colonial government? This neutral ground was afterward given away in large tracts to the Dutch boors, so as again to bring them into contact with the Caffres."

"Is it possible?"

"Yes; to men who had always been opposed to the English government, who had twice risen in rebellion against them, and who had tried to bring in the Caffres to destroy the colony. Neither were the commandoes, or excursions against the Caffres, put an end to: Makomo, the son of Gaika, our late ally, has, I hear, been the party now attacked. I trust, however, that we may soon have affairs going on in a more favorable and reputable manner; indeed, I am sure that, now the government at home have been put in possession of the facts, such will be the case.

"I have now given you a very brief insight into the history of the Cape up to the present time. There are many points which I have passed over, not wishing to diverge from a straightforward narrative; but upon any questions you may wish to ask, I shall be most happy to give you all the information in my power. I can not, however, dismiss the subject without making one remark, which is, that it is principally, if not wholly, to the missionaries, to their exertions and to their representations, that what good has been done is to be attributed. They are entitled to the greatest credit and the warmest praise;

and great as has been the misrule of this colony for many years, it would have been much greater and much more disgraceful, if it had not been for their efforts. Another very important alteration has been taking place in the colony, which will eventually be productive of much good. I refer to the British immigration, which every year becomes more extensive; and as soon as the British population exceeds and masters that of the old Dutch planters and boors, we shall have better feeling in the colony. Do not suppose that all the Dutch boors are such as those whose conduct I have been obliged to point out. There are many worthy men, although but few educated or enlightened.

"I know from my own observation that the failings and prejudices against the natives are fast fading away, and that lately the law has been able to hold its ground, and has been supported by the people inhabiting the districts. The Dutch, with all their prejudices and all their vices, will soon be swallowed up by the inundation of English settlers, and will gradually be so incorporated and intermingled by marriage that no distinction will be known. Time, however, is required for such consolidation and cementation; that time is arriving fast, and the future prospects of the Cape are as cheering, as you may think, from my narrative, they have been disheartening and gloomy."

"I trust in God that such will be the case," replied Alexander. "If this wind continues, in a few days we shall be at the Cape, and I shall be most anxious to hear how affairs are going on."

"I had a letter just before I set out from England, stating that the Zoolu tribes, to the northward of the Caffres, are in an unquiet state; and as you must pass near to these tribes on your journey, I am anxious to know the truth. At all events, Chaka is dead; he was murdered about two years back by his own relations."

"Who was Chaka?" inquired Alexander.

"That I have yet to tell you; at present we have only got as far as the Caffres, who are immediately on our frontiers."

CHAPTER VII

The wind continued fair, and the vessel rapidly approached the Cape. Alexander, who had contracted a great friendship for Mr. Swinton, had made known to him the cause of his intended journey into the interior, and the latter volunteered, if his company would not be displeasing, to accompany Alexander on his tedious and somewhat perilous expedition.

Alexander gladly accepted the offer, and requested Mr. Swinton would put himself to no expense, as he had unlimited command of money from his grand-uncle, and Mr. Swinton's joining the caravan would make no difference in his arrangements.

After it had been agreed that they should travel together, the continued subject of discourse and discussion was the nature of the outfit, the number of wagons, their equipment, the stores, the number of horses and oxen which should he provided; and they were busy every day adding to their memoranda as to what it would be advisable to procure for their journey.

Mr. Fairburn often joined in the discussion, and gave his advice, but told them that, when they arrived at Cape Town, he might be more useful to them. Alexander, who, as we have before observed, was a keen hunter, and very partial to horses and dogs, promised himself much pleasure in the chase of the wild animals on their journey, and congratulated himself upon being so well provided with guns and rifles, which he had brought with him, more with the idea that they might be required for self-defense than for sport.

At last, "Land, ho!" was cried out by the man who was at the mast-head in the morning watch, and soon afterward, the flat top of Table Mountain was distinctly visible from the deck. The *Surprise*, running before a fresh breeze, soon neared the land, so that the objects on it might be perceived with a glass. At noon they were well in for the bay, and before three o'clock the *Surprise* was brought to an anchor between two other merchant vessels, which were filling up their home cargoes.

After a three months' voyage, passengers are rather anxious to get on shore; and therefore before night all were landed, and Alexander found himself comfortably domiciled in one of the best houses in Cape Town; for Mr. Fairburn had, during the passage, requested Alexander to take up his abode with him.

Tired with the excitement of the day, he was not sorry to go to bed early, and he did not forget to return his thanks to Him who had preserved him through the perils of the voyage.

The next morning Mr. Fairburn said to Alexander –

"Mr. Wilmot, I should recommend you for the first ten days to think nothing about your journey. Amuse yourself with seeing the public gardens, and other things worthy of inspection; or, if it pleases you, you can make the ascent of Table Mountain with your friend Swinton. At all events, do just as you please; you will find my people attentive, and ready to obey your orders. You know the hours of meals; consider yourself at home, and as much master here as I am. As you may well imagine, after so long an absence, I have much to attend to in my official capacity, and I think it will be a week or ten days before I shall be comfortably reseated in my office, and have things going on smoothly, as they ought to do. You must therefore excuse me if I am not quite so attentive a host at first as I should wish to be. One thing only I recommend you to do at present, which is, to accompany me this afternoon to Government-house, that I may introduce you to the governor. It is just as well to get over that mark of respect which is due to him, and then you will be your own master."

Alexander replied with many thanks. He was graciously received by the governor, who promised him every assistance in his power in the prosecution of his journey. Having received an invitation for dinner on the following day, Alexander bowed and took his leave in company with Mr. Fairburn.

On the following day Alexander was visited by Mr. Swinton. Mr. Swinton was accompanied by a major in the Bengal Cavalry, whom he introduced as Major Henderson. He had arrived a few days before from Calcutta, having obtained leave of absence for the recovery of his health, after a smart jungle-fever, which had nearly proved fatal. The voyage, however, had completely reinstated him, and he appeared full of life and spirits. They walked together to the Company's gardens, in which were a few lions, and some other Cape animals, and the discourse naturally turned upon them. Major Henderson described the hunting in India, especially the tiger-hunting on elephants, to which he was very partial; and Alexander soon discovered that he was talking to one who was passionately fond of the sport. After a long conversation they parted, mutually pleased with each other. A day or two afterward, Mr. Swinton, who had been talking about their intended journey with Alexander, said to him: –

"You must not be surprised at the off-hand and unceremonious way we have in the colonies. People meeting abroad, even Englishmen occasionally, throw aside much ceremony. I mention this, because Major Henderson intends to call this afternoon, and propose joining our party into the interior. I do not know much of him, but I have heard much said in his favor, and it is easy to see by his manners and address that he is a gentleman. Of course, when he stated his intention, I could do nothing but refer him to you, which I did. What do you think, Wilmot?"

"I think very well of Major Henderson, and I consider that, as the journey must be one of some peril, the more Europeans the better, especially when we can find one who is used to danger from his profession, and also to dangerous hunting, which we must also expect. So far from not wishing him to join us, I consider him a most valuable acquisition, and am delighted at the idea."

"Well, I am glad to hear you say so, for I agree with you. He is hunting mad, that is certain, and I hear, a most remarkable shot. I think with you he will be an acquisition. It appears that it was his intention to have gone into the interior, even if he went by himself; and he has two Arab horses which he brought with him from India with that view."

"If you see him before he comes, you may say that you have stated his wishes to me, and that I am quite delighted at his joining our party, – it being perfectly understood that he is at no expense for any thing connected with the outfit."

"I will tell him so," replied Swinton; "and I think the sooner we begin to collect what is necessary the better. We must have Major Henderson in our councils. Depend upon it, he will be very useful and very active; so, for the present, farewell."

Mr. Swinton and Major Henderson called together that afternoon, and the latter, as soon as he was admitted into the party, began to talk over the plans and preparations.

"My suite is not very large," said he; "I have two horses and two dogs, a Parsee servant, and a Cape baboon. I should like to take the latter with us as well as my servant. My servant, because he is a good cook; and my monkey, because, if we are hard put to it, she will show us what we may eat and what we may not; there is no taster like a monkey. Besides, she is young and full of tricks, and I like something to amuse me."

"The baboons have another good quality: they give notice of danger sooner than a dog," observed Swinton. "I think, Wilmot, we must admit the monkey into the party."

"I shall be most happy," replied Alexander, laughing; "pray give her my compliments, Major Henderson, and say how happy I shall be."

"I call her Begum," said Major Henderson; "because she is so like the old Begum princess whom I was once attending, when in India with my troop, as guard of honor. You must look out for some good horses, Mr. Wilmot; you will want a great many, and if you do not wish them to have sore backs, don't let the Hottentots ride them."

"We have been discussing the point, Major Henderson, as to whether it will not be better to go round in a vessel to Algoa Bay, complete our equipment there, and make that our starting place."

"If you do, you will save a long journey by land, and find yourself not very far from what I understand are the best of hunting-grounds, near to the country of the Vaal River."

The topics then dwelt upon were what articles they should procure in Cape Town, and what they should defer providing themselves with until their arrival at Algoa Bay. They agreed to provide all their stores at Cape Town, and as many good horses as they could select; but the wagons and oxen, and the hiring of Hottentots, they put off until they arrived at Algoa Bay.

Mr. Fairburn was now more at leisure, and Alexander had more of his society. One evening after dinner Mr. Fairburn had opened a map of the country, to give Alexander some information relative to his projected journey. He pointed out to him the track which appeared most advisable through the Caffre country, and then observed that it was difficult to give any advice as to his proceedings after he had passed this country, governed by Hinza, as every thing would depend upon circumstances.

"Do you know any thing of the country beyond?"

"Not much; we know that it was overrun by the Zoolus, the tribe of which Chaka was the chief; and last year our troops went to the assistance of the Caffres, who were attacked by another tribe from the northward, called the Mantatees. These were dispersed by our troops with immense slaughter. The Zoolu country, you perceive, is on the east side of the great chain of mountains, and to the northward of Port Natal. The Mantatees came from the west side of the mountains, in about the same parallel of latitude. It is impossible to say what may be going on at present, or what may take place before you arrive at your destination, as these northern irruptions are continual."

"You promised me the history of that person, Chaka."

"You shall have it now: he was the king of the Zoolu nation – I hardly know what to call him. He was the Nero and the Napoleon of Africa; a monster in cruelty and crime, yet a great warrior and conqueror. He commenced his career by murdering his relatives to obtain the sovereignty. As soon as he had succeeded, he murdered all those whom he thought inimical to him, and who had been friends to his relatives."

"But are the Zoolus Caffres?"

"No; but there are many races to the northward which we consider as Caffre races. You may have observed, in the history of the world, that the migrations of the human race are generally from the north to the south: so it appears to have been in Africa. Some convulsion among the northern tribes, probably a pressure from excessive population, had driven the Zoolus to the southward, and they came down like an inundation, sweeping before them all the tribes that fell in their path. Chaka's force consisted of nearly 100,000 warriors, of whom 15,000 were always in attendance to execute his orders. In every country which he overran he spared neither age nor sex; it was one indiscriminate slaughter."

"What a monster!"

"He ruled by terror, and it is incredible that his orders met with such implicit obedience. To make his army invincible, he remodeled it, divided it into companies, distinguished by the color of their shields, and forbade them to use any other weapon but a short stabbing-spear, so that they always fought at close quarters. He weeded his army by picking out 1000 of his veteran warriors, who had gained his victories, and putting them to death. Any regiment sent out to battle, if they were defeated, were instantly destroyed on their return; it was, therefore, victory or death with them; and the death was most cruel, being that of impalement. Well he was surnamed 'the Bloody,'"

"Yes, indeed."

"His tyranny over his own people was dreadful. On one occasion, a child annoyed him; he ordered it to be killed; but the child ran among seventy or eighty other children, and could not be distinguished, so he ordered the whole to be put to death. He murdered two or three hundred of his wives in one day. At the slightest suspicion he would order out his chiefs to execution, and no one knew when his turn might come. His will was law: every one trembled and obeyed. To enter into a detail of all his cruelties would fill volumes; it will be sufficient to mention the last act of his life. His mother died, and he declared that she had perished by witchcraft. Hundreds and hundreds were impaled, and, at last, tired of these slow proceedings, he ordered out his army to an indiscriminate slaughter over the whole country, which lasted for fourteen days."

"How horrible!"

"He was a demon who reveled in blood; but his own turn came at last. He was murdered by his brother Dingaam, who knew that he was about to be sacrificed; and thus perished the bloody Chaka. His brother Dingaam is now on the Zoolu throne, and appears inclined to be quiet. There is another great warrior chief named Moselekatsee, who revolted from Chaka, and who is much such another character; but our accounts of these people are vague at present, and require time to corroborate their correctness.

You will have to act and decide when you arrive there, and must be guided by circumstances. With the caravan you propose to travel with, I think there will not be much danger; and if there is, you must retreat. The favor of these despots is easily to be obtained by judicious presents, which of course you will not be unprovided with. I have ordered your letters to the authorities to be made out, and you will have the governor's signature to them. When do you propose to, start?"

"We shall be ready in a few days, and have only to find a vessel going to Algoa Bay."

"You will be asked to take charge of several articles which are to be sent to the missionary station which you will pass on your way. I presume you have no objection?"

"Certainly not; they deserve every encouragement, and any kindness and attention I can show them will give me great pleasure."

Alexander received many proposals from different parties who wished to join the expedition, but they were all civilly declined. In a few days a vessel arrived, which was about to go round to the settlement at Algoa Bay. Their stores, horses, and dogs, not forgetting Begum the baboon, were all embarked, and, taking leave of Mr. Fairburn and the governor, Alexander, Major Henderson, and Mr. Swinton embarked, and on the evening of the fourth day found themselves safe at anchor in company with ten or twelve vessels which were lying in Algoa Bay.

CHAPTER VIII

The vessels which lay at anchor in Algoa Bay had just arrived from England, with a numerous collection of emigrants, who, to improve their fortunes, had left their native land to settle in this country. Many had landed, but the greater proportion were still on board of the vessels. The debarkation was rapidly going on, and the whole bay was covered with boats landing with people and stores, or returning for more. The wind blowing from the westward, there was no surf on the beach; the sun was bright and warm, and the scene was busy and interesting; but night came on, and the panorama was closed in.

Alexander and his companions remained on the deck of their vessel till an undisturbed silence reigned where but an hour or two before all was noise and bustle. The stars, so beautiful in the southern climes, shone out in cloudless brilliancy; the waters of the bay were smooth as glass, and reflected them so clearly that they might have fancied that there was a heaven beneath as well as above them. The land presented a dark opaque mass, the mountains in the distance appearing as if they were close to them, and rising precipitately from the shore. All was of one somber hue, except where the lights in the houses in the town twinkled here and there, announcing that; some had not yet dismissed their worldly cares, and sought repose from the labors of the day. Yet all was silent, except occasionally the barking of a dog, or the voice of the sentry in Fort Frederick, announcing that "all was well."

"What a gathering in a small space of so many people with so many different histories, so many causes for leaving their native land, and with so many different fortunes in store for them, must there be on board of an emigrant ship," observed Mr. Swinton.

"Yet all united in one feeling, and instigated by the same desire, – that of independence, and, if possible, of wealth," rejoined Major Henderson.

"Of that there can be no doubt," said Alexander; "but it must be almost like beginning a new life; so many ties broken by the vast ocean which has separated them; new interests usurping the place of old ones; all novelty and adventure to look forward to; new scenes added to new hopes and new fears; but we must not remain too long even to watch these beautiful heavens, for we must rise at daylight, so I shall set the example, and wish you both good-night."

At daylight on the following morning the long-boat was hoisted out, and the horses safely conveyed on shore. After a hasty breakfast, Alexander and his two companions landed, to see if it were possible to obtain any roof under which they could shelter themselves; but the number of emigrants who had arrived put that out of the question, every house and every bed being engaged. This was a great disappointment, as they had no wish to return on board and reoccupy the confined space which had been allotted to them.

Having found accommodation for their horses, they proceeded to examine the town and resume their search for lodgings. The streets presented a bustling and animated scene; wagons with goods, or returning empty with their long teams of oxen; horses, sheep, and other animals, just landed; loud talking; busy inquirers; running to and fro of men; Hottentots busy with the gods, or smoking their pipes in idle survey; crates and boxes, and packages of all descriptions, mixed up with agricultural implements and ironware, lining each side of the road, upon which were seated wives and daughters watching the property, and children looking round with astonishment, or playing or crying.

Further out of the town were to be seen tents pitched by the emigrants, who had provided themselves with such necessaries before they had quitted England, and who were bivouacking like so many gipsies, independent of lodgings and their attendant expenses, and cooking their own provisions in kettles or frying-pans. As Alexander perceived the latter, he said, "At all events, we have found lodgings now; I never thought of that."

The Mission

"How do you mean?"

"I have two tents in the luggage I brought from Cape Town; we must get them on shore, and do as these people have done."

"Bravo! I am glad to hear that," replied Major Henderson; "any thing better than remaining on board to be nibbled by the cockroaches. Shall we return at once?"

"By all means," said Mr. Swinton; "we have but to get our mattresses and a few other articles."

"Leave my man to do all that," said the Major; "he is used to it. In India we almost live in tents when up the country. But here comes one that I should know; – Maxwell, I believe?"

"Even so, my dear Henderson," replied the military officer who had been thus addressed; "why, what brought you here? – surely you are not a settler?"

"No; I am here because I am not a settler," replied Henderson, laughing; "I am always on the move; I am merely on my own way with my two friends here to shoot a hippopotamus. Allow me to introduce Mr. Wilmot and Mr. Swinton. But I see you are on duty; are you in the fort?"

"Yes; I came from Somerset about a month back. Can I be of any use to you?"

"That depends upon circumstances; we are now going on board for our tents, to pitch them on the hill there, as we can get no lodgings."

"Well, I can not offer you beds in the fort, but I think if you were to pitch your tents outside the fort, on the glacis, you would be better than on the hill; your baggage would be safer, and I should be more able to render you any attention or assistance you may require."

"An excellent idea; if it were only on account of the baggage," replied Henderson; "we accept your offer with pleasure."

"Well then, get them on shore as quick as you can; my men will soon have them out for you and assist in transporting your luggage; and don't distress yourself about your dinner, I will contrive to have something cooked for you."

"A friend in need is a friend indeed, my good fellow. We will accept your offers as freely as they are made: so farewell for an hour or so."

As they parted with Captain Maxwell, Henderson observed, "That was a lucky meeting, for we shall now get on well. Maxwell is an excellent fellow, and he will be very useful to us in making our purchases, as he knows the people and the country: and our luggage will be safe from all pilferers."

"It is indeed very fortunate," replied Mr. Swinton. "Where did you know Captain Maxwell?"

"In India. We have often been out hunting tigers together. How he would like to be of our party; but that is of course impossible."

"But how shall we manage about our living, Major Henderson?" observed Wilmot; "it will never do to quarter ourselves on your friend."

"Of course not; we should soon eat up his pay and allowance. No, no; we will find dinners, and he will help us to cook them first and eat them afterward."

"Upon such terms, I shall gladly take up my quarters in the fort," replied Alexander. "But which is our boat out of all these?"

"Here, sir," cried out one of the sailors; "come along, my lads," continued he to the other men, who were lounging about, and who all jumped into the boat, which pushed off, and they were soon on board of the ship.

As the master of the vessel was equally glad to get rid of his passengers and their luggage as they were to leave, the utmost expedition was used by all parties, and in a few hours everything was landed, Begum, the baboon, being perched upon the stores conveyed in the last boat. A party of soldiers sent down by Captain Maxwell assisted the seamen to carry the various packages up to the fort, and before the evening closed in, the tents were pitched, their beds made up, and their baggage safely housed, while they were amusing themselves after dining with Captain Maxwell, leaning on the parapet and watching the passing and repassing of the boats which were unlading the vessels.

As there was little chance of rain in the present season, they lay down on their mattresses in perfect security and comfort, and did not wake up the next morning until breakfast was ready. After breakfast they sallied out with Captain Maxwell to look after wagons and oxen, and as, on the arrival of the emigrants, a number of wagons had been sent down to take them to their destinations, Captain Maxwell soon fell in with some of the Dutch boors of the interior with whom he had been acquainted, and who had come down with their wagons; but previous to making any bargains, Alexander went with Captain Maxwell to the landroost, for whom he had brought a letter from the governor.

This gentleman immediately joined the party, and through his intervention, before night, four excellent wagons with their tilts and canvas coverings, and four span of oxen of fourteen each, were bought and promised to be brought down and delivered up in good order, as soon as they had carried up the freights with which they were charged.

As these wagons could not return under four days, the next object that they had in view was to procure some more horses, and here they met with difficulty; for Major Henderson, who, as an excellent judge of horses, was requested to select them, would not accept of many that were offered. Still they had plenty of time, as the wagons would require fitting out previous to their departure, and this would be a work of some days; and many articles which they had decided to procure at Algoa Bay, instead of the Cape, were now to be sought for and selected.

At the time appointed, the wagons and teams were delivered over and paid for. Carpenters were then engaged, and the wagons were fitted out with lockers all round them, divided off to contain the luggage separate, so that they might be able to obtain in a minute any thing that they might require. While this work was proceeding, with the assistance of the landroost, they were engaging Hottentots and other people to join the expedition, some as drivers to the wagons, others as huntsmen, and to perform such duties as might be required of them. Some very steady brave men were selected, but it was impossible to make up the whole force which they wished to take of people of known character; many of them were engaged rather from their appearance, their promises, and the characters they obtained from others or gave themselves, than from any positive knowledge of them. This could not be avoided; and as they had it in their power to dismiss them for bad conduct, it was to be presumed that they could procure others.

It was more than three weeks before every thing was ready for their departure, and then the caravan was composed as follows: –

The persons who belonged to it were our three gentlemen; the servant of Major Henderson; eight drivers of the teams of oxen; twelve Hottentot and other hunters (for some of them were of a mixed race); two Hottentots who had charge of the horses, and two others who had charge of a flock of Cape sheep, which were to follow the caravan, and serve as food until they could procure oxen by purchase or game with their guns: so that the whole force of the party amounted to twenty men: two Hottentot women, wives of the principal men, also accompanied the caravan to wash and assist in cooking.

The animals belonging to the caravan consisted of fifty-six fine oxen, which composed the teams; twelve horses, as Major Henderson could only procure six at Algoa Bay, or they would have purchased more; thirteen dogs of various sizes, and Begum, the baboon, belonging to Captain Henderson: to these were to be added the flock of sheep.

The wagons were fitted out as follows, chiefly under the direction of Major Henderson and Mr. Swinton.

The first wagon, which was called Mr. Wilmot's wagon, was fitted up with boxes or lockers all round, and contained all the stores for their own use, such as tea, sugar, coffee, cheeses, hams, tongues, biscuits, soap, and wax candles, wine and spirits in bottles, besides large rolls of tobacco for the Hottentots or presents, and Alexander's clothes; his mattress lay at the bottom of the wagons, between the lockers. The wagon was covered with a double sail-cloth tilt, and with curtains before and behind; the carpenter's tools were also in one of the lockers of this wagon.

The second wagon was called Mr. Swinton's wagon; it was fitted up with lockers in the same way as the other, but it had also a large chest with a great quantity of drawers for insects, bottles of spirits for animals, and every thing necessary for preserving them; a ream or two of paper for drying plants, and several other articles, more particularly a medicine-chest well filled, for Mr. Swinton was not unacquainted with surgery and physic. The other lockers were filled with a large quantity of glass beads and cutlery for presents, several hundred pounds of bullets, ready cast, and all the kitchen ware and crockery. It had the same covering as the first, and Mr. Swinton's mattress was at night spread in the middle between the lockers.

The third wagon was called the armory, or the Major's wagon; it was not fitted up like the two first. The whole bottom of it was occupied with movable chests, and four large casks of spirits, and the Major made up his bed on the top of the chests. In the chests were gunpowder in bottles and a quantity of small shot for present use; tobacco in large rolls; 1 cwt. of snuff; all the heavy tools, spades, shovels, and axes, and a variety of other useful articles.

The tilt-frame was much stouter than that of the two other wagons, for the hoops met each other so as to make it solid. It was covered with a tarred sail-cloth so as to be quite water-proof, and under the tilt-frame were suspended all the guns, except the two which Alexander and Mr. Swinton retained in their own wagons in case of emergency. The back and front of this wagon were closed with boards, which were let down and pulled up on hinges, so that it was a little fortress in case of need; and as it

The Mission

could be locked up at any time, the Hottentots were not able to get at the casks of spirits without committing a sort of burglary. Begum was tied up in this wagon at night.

The fourth wagon was called the store wagon, and contained several articles which were not immediately wanted; such as casks of flour and bags of rice: it also held most of the ammunition, having six casks of gunpowder, a quantity of lead, two coils of rope, iron bars, bags of nails of various sizes, rolls of brass wire, and the two tents, with three chairs and a small table. Like the wagon of Major Henderson, it was covered with water-proof cloth.

Such was the fit-out which was considered necessary for this adventurous expedition, and the crowds who came to see the preparations for the great hunting-party, as it was called, were so great and so annoying that the utmost haste was made to quit the town. At last the wagons were all loaded, the Hottentots collected together from the liquor-shops, their agreements read to them by the landroost, and any departure from their agreements, or any misconduct, threatened with severe punishment.

The horses and oxen were brought in, and the next morning was fixed for their departure. Having taken leave of the landroost and other gentlemen of the town, who had loaded them with civilities, they retired to the fort, and passed the major part of the night with Captain Maxwell; but to avoid the crowd which would have accompanied them, and have impeded their progress, they had resolved to set off before daylight. At two o'clock in the morning the Hottentots were roused up, the oxen yoked, and an hour before day-break the whole train had quitted the town, and were traveling at a slow pace, lighted only by the brilliant stars of the southern sky.

CHAPTER IX

The plans of our travelers had been well digested. They had decided that they would first prosecute the object of their journey by proceeding straight through the Caffre country to the borders of the Undata River, near or whereabout it was reported that the descendants of the whites would be found located; and as soon as Alexander had accomplished his mission, that they would cross the chain of mountains, and return through the Bushmen and the Koranna country. Their reason for making this arrangement was, that throughout the whole of the Caffre country, with the exception of lions and elephants in the forest, and hippopotami in the rivers, there was little or no game to be found, the Caffres having almost wholly destroyed it.

This plan had been suggested by Major Henderson, and had been approved by Alexander and Mr. Swinton, – Alexander being equally desirous as the Major to have plenty of field-sport, and Mr. Swinton anxious to increase his stock and knowledge of the animal kingdom. There was little to be feared in their advance through the Caffre country, as the missionaries had already planted two missions, one at Butterworth and the other at Chumie; and the first of these Alexander had decided upon visiting, and had, in consequence, several packages in his wagon, which had been entrusted to his care.

It was on the 7th of May, 1829, that the caravan quitted Algoa Bay for Graham's Town. The weather had been for some weeks fine, the heavy rains having ceased, and the pasturage was now luxuriant; the wagons proceeded at a noiseless pace over the herbage, the sleepy Hottentots not being at all inclined to exert themselves unnecessarily. Alexander, Swinton, and Henderson were on horseback, a little ahead of the first wagon.

"I don't know how you feel," said the Major; "but I feel as if I were a prisoner just released from his chains. I breathe the air of independence and liberty now. After the bustle, and noise, and crowding together of the town, to find ourselves here so quiet and solitary is freedom."

"I had the same feeling," replied Alexander; "this wide-extended plain, of which we can not yet discern the horizontal edge; these brilliant stars scattered over the heavens, and shining down upon us; no sound to meet our ears but the creaking of the wagon-wheels in the slow and measured pace, is to me delightful. They say man is formed for society, and so he is; but it is very delightful occasionally to be alone."

"Yes; alone as we are," replied Swinton, laughing; "that is, with a party of thirty people, well armed, in search of adventure. To be clear of the bustle of the town, and no longer cooped up in the fort, is pleasant enough; but, I suspect, to be quite alone in these African wilds would be any thing but agreeable."

"Perhaps so."

"Neither would you feel so much at ease if you knew that your chance of to-morrow's dinner was to depend wholly upon what you might procure with your gun. There is a satisfaction in knowing that you have four well-filled wagons behind you."

"I grant that also," replied the Major; "but still there is solitude even with this company, and I feel it."

"A solitary caravan – but grant that there is some difference between that and a solitary individual," rejoined Swinton; "however, we have not come to solitude yet, for we shall find Dutch boors enough between this and Graham's Town."

"I think, Wilmot," observed Henderson, "that I should, if I were you, proceed by slow stages at first, that we may get our men into some kind of order and discipline, and also that we may find out whether there are any who will not suit us; we can discharge them at Graham's Town, and procure others in their place, at the same time that we engage our interpreters and guides."

"I think your plan very good," replied Alexander; "besides, we shall not have our wagons properly laden and arranged until we have been out three or four days."

"One thing is absolutely necessary, which is, to have a guard kept every night," said Swinton; "and there ought to be two men on guard at a time; for one of them is certain to fall asleep, if not both. I know the Hottentots well."

"They will be excellent guards, by your account," said Alexander; "however, the dogs will serve us more faithfully."

"I do not mean my remark to include all Hottentots; some are very faithful, and do their duty; but it comprehends the majority."

"Are they courageous?" inquired Alexander.

"Yes, certainly, they may be considered as a brave race of men; but occasionally there is a poltroon, and, like all cowards, he brags more than the rest."

"I've a strong suspicion that we have one of that kind among our hunters," replied Henderson; "however, it is not fair to prejudge; I may be mistaken."

"I think I know which you refer to, nevertheless," said Alexander; "it is the great fellow that they call Big Adam."

"You have hit upon the man, and to a certain degree corroborated my opinion of him. But the day is dawning, the sun will soon be above those hills."

"When we stop, I will have some grease put to those wagon-wheels," said Alexander.

"I fear it will be of little use," replied the Major; "creak they will. I don't know whether the oxen here are like those in India; but this I know, that the creaking of the carts and hackeries there is fifty times worse than this. The natives never grease the wheels; they say the oxen would not go on if they did not hear the music behind them."

"Besides, the creaking of the wheels will by and by be of service; when we are traveling through grass higher than our heads, we shall not be able to stop behind a minute, if we have not the creaking of the wheels to direct us how to follow."

"Well, then, I suppose we must save our grease," said Alexander.

"In a very few days you will be so accustomed to it," said the Major, "that if it were to cease, you would feel the loss of it."

"Well, it may be so; use is second nature; but at present I feel as if the loss would be gain. There is the sun just showing himself above the hill. Shall we halt or go on?"

"Go on for another hour, and the men can thus examine the traces and the wagons by daylight, and then, when we stop, we can remedy any defects."

"Be it so; there is a house, is there not, on the rising ground, as far as you can see?"

"Yes, I think so," replied the Major.

"I know it very well," said Swinton; "it is the farm of a Dutch boor, Milius, whom we saw at Algoa Bay. I did not think that we had got on so fast. It is about three miles off, so it will just be convenient for our breakfast. It will take us a good hour to arrive there, and then we will unyoke the oxen. How many have we yoked?"

"Ten to each wagon. The other sixteen are following with the sheep and horses; they are as relays."

"Let us gallop on," said the Major.

"Agreed," replied the others; and putting spurs to their horses, they soon arrived at the farmhouse of the Dutch planter.

They were saluted with the barking and clamor of about twenty dogs, which brought out one of the young boors, who drove away the dogs by pelting them with bullock-horns, and other bones of animals which were strewed about. He then requested them to dismount. The old boor soon appeared, and gave them a hearty welcome, handing down from the shelf a large brandy-bottle, and recommending a dram, of which he partook himself, stating that it was good brandy, and made from his own peaches.

Shortly afterward the wife of the boor made her appearance, and having saluted them, took up her station at a small table, with the tea apparatus before her. That refreshing beverage she now poured out for the visitors, handing a box, with some sugar-candy in it, for them to put a bit into their youths, and keep there as they drank their tea, by way of sweetening it. The old boor told them he had expected them, as he had been informed that they were to set out that day; but he had concluded that they would arrive in the afternoon, and not so early.

We may as well here give a description of a Dutch farmer's house at the Cape settlement.

It was a large square building, the wall built up of clay, and then plastered with a composition made by the boors, which becomes excessively hard in time; after which it is whitewashed. The roof was thatched with a hard sort of rushes, more durable and less likely to catch fire than straw. There was no ceiling under the roof, but the rafters overhead were hung with a motley assemblage of the produce of the chase and farm, as large whips made of rhinoceros-hide, leopard and lion skins, ostrich eggs and feathers, strings of onions, rolls of tobacco, bamboos, etc.

The house contained one large eating-room, a small private room, and two bedrooms. The windows were not glazed, but closed with skins every night. There was no chimney or stove in the house, all the cooking being carried on in a small outhouse.

The furniture was not very considerable: a large table, a few chairs and stools, some iron pots and kettles, a set of Dutch teacups, a teapot, and a brass kettle, with a heater. The large, brass-clasped, family Dutch Bible occupied a small table, at which the mistress of the house presided, and behind her chair were the carcasses of two sheep, suspended from a beam.

Inquiries about the news at the Cape, and details of all the information which our travelers could give, had occupied the time till breakfast was put on the table. It consisted of mutton boiled and stewed, butter, milk, fruits, and good white bread. Before breakfast was over the caravan arrived, and the oxen were unyoked. Our travelers passed away two hours in going over the garden and orchards, and visiting the cattlefolds, and seeing the cows milked. They then yoked the teams, and wishing the old boor a farewell, and thanking him for his hospitality, they resumed their journey.

"Is it always the custom here to receive travelers in this friendly way?" observed Alexander, as they rode away.

"Always," replied Swinton; "there are no inns on the road, and every traveler finds a welcome. It is considered a matter of course."

"Do they never take payment?"

"Never, and it must not be offered; but they will take the value of the corn supplied to your horses, as that is quite another thing. One peculiarity you will observe as you go along, which is, that the Dutch wife is a fixture at the little tea-table all day long. She never leaves it, and the tea is always ready for every traveler who claims their hospitality; it is an odd custom."

"And I presume that occasions the good woman to become so very lusty."

"No doubt of it; the whole exercise of

the day is from the bedroom to the teapot, and back again," replied Swinton, laughing.

"One would hardly suppose that this apparently good-natured and hospitable people could have been guilty of such cruelty to the natives as Mr. Fairburn represented."

"Many of our virtues and vices are brought prominently forward by circumstances," replied Swinton. "Hospitality in a thinly-inhabited country is universal, and a Dutch boor is hospitable to an excess. Their cruelty to the Hottentots and other natives arises from the prejudices of education: they have from their childhood beheld them treated as slaves, and do not consider them as fellow-creatures. As Mr. Fairburn truly said, nothing demoralizes so much, or so hardens the heart of man, as slavery existing and sanctioned by law."

"But are not the Dutch renowned for cruelty and love of money?"

"They have obtained that reputation, and I fear there is some reason for it. They took the lead, it must be remembered, as a commercial nation, more commercial than the Portuguese, whose steps they followed so closely: that this eager pursuit of wealth should create a love of money is but too natural, and to obtain money, men, under the influence of that passion, will stop at nothing. Their cruelties in the East are on record; but the question is, whether the English, who followed the path of the Dutch, would not, had they gone before them, have been guilty of the same crimes to obtain the same ends? The Spaniards were just as cruel in South America, and the Portuguese have not fallen short of them; nay, I doubt if our own countrymen can be acquitted in many instances. The only difference is, that the other nations who preceded them in discoveries had greater temptation, because there were more riches and wealth to be obtained."

"Your remarks are just; well may we say in the Lord's Prayer, 'Lead us not into temptation,' for we are all too frail to withstand it."

At noon they again unyoked, and allowed the cattle to graze for an interval; after which they proceeded till an hour before dark, when they mustered the men, and gave them their several charges and directions. At Alexander's request the Major took this upon himself, and he made a long speech to the Hottentots, stating that it was their intention to reward those who did their duty, and to punish severely those who did not. They then collected wood for the fires, and had their supper, – the first meal which they had taken out of doors. Mahomed, the Parsee servant of Major Henderson, cooked very much to their satisfaction; and having tied the oxen to the wagons, to accustom them to the practice, more than from any danger to be apprehended, the watch was set to keep up the fires: they then all retired to bed, the gentlemen sleeping in their wagons, and the Hottentots underneath them, or by the sides of the fires which had been lighted.

It will be unnecessary to enter into a detail of the journey to Graham's Town, which was performed without difficulty. They did not arrive there until eight days after their departure from Algoa Bay, as they purposely lost time on the road, that things might find their places. At Graham's Town they received every kindness and attention from the few military who were there and the landroost. Here they dismissed three of the men, who had remained drunk in the liquor-houses during their stay, and hired nine more, who were well recommended; among these were two perfectly well acquainted with the Caffre language and country; so that they were serviceable both as interpreters and guides. The day after their arrival, when they were out in the skirts of the town, Mr. Swinton perceived something moving in the bushes. He advanced cautiously, and discovered that it was a poor little Bushman boy, about twelve years old, quite naked, and evidently in a state of starvation, having been left there in a high fever by his people. He was so weak that he could not stand, and Mr. Swinton desired the Hottentot who was with him to lift him up, and carry him to the wagons. Some medicine and good food soon brought the little fellow round again, and he was able to walk about. He showed no disposition to leave them; indeed he would watch for Mr. Swinton, and follow him as far as he could. The child evidently appeared to feel attachment and gratitude, and when they were about to depart, Mr. Swinton, through the medium of one of the Hottentots who could speak the language, asked him if he would like to stay with them. The answer was in the affirmative, and it was decided that he should accompany them, the Major observing that he would be a very good companion for Begum.

"What name shall we give him?" said Swinton.

"Why, as my baboon is by title a princess, I think we can not create him less than a prince. Let us call him Omrah."

"Omrah be it then," replied Mr. Swinton, "until we can name him in a more serious way."

So Omrah was put into the wagon, with Begum to amuse him, and our travelers took their departure from Graham's Town.

CHAPTER X

It was in the afternoon that they moved from Graham's Town. They had intended to have started earlier, but they found it impossible to collect the Hottentots, who were taking their farewells of their wives and their liquor-shops. As it was, most of them were in a state of intoxication, and it was considered advisable to get them out of the town as soon as possible. Late in the evening they arrived at Hermann's Kraal, a small military fort, where they remained for the night to give the Hottentots an opportunity of recovering from the effects of the liquor. The next morning they again started, and the landscape now changed its aspect, being covered with thick bushes, infested with wild beasts.

A barren and sterile country was soon spread before them, the sun was oppressively hot, and not a sign of water was to be observed in any direction. At last they arrived at a muddy pool, in which elephants had evidently been enjoying themselves, and the oxen and horses were but too glad to do the same. At night they halted as before, having lighted fires to keep off the wild beasts and the elephants.

The following morning they renewed their journey at daylight, and the scene again changed; they now plunged into the dense forests bordering on the great Fish River, which they forded in safety. The prospects all around were very beautiful, the river smoothly gliding through stupendous mountains and precipices, with verdant valleys on each side of its banks. In the afternoon they arrived at Fort Wiltshire, the outermost defense of the colony, situated on the banks of the Keiskamma. English troops were stationed there, to prevent any marauding parties from passing the river, or to intercept them on their return with their booty.

As this was the last spot where they could expect to see any of their countrymen, and they were kindly received by the officers, they agreed to remain two days, that they might obtain all the information which they could, and rearrange the stowing of the wagons before they started. The original plan had been to direct their course to Chumie, the first missionary station, which was about twenty-five miles distant; but as it was out of their way, they now resolved to proceed direct to Butterworth, which was forty miles further in the Caffre country, and the more distant of the two missions. Our party took leave of their kind entertainers, and, having crossed without difficulty at the ford the Keiskamma river, had passed the neutral ground, and were in the land of the Caffres.

Up to the present they had very little trouble with the Hottentots whom they had hired. As long as they were within reach of the law they behaved well; but now that they had passed the confines of the Cape territory, some of them began to show symptoms of insubordination. The dismissal of one, however, with an order to go back immediately, and threatening to shoot him if he was ever seen in the caravan, had the desired effect of restoring order. The country was now a series of hills and dales, occasionally of deep ravines, and their route lay through the paths made by the elephants, which were numerous. A Hottentot of the name of Bremen, who was considered as their best man and most practiced hunter, begged Alexander and his companions to be careful how they went along, if they preceded the rest on horseback; as the elephants always return by the same path at evening or after nightfall, in whatever direction they may have been feeding, and it is very dangerous to intercept them.

For two days they continued their course in nearly a straight line for the missionary establishment. On the second evening, just about dusk, as they were crossing a woody hill, by the elephants' path, being then about 200 yards in advance of the wagons, they were saluted with one of the most hideous shrieks that could be conceived. Their horses started back; they could see nothing, although the sound echoed through the hills for some seconds.

"What was that?" exclaimed Alexander.

"Shout as loud as you can," cried the

Major; "and turn your horses to the wagons."

Alexander and Swinton joined the Major in the shout, and were soon accompanied by the whole mass of Hottentots, shouting and yelling as loud as they could.

"Silence, now," cried the Major; every one was hushed, and they listened for a few seconds.

"It was only one, sir, and he is gone," said Bremen. "We may go on."

"Only one what?" inquired Alexander.

"An elephant, sir," replied the Hottentot; "it's well that he did not charge you; he would have tumbled you down the precipice, horse and all. There must be a herd here, and we had better stop as soon as we are down the other side of the hill."

"I think so too," replied the Major.

"I shall not get that shriek out of my ears for a month," said Alexander; "why, the roar of a lion can not be so bad."

"Wait till you hear it," replied Swinton.

They had now arrived at the bottom of the hill which they had been passing, and by the light of the stars they selected a spot for their encampment. Whether they were near to any Caffre kraals or not it was impossible to say; but they heard no barking of dogs or lowing of oxen. Having collected all the cattle, they formed a square of the four wagons, and passed ropes from the one to the other; the horses and sheep were driven within the square, and the oxen were, as usual, tied up to the sides of the wagons.

It should here be observed, that the oxen were turned out to graze early in the morning, yoked in the afternoon, and they traveled then as far as they could after nightfall, to avoid the extreme heat of the day, the continual visits of the Carries, and the risk of losing the cattle if they were allowed to be loose and fed during the night.

On the night we have been referring to, a more than usual number of fires were lighted, to keep off the elephants and other wild animals. The hyenas and wolves were very numerous, and prowled the whole night in hopes of getting hold of some of the sheep; but as yet there had not been seen or heard a lion, although an occasional track had been pointed out by the Hottentots.

When the Hottentots had finished their labor, our travelers had to wait till the fires were lighted and a sheep killed before they could have their suppers cooked by Mahomed. Begum, the baboon, had been released from her confinement since their crossing the Fish River, and as usual, when they sat down, came and made one of the party, generally creeping in close to her master until supper was served, when she would have her finger in every dish, and steal all she could, sometimes rather to their annoyance.

Our little Bushman had now quite recovered not only his strength but his gayety, and was one of the most amusing little fellows that could be met with.

He could not make himself understood

except to one or two of the Hottentots; but he was all pantomime, trying, by gestures and signs, to talk to Mr. Swinton and his companions. He endeavored to assist Mahomed as much as he could, and appeared to have attached himself to him, for he kept no company with the Hottentots. He was not more than three feet and a half high, and with limbs remarkably delicate, although well made. His face was very much like a monkey's, and his gestures and manners completely so; he was quite as active and full of fun. The watch had been set as soon as the fires were lighted; and close to where Alexander and the others were seated, Big Adam, the Hottentot we have mentioned as having raised doubts in the mind of the Major as to his courage, had just mounted guard, with his gun in his hand. Omrah came up to where they were sitting, and they nodded and smiled at him, and said, "How do you do?" in English.

The boy, who had already picked up a few sentences, answered in the same words, "How do you do?" and then pointing to Big Adam, whose back was turned, he began making a number of signs, and nodding his head; at last he bent down, putting his arm in front of him, and raising it like an elephant's trunk, walking with the measured steps of that animal, so as fully to make them Understand that he intended to portray an elephant.

Having so done, he went up behind Big Adam, and gave a shriek so exactly like that which the elephant had given an hour before, that the Hottentot started up, dropped his musket, and threw himself flat on the ground, in order that the supposed animal might pass by him unperceived.

The other Hottentots had been equally startled, and had seized their muskets, looking in every direction for the approach of the animal; but the convulsions of laughter which proceeded from the party soon told them that there was nothing to apprehend, and that little Omrah had been playing his tricks. Big Adam rose up, looking very foolish; he had just before been telling his companions how many elephants he had killed, and had been expressing his hopes that they soon should have an elephant-hunt.

"Well," observed Swinton, after the laugh was over, "it proves that Adam is an elephant-hunter, and knows what to do in time of danger."

"Yes," replied the Major; "and it also proves that our opinion of him was just, and that with him the best part of valor is discretion."

"The most wonderful escape from an elephant which we have on record here," observed Swinton, "is that of Lieutenant Moodie; did you ever hear of it? I had it from his own lips."

"I never did, at all events," said Alexander; "and if the Major has, he will listen very patiently, to oblige me."

"I have never heard the precise particulars, and shall therefore be as glad to be a listener as Wilmot."

"Well, then, I will begin. Lieutenant Moodie was out elephant-hunting with a party of officers and soldiers, when one day he was told that a large troop of elephants was close at hand, and that several of the men were out, and in pursuit of them. Lieutenant Moodie immediately seized his gun, and went off in the direction where he heard the firing.

"He had forced his way through a jungle, and had just come to a cleared spot, when he heard some of his people calling out, in English and Dutch, 'Take care, Mr. Moodie, take care,' As they called out, he heard the crackling of branches broken by the elephants as they were bursting through the wood, and then tremendous screams, such as we heard this night. Immediately afterward four elephants burst out from the jungle, not two hundred yards from where he stood. Being alone on the open ground, he knew that if he fired and did not kill, he could have no chance; so he hastily retreated, hoping that the animals would not see him. On looking back, however, he perceived, to his dismay, that they were all in chase of him, and rapidly gaining on him; he therefore resolved to reserve his fire till the last moment, and, turning toward some precipitous rocks, hoped to gain them before the elephants could come up with him. But he was still at least fifty paces from the rocks, when he found that the elephants were within half that distance of him, – one very large animal, and three smaller, – all in a row, as if determined that he should not escape, snorting so tremendously that he was quite stunned with the noise."

"That's what I call a very pretty position," observed the Major. "Go on, Swinton; the affair is becoming a little nervous."

"As his only chance, Lieutenant Moodie turned round, and leveled his gun at the largest elephant; but unfortunately the powder was damp, and the gun hung fire, till he was in the act of taking it from his shoulder, when it went off, and the ball merely grazed the side of the elephant's head. The animal halted for an instant, and then made a furious charge upon him. He fell; whether struck down by the elephant's trunk he can not say. The elephant then thrust at him as he lay, with his tusk; fortunately it had but one, and more fortunately it missed its mark, plowing up the ground within an inch of Mr. Moodie's body.

"The animal then caught him up with its trunk by his middle, and dashed him down between his fore-feet to tread him to death. Once it pressed so heavily on his chest, that all his bones bent under the weight, but somehow or other, whether from the animal being in a state of alarm, it never contrived to have its whole weight upon him; for Mr. Moodie had never lost his recollection, and kept twisting his body and his limbs, so as to prevent it from obtaining a direct tread upon him. While he was in this state of distress, another officer and a Hottentot hunter came up to his assistance, and fired several shots at the animal, which was severely wounded, and the other three took to their heels. At last the one which had possession of Mr. Moodie turned round, and giving him a cuff with its fore-feet followed the rest. Mr. Moodie got up, picked up his gun, and staggered away as fast as his aching bones would permit him. He met his brother, who had just been informed by one of the Hottentots, who had seen him under the elephant, that he was killed."

The Mission

"Well, that was an escape," observed Wilmot.

"What made it more remarkable was, that he had hardly time to explain to his brother his miraculous preservation, before he witnessed the death of one of the hunters, a soldier, who had attracted the notice of a large male elephant which had been driven out of the jungle. The fierce animal gave chase to him, and caught him immediately under the height where Mr. Moodie and his brother were standing, carried the poor fellow for some distance on his trunk, then threw him down, and stamping upon him until he was quite dead, left the body for a short time. The elephant then returned, as if to make sure of its destruction; for it kneeled down on the body, and kneaded it with his fore-legs; then, rising, it seized it again with its trunk, carried it to the edge of the jungle, and hurled it into the bushes."

"Dreadful! I had no idea that there was such danger in an elephant-hunt; yet I must say," continued Alexander, "that, although it may appear foolishness, it only makes me more anxious to have one."

"Well, as we advance, you will have no want of opportunity; but it will be better to get the Caffres to join us, which they will with great delight."

"Why, they have no weapons, except their spears."

"None; but they will attack him with great success, as you will see; they watch their opportunity as he passes, get behind, and drive their spears into his body until the animal is exhausted from loss of blood, and they are so quick that the elephant seldom is able to destroy one of them. They consider the elephant of as high rank as one of their kings, and it is very laughable to hear them, as they wound him, beg pardon of him, and cry out, 'Great man, don't be angry; great captain, don't kill us,'"

"But how is it that they can approach so terrible an animal without destruction?"

"It is because they do approach quite close to him. An elephant sees but badly, except straight before him, and he turns with difficulty. The Caffres are within three feet of his tail or flank when they attack, and they attack him in the elephant-paths, which are too narrow for the animal to turn without difficulty; the great risk that they run is from another elephant breaking out to the assistance of the one attacked."

"The animals do assist each other, then?"

"Yes; there was a remarkable instance of it in the affair of Lieutenant Moodie. I mentioned that it was a large male elephant which killed the soldier just after Mr. Moodie's escape. Shortly afterward a shot from one of the hunters broke the fore-leg of this animal, and prevented him from running, and there it stood to be fired at. The female elephant, which was in the jungle, witnessing the distress of its mate, regardless of her own danger, immediately rushed out to his assistance, chasing away the hunters, and walked round and round her mate, constantly returning to his side, and caressing him. When the male attempted to walk, she had the sagacity to place her flank against the wounded side, so as to support him, and help him along. At last the female received a severe wound, and staggered into the bush, where she fell; and the male was soon after laid prostrate by the side of the poor soldier whom he had killed."

"There is something very touching in the last portion of your story, Swinton," observed Alexander; "it really makes one feel a sort of respect for such intelligent and reasoning animals."

"I think the first portion of the story ought to teach you to respect them also," said the Major. "Seriously, however, I quite agree with you; their sagacity, as my Indian experience has taught me, is wonderful; – but here comes supper, and I am not sorry for it."

"Nor I," replied Alexander. "To-morrow we shall be at the missionary station, if the guides are correct. I am very anxious to get there, I must say. Does not the chief of the Amakosa tribe live close to the Mission-house, – Hinza, as they call him?"

"Yes," replied Swinton, "he does, and

we must have a present ready for him, for I think it would be advisable to ask an escort of his warriors to go with us after we leave the Mission."

"Yes, it will be quite as well," replied the Major, "and then we shall have some elephant-hunting: but Bremen tells me that there are plenty of hippopotami in the river there, close to the Mission."

"Water-elephants," replied Swinton; "I suppose you will not leave them alone?"

"Certainly not if our commander-in-chief will allow us to stop."

"I think your commander-in-chief," replied Wilmot, "is just as anxious to have a day's sport with them as you are, Major; so you will certainly have his permission."

"I think we ought to put Omrah on a horse. He is a nice light weight for a spare horse, if required."

"Not a bad idea," replied Alexander. "What a tiger he would make for a cab in the park!"

"More like a monkey," replied the Major; "but it is time to go to bed; so, good-night."

CHAPTER XI

The caravan proceeded on the following morning, and by noon they arrived at the Mission station of Butterworth, which was about one hundred and forty miles from the colonial boundaries. This station had only been settled about three years, but even in that short time it wore an air of civilization strongly contrasted with the savage country around it. The Mission-house was little better than a large cottage, it is true, and the church a sort of barn; but it was surrounded by neat Caffre huts and gardens full of produce.

On the arrival of the caravan, Mr. S., the missionary, came out to meet the travelers, and to welcome them. He had been informed that they would call at the station, and bring some articles which had been sent for. It hardly need be said that, meeting at such a place, and in such a country, the parties soon became on intimate terms. Mr. S. offered them beds and accommodation in his house, but our travelers refused; they were well satisfied with their own;

and having unyoked their oxen, and turned them out to graze with those belonging to the station, they accepted the missionary's invitation to join his repast.

Alexander having stated the object of his expedition, requested the advice of Mr. S. as to his further proceedings, and asked him whether it would not be advisable to see the Caffre king, and make him a present. This Mr. S. strongly advised them to do; and to ask for a party of Caffres to accompany the caravan, which would not only insure them safety, but would prove in many respects very useful. All that would be necessary would be to find them in food and to promise them a present, if they conducted themselves well. "You are aware," continued he, "that Hinza's domain only extends as far as the Bashee or St. John's River, and you will have to proceed beyond that; but with some of the Caffre warriors you will have no difficulty, as the tribes further will not only fear your strength, but also the anger of Hinza, should they commit any depredation. But things, I regret to say, do not look very peaceable just now."

"Indeed! what is the quarrel, and with whom?"

"Hinza has quarreled with a powerful neighboring chief of the name of Voosani, who reigns over the Tambookie tribes, about some cattle, which are the grand cause of quarrels in these countries, and both parties are preparing for war. But whether it will take place is doubtful, as they are both threatened with a more powerful enemy, and may probably be compelled to unite, in order to defend themselves."

"And who may that be?"

"Quetoo, the chief of the Amaquibi, is in arms with a large force, and threatens the other tribes to the northward of us; if he conquers them, he will certainly come down here. He was formerly one of Chaka's generals, and is, like him, renowned for slaughter. At present he is too far to the northward to interfere with you, but I should advise you to lose no time in effecting your mission; for should he advance, you will be compelled to retreat immediately. I had better send to Hinza to-morrow to let him know that strangers have come and wish to see him, that they may make him a present. That notice will bring him fast enough; not but that he well knows you are here, and has known that you have been in his country long ago."

"It will be as well, after the information you have given us," said Mr. Swinton.

"What is your opinion of the Caffres, Mr. S., now that you have resided so long with them?"

"They are, for heathens, a fine nation, – bold, frank, and, if any thing is confided to them, scrupulously honest; but cattle-stealing is certainly not considered a crime among them, although it is punished as one. Speaking as a minister of the Gospel, I should say they are the most difficult nation to have any thing to do with that it ever has been my lot to visit. They have no religion whatever; they have no idols; and no idea of the existence of a God. When I have talked to them about God, their reply is, 'Where is he? show him to me.'"

"But have they no superstitions?"

"They believe in necromancy, and have their conjurers, who do much harm, and are our chief opponents, as we weaken their influence, and consequently their profits. If cattle are stolen, they are referred to. If a chief is sick, they are sent for to know who has bewitched him; they must of course mention some innocent person, who is sacrificed immediately. If the country is parched from want of rain, which it so frequently is, then the conjurers are in great demand: they are sent for to produce rain. If, after all their pretended mysteries, the rain does not fall so as to save their reputation, they give some plausible reason, generally ending, however, in the sacrifice of some innocent individual; and thus they go on, making excuses after excuses until the rain does fall, and they obtain all the credit of it. I need hardly say that these people are our greatest enemies."

"Are you satisfied with the success which you have had?"

"Yes, I am, when I consider the difficulty to be surmounted. Nothing but the Divine assistance could have produced such effects as have already taken place. The chiefs are to a man opposed to us."

"Why so?"

"Because Christianity strikes at the root of their sensuality; it was the same when it was first preached by our Divine Master. The riches of a Caffre consist not only in his cattle, but in the number of his wives, who are all his slaves. To tell them that polygamy is unlawful and wrong, is therefore almost as much as to tell them that it is not right to hold a large herd of cattle; and as the chiefs are of course the opulent of the nation, they oppose us. You observe in Caffreland, as elsewhere, it is 'hard for a rich man to enter into the kingdom of heaven.' I have asked the chiefs why they will not come to church, and their reply has been, 'The great word is calculated to lessen our pleasures and diminish the number of our wives; to this we can never consent,'"

"But still you say you have made some progress."

"If I have, let it be ascribed to the Lord,

and not to me and my otherwise useless endeavors; it must be His doing; and without His aid and assistance, the difficulties would have been insurmountable. It is for me only to bear in mind the scriptural injunction, 'In the morning sow thy seed, and in the evening withhold not thy hand; for thou knowest not whether shall prosper, either this or that, or whether they both shall be alike good.'"

"But have they no idea whatever of a Supreme Being, either bad or good? have they no idea, as some of the African tribes have, of the devil?"

"None; and in their language they have no word to express the idea of the Deity; they swear by their kings of former days as great chiefs, but no more. Now if they had any religion whatever, you might, by pointing out to them the falsity and absurdity of that religion, and putting it in juxtaposition with revealed Truth, have some hold upon their minds; but we have not even that advantage."

"But can not you make an impression upon their minds by referring to the wonders of nature, – by asking them who made the sun and stars? Surely they might be induced to reflect by such a method."

"I have tried it a hundred times, and they have laughed at me for my fables, as they have termed them. One of the chiefs told me to hold my tongue, that his people might not think me mad. The Scriptures, indeed, teach us that, without the aid of direct revelation, men are also without excuse if they fail to attain to a certain knowledge of the Deity, – 'even his eternal power and God-head,' – by a devout contemplation of the visible world, which with all its wonders is spread out before them as an open volume. But beyond this, all knowledge of the origin or manner of creation is derived, not from the deductions of human reasoning, but from the Divine testimony; for it is expressly said, 'Through faith we understand that the worlds were made by the word of God.'"

"Nevertheless you must admit that, among the civilized nations of Europe, many who deny revelation, and treat the

Bible as a fable, acknowledge that the world must have been made by a Supreme Power."

"My dear sir, many affect to deny the truth of revelation out of pride and folly, who still in their consciences can not but believe it. Here, there being no belief in a Deity, they will not be persuaded that the world was made by one. Indeed, we have much to contend with, and perhaps one of the greatest difficulties is in the translation of the Scriptures. I sit down with an interpreter who can not read a single word, and with perhaps a most erroneous and imperfect knowledge of divine things. We open the sacred volume, and it is first translated into barbarous Dutch to the Caffre interpreter, who then has to tell us how that Dutch is to be put into the Caffre language. Now you may imagine what mistakes may arise. I have found out lately that I have been stating the very contrary to what I would have said. With this translation, I stand up to read a portion of the Word of God, for my interpreter can not read, and hence any slight defect or change in a syllable may give altogether a different sense from what I desire to inculcate."

"That must indeed be a great difficulty, and require a long residence and full acquaintance with the language to overcome."

"And even then not overcome, for the language has no words to express abstract ideas; but the Lord works after His own way, and at His own season."

"You do not then despair of success?"

"God forbid; I should be indeed a most unworthy servant of our Divine Master, if I so far distrusted His power. No; much good has been already done, as you will perceive when we meet to-morrow to perform Divine service; but there is much more to do, and, with His blessing, will in His own good time be perfected; but I have duties to attend to which call me away for the present; I shall therefore wish you good-night. At all events, the Mission has had one good effect: you are perfectly safe from Caffre violence and Caffre robbery. This homage is paid to it even by their kings and chiefs."

"I will say, that if we are only to judge by the little we have seen, the Mission appears to have done good," observed the Major. "In the first place, we are no longer persecuted, as we have been during our journey, for presents; and, as you may observe, many of the Caffres about are clothed in European fashions, and those who have nothing but their national undress, I may call it, wear it as decently as they can."

"I made the same observation," said Alexander. "I am most anxious for to-morrow, as I wish to see how the Caffres behave; and really, when you consider all the difficulties which Mr. S. has mentioned, it is wonderful that he and those who have embraced the same calling should persevere as they do."

"My dear Wilmot," replied Mr. Swinton, "a missionary, even of the most humble class, is a person of no ordinary mind; he does not rely upon himself or upon his own exertions, – he relies not upon others, or upon the assistance of this world; if he did, he would, as you say, soon abandon his task in despair. No; he is supported, he is encouraged, he is pressed on by faith – faith in Him who never deserts those who trust and believe in Him; he knows that, if it is His pleasure, the task will be easy, but at the same time that it must be at His own good time. Convinced of this, supported by this, encouraged by this, and venturing his life for this, he toils on, in full assurance that if he fails another is to succeed, – that if he becomes a martyr, his blood will moisten the arid soil from which the future seed will spring. A missionary may be low in birth, low in education, as many are; but he must be a man of exalted mind, – what in any other pursuit we might term an enthusiast; and in this spreading of the Divine word, he merits respect for his fervor, his courage, and self-devotion; his willingness, if the Lord should so think fit, to accept the crown of martyrdom."

"You are right, Swinton; nothing but what you have described could impel a man to pass a life of privation and danger among a savage race – leaving all, and following his Master in the true apostolic sense. Well, they will have their reward."

The Mission

"Yes, in heaven, Wilmot; not on earth," replied Swinton.

The next day, being the Sabbath, with the assistance of Mahomed, who was valet as well as cook to the whole party, they divested themselves of their beards, which had not been touched for many days, and dressed themselves in more suitable apparel than their usual hunting costume, – a respect paid to the Sabbath by even the most worldly and most indifferent on religious points. The bell of the Mission church was tolled, and the natives were seen coming from all directions. Our party went in, and found Mr. S. already there, and that seats had been provided for them. The numbers of natives who were assembled in the church were about 200, but many more were at the windows, and sitting by the open door.

Many of them were clothed in some sort of European apparel; those who were not, drew their krosses close round them, so as to appear more covered. A hymn in the Caffre language was first sung, and then prayers, after which the Litany and responses; the

Commandments were repeated in the same language. Mr. S. then read a chapter in the Bible, and explained it to the assembly. Profound silence and quiet attention generally prevailed, although in some few instances there was mockery from those outside. Mr. S. gave the blessing, and the service was ended.

"You have already done much," observed Mr. Swinton. "I could hardly have believed that a concourse of savages could have been so attentive, and have behaved with such decorum."

"It certainly is the most difficult point gained, – to command their attention, I mean," replied Mr. S.; "after that, time and patience, with the assistance of God, will effect the rest."

"Do you think that there are many who, if I may use the term, feel their religion?"

"Yes, many; and prove it by traveling about and sowing the seed. There are many who not only are qualified so to do, but are incessantly laboring to bring their countrymen to God."

"That must be very satisfactory to you."

"It is; but what am I, and the few who labor with me, to the thousands and thousands who are here in darkness and require our aid? There are now but three missions in all Caffreland; and there is full employment for two hundred, if they could be established. But you must excuse me, I have to catechise the children, who are my most promising pupils. We will meet again in the evening, for I have to preach at a neighboring village. Strange to say, many who doubt and waver will listen to me there; but they appear to think that there is some witchcraft in the Mission church, or else are afraid to acknowledge to their companions that they have been inside of it."

The missionary then left them, and Alexander observed –

"I don't know how you feel? but I assure you it has been a great pleasure to me to have found myself in this humble church, and hearing Divine service in this wild country."

Both Swinton and Major Henderson

expressed the same opinion.

"I am not afraid of being laughed at," continued Alexander, "when I tell you that I think it most important, wherever we may be during our travels, to keep the Sabbath holy, by rest and reading the service."

"With pleasure, as far as I am concerned, and I thank you for the proposal," replied Swinton.

"And I am equally pleased that you have proposed it, Wilmot," said Major Henderson; "even we may be of service to the good cause, if, as we pass through the land, the natives perceive that we respect the Sabbath as the missionary has requested them to do. We are white men, and considered by them as superior; our example, therefore, may do good."

The evening was passed away very agreeably with Mr. S., who was inexhaustible in his anecdotes of the Caffres. He informed them that Hinza intended to call the next morning to receive his presents, and that he would be interpreter for them if they wished it.

The Mission

Alexander, having thanked the missionary, said, "I think you mentioned, sir, that some of your brother missionaries have their wives with them. Since you have told me so much of the precarious tenure by which you hold your ground here, and I may add your lives, I think that the wives of the missionaries must have even more to encounter than their husbands."

"You are right, sir," replied the missionary; "there is no situation so trying, so perilous, and I may say, so weary to the mind and body, as that of a female missionary. She has to encounter the same perils and the same hardships as her husband, without having the strength of our sex to support them; and what is more painful than all, she is often left alone in the Mission-house, while her husband, who has left her, is proceeding on his duty, at the hourly peril of his life. There she is alone, and compelled to listen to all the reports and falsehoods which are circulated; at one moment she is told that her husband has been murdered; at another, that he is still alive. She has no means of hearing from him, as there is no communication throughout the country; thus is she left in this horrible state of suspense and anxiety, perhaps for many weeks. I have a letter from a brother missionary which is in my writing-desk, wherein the case in point is well portrayed; I will get it, and read that portion to you." Mr. S. went to the other end of the room, and came back with a letter, from which he read as follows: –

"Having been detained among those distant tribes for nearly two months, report upon report had been circulated that the interpreters and guides, as well as myself, had all been murdered. On my arrival within forty miles of the station, I was informed that all doubt upon the subject had been removed by a party of natives who had passed the Mission station, and who pretended an acquaintance with all the particulars of the massacre. We had been traveling the whole day, and night had come on; I was most anxious to proceed, that I might relieve the mind of my dear wife, but the earnest remonstrances of my little party, who represented it as certain death to all of us to cross the plains, which were infested with lions and other savage beasts who were prowling in every direction, at length induced me to wait till the next day. But scarcely had day begun to dawn when I sallied forth, without either arms or guide, except a pocket compass, leaving my fellow-travelers to bring on the wagon as soon as they should arouse from their slumbers. This impatience had, however, well-nigh cost me my life; for having to wade through many miles of deep sand with a vertical sun over my head, I had not accomplished half the journey before my strength began to fail, and an indescribable thirst was induced. Nevertheless, I reached the Mission in safety, and with truly grateful feelings to the Preserver of men. A few minutes prior to my arrival, the wife of one of my brother missionaries, little imagining that I was at hand and alive, had entered our dwelling, to apprise my wife of the latest intelligence, confirming all that had been said before respecting my fate, and to comfort her under the distressing dispensation. At this affecting crisis, while both were standing in the center of the room, the one relating, the other weeping, I opened the door, bathed in perspiration, covered with dust, and in a state of complete exhaustion. 'Oh, dear!' cried our friend; 'is it he – or is it his spirit?' I must, my dear sir, leave to your imagination the scene that followed."

"Yes, sir," said Mr. S., folding up the letter, "a missionary's wife, who follows him into such scenes and such perils and privations, does, indeed, 'cleave to her husband.'"

"Indeed she does," replied Mr. Swinton; "but we will tax you no longer, my dear sir. Good-night."

CHAPTER XII

On the following day, a little before noon, loud shouts and men dancing and calling out the titles of the king of the Caffres announced his approach. These men were a sort of heralds, who invariably preceded him on a visit of ceremony. A band of warriors armed with their assaguays and shields, next made their appearance, and then Hinza, accompanied by fifty of his chief councilors: with the exception of their long krosses of beast-skins thrown over their shoulders, they were all naked, and each daubed with grease and red ocher. As soon as they arrived in front of the Mission-house, they sat down in a circle on each side of the Caffre king, who was treated with marked respect by all, and by the common people in particular, who assembled on his presence. Every one who happened to pass by gave what was termed a 'salute' of honor to the king, who did not appear to consider that it required any acknowledgment on his part.

Our travelers, accompanied by the

missionary, advanced into the circle, and saluted his majesty. Mr. S. then explained the object of their journey, and their wish that a small party of the king's warriors should accompany them on their expedition. As soon as the speech was ended, a few pounds of colored beads, a roll of tobacco, two pounds of snuff, and some yards of scarlet cloth, were laid before his majesty as a present. Hinza nodded his head with approval when the articles were spread before him, and then turned to his councilors, with whom he whispered some time, and then he replied "that the strange white men should pass through his country without fear, that his warriors should accompany them as far as they wished to go; but," he added, "do the strangers know that there is disorder in the country beyond?"

Mr. S. replied that they did, and were anxious to go, and return as soon as possible, on that account.

Hinza replied, "It is well; if there is danger, my warriors will let them know – if it is necessary, they will fight for them – if the enemy is too strong, the white men must return."

Hinza then ordered some of his councilors to take charge of the presents, and inquired of Mr. S. how many warriors they wished to have, and when they wished to go.

The reply was, that fifty warriors would be sufficient, and that they wished to depart on the following morning. "It is well," replied Hinza; "fifty warriors are enough, for my men eat a great deal – they shall be ready."

The council then broke up, and the king, having shaken hands with our travelers, departed with his train: toward the evening an old cow was sent to them as a present from his majesty. The Hottentots soon cut it up and devoured it. Every thing was now arranged for their immediate departure.

The next morning, at break of day, the band of Caffre warriors were all in readiness, each with his shield and three assaguays in his hand. They were all fine, tall young men, from twenty to thirty years of age. Alexander desired Mr. S. to tell them that, if they behaved well and were faithful, they should every one receive a present when they were dismissed; a notification which appeared to give general satisfaction. The oxen had already been yoked, and taking leave of the worthy missionary, our travelers mounted their horses and resumed their journey. For the whole day they proceeded along the banks of the Kae River, which ran its course through alternate glens and hills clothed with fine timber; and as they were on an eminence, looking down upon the river, the head Caffre warrior, who had, with the others, hung up his shield at the side of the wagon, and now walked by our travelers with his assaguay in his hand, pointed out to them, as the sun was setting behind a hill, two or three large black masses on the further bank of the river.

"What are they, and what does he say?"

"Sea-cows," replied the interpreter.

"*Hippopotami!* We must have a shot at them, Wilmot," cried the Major.

"To be sure; tell them we will stop and kill one if we can," said Wilmot to the interpreter.

"We shall want one to feed our army," said Swinton laughing, "or our sheep will soon be devoured."

The Caffres were all immediately in motion, running down to the bank of the river, about a quarter of a mile distant; they swam across, and there remained waiting till our travelers should give the word.

The animals lay on a muddy bank, at a turn of the river, like so many swine asleep, some of them out, and some partly in and partly out of the water. As they were huddled together, they looked more like masses of black rock than any thing else. Two lay considerably apart from the others, and it was toward these two that the Caffres, who had crossed the river, crept until they were in the high reeds, but a few yards from them. Henderson and Wilmot, with some of the Hottentots, descended the ravine on their side of the river, opposite to where the animals lay, and as soon as they were on the bank, being then within one hundred yards of them, they leveled and fired. At the report, all the animals started up from their beds as if astonished at the noise, which they had not been accustomed to. Three or four instantly plunged into the deep water, but the others, apparently half asleep, stood for a few seconds, as if not knowing what course to take: two of them were evidently wounded, as they rushed into the water; for they did not remain below, but rose to the surface immediately, as if in great agony. They appeared anxious to get out of the water altogether, and tried so to do, but fearing the people on the river's bank, they darted in again. In the mean time, at the first report of the guns, the two which lay apart from the others with their heads toward the river, as soon as they rose on their legs, were pierced with several assaguays by the concealed Caffres, and plunged into the water with the spears remaining in their bodies. These also rose, and floundered like the others; and as their heads appeared above, they were met with the unerring rifle of the Major and whole volleys from Wilmot and the Hottentots, till, exhausted from loss of blood, they floated dead upon the surface.

The Caffres waited till the bodies had

been borne some hundred yards down the stream, that they might not be attacked when in the water by the remainder of the herd, and then swam off, and pushed the bodies on shore. This was a very seasonable supply of provisions for so large a band of people; but those who belonged to the caravan were not the only parties who benefited: all the Caffres of the surrounding hamlets hastened to the river, and carried off large quantities of the flesh of the animals; there was, however, more than enough for all, and for the wolves and hyenas after they had taken what they chose. It was so late before the animals were cut up, that they decided upon remaining where they were that night; for now that they had the Caffre warriors with them, they had no fear as to losing their oxen, the king having stated that his men should be responsible for them.

Large fires were lighted, and the Caffres and Hottentots, all mingled together, were busy roasting, boiling, and frying the flesh of the hippopotamus, and eating it as fast as it was cooked, so that they were completely gorged before they lay down to sleep; Wilmot had also given them a ration of tobacco each, which had added considerably to the delight of the feast.

"It is not bad eating by any means," said the Major, as they were at supper.

"No; it is something like old veal," replied Swinton. "Now, what is Omrah about? He is after some mischief, by the way he creeps along."

"A monkey is a fool to that boy," observed the Major, "and he appears to know how to imitate every animal he has ever heard."

"Did you hear the dance he led some of the Hottentots on Sunday evening, when we were at the Mission?"

"No; what was that?"

"Bremen told me of it; I thought he would have died with laughing. You are aware that there is a species of bird here which they call the honey-bird, – by naturalists, the *Cuculus indicator*; do you not remember I showed you a specimen which I was preserving?"

"You have showed us so many specimens, that I really forget."

"Well, I should have given you at the same time the natural history of the bird. It is very partial to honey, upon which it lives as much as it can; but as the bees make their hives in the trunks of old decayed trees, and the hole they enter by is very small, the bird can not obtain it without assistance. Its instinct induces it to call in the aid of man, which it does by a peculiar note, like cher-cher-cher, by which it gives notice that it has found out a beehive. The natives of Africa well know this, and as soon as the bird flies close to them, giving out this sound, they follow it; the bird leads them on, perching every now and then, to enable them to keep up with it, until it arrives at the tree, over which it flutters without making any more noise."

"How very curious!"

"Little Bushman knows this as well as the Hottentots, and hearing that they were going out in search of honey he went before them into the wood, concealing himself, and imitating the note of the bird so exactly, that the Hottentots went on following it for several miles, wondering how it was that the bird should lead them such a distance, but unwilling to give up the pursuit. About sunset, he had brought them back to the very edge of the wood from whence they had started, when he showed himself about one hundred yards ahead of them, dancing, capering, and tumbling so like Begum, that they thought it was her before them, and not him. He gained the caravan again without their knowing who played them the trick; but he told Swanevelt, who speaks his language, and Swanevelt told Bremen."

"Capital!" said the Major; "well, he is after some trick now, depend upon it."

"He has a great talent for drawing," observed Alexander.

"A very great one; I have given him a pencil and occasionally a piece of paper, and he draws all the birds, so that I can recognize them; but you must know that all the Bushmen have that talent, and that their caves are full of the sketches of all sorts of animals, remarkably characteristic. The organ of imitation is very strongly developed in the Bushmen, which accounts for their talents as draftsmen, and Omrah's remarkable imitative powers."

"Do you then believe in phrenology, Swinton!" said Alexander.

"I neither believe nor disbelieve in that and many more modern discoveries of the same kind; I do not think it right to reject them or to give blind credence. Not a day passes but some discovery excites our wonder and admiration, and points out to us how little we do know. The great fault is, that when people have made a discovery to a certain extent, they build upon it, as if all their premises were correct; whereas, they have, in fact, only obtained a mere glimmering to light them to a path which may some future day lead to knowledge. That the general principles of phrenology are correct maybe fairly assumed, from the examination of the skulls of men and animals, and of different men; but I give no credence to all the divisions and subdivisions which have, in my opinion, been most presumptuously marked out by those who profess, and of course fully believe, the full extent of these supposed discoveries."

"And mesmerism?" said Alexander.

"I make the same reply; there is *something* in it, that is certain, but nothing yet sufficiently known to warrant any specific conclusion to be drawn."

"There is a great deal of humbug in it," said the Major.

"So there is in all sciences; when truth fails them and they are at fault, they fill up the hiatus with supposition; which is, as you term it, humbug."

"Well, I vote that we return to our wagons; every body appears fast asleep except us three."

Such was not, however, the case; for they had not been half an hour on their mattresses, before they were awakened by loud cries of "help," which made them seize the irguns and jump out of the wagons without waiting for their clothes.

The Hottentots and Caffres were so full of hippopotamus flesh, that the noise did not awake but a small portion of them, and these only turned round and stared about without getting up, with the exception of Bremen, who was on his feet and, with his gun in his hand, running in the direction of the cries. He was followed by our travelers, and they soon came up with the object of their search, which proved to be no other than Big Adam, the Hottentot; and as soon as they perceived his condition, which they could do by the light of the fires still burning, they all burst out laughing so excessively that they could not help him.

That it was the work of little Omrah there was no doubt, for Big Adam had not forgotten the former trick the boy had played him, and had more than once, when he caught the boy, given him a good cuffing. Big Adam was on the ground, dragged away by two of the largest dogs. Omrah had taken the bones he could find with most flesh upon them belonging to the hippopotamus, and had tied them with leathern thongs to the great toes of Big Adam as he lay snoring after his unusual repast. He had then waited till all were asleep, and had let loose the two largest dogs, which were always tied with the others under the wagons, and not over-fed, to make them more watchful.

The dogs had prowled about for food, and had fallen in with these large bones, which they immediately seized, and were dragging away, that they might make their repast without interruption; but in attempting to drag away the bones, they had dragged Big Adam some yards by his great toes, and the pain and fright – for the Hottentot thought they were hyenas or wolves – had caused him thus to scream for help. Bremen divided the thongs with his knife, and the dogs ran off growling with the bones, and Adam stood again upon his feet, still so much terrified as not to be able to comprehend the trick which had been played him. Our travelers, having indulged their mirth, retired once more to their resting-places. The Major found

Omrah and Begum both in their corners of the wagon, the former pretending to be fast asleep, while the latter was chattering and swearing at the unusual disturbance.

At daylight next morning they resumed their journey. Big Adam walked rather stiff, and looked very sulky. Omrah had perched himself on a tilt of the baggage-wagon with Begum, and was quite out of the Hottentot's reach; for Bremen had told the others what had happened, and there had been a general laugh against Big Adam, who vowed vengeance against little Omrah. The country was now very beautiful and fertile, and the Caffre hamlets were to be seen in all directions. Except visits from the Caffres, who behaved with great decorum when they perceived that the caravan was escorted by the king's warriors, and who supplied them nearly every day with a bullock for the use of the people, no adventure occurred for four days, when they crossed the Bashee or St. John's River, to which the territories of Hinza extended; but although the tribes beyond did not acknowledge his authority, they respected the large force of the caravan, and were much pleased at receiving small presents of tobacco and snuff.

Milk, in baskets, was constantly brought in by the women; for the Caffres weave baskets of so close a texture, that they hold any liquid, and are the only utensil used for that purpose. At the Bashee River, after they had passed the ford, they remained one day to hunt the hippopotami, and were successful; only Major Henderson, who was not content to hunt during the day, but went out at night, had a narrow escape. He was in one of the paths, and had wounded a female, and was standing, watching the rising to the surface of the wounded animal, for it was bright moonlight, when the male, which happened to be feeding on the bank above, hearing the cry of the female, rushed right down the path upon the Major. Fortunately for him, the huge carcass of the animal gave it such an ungovernable degree of velocity, as to prevent it turning to the right hand or left. It passed within a yard of the Major, sweeping the bushes and underwood, so as to throw him down as it passed. The Major got up again, it may be truly said, more frightened than hurt; but at all events he had had enough of hippopotamus-hunting for that night, for he recovered his gun, and walked back to the wagon, thanking Heaven for his providential escape.

The next morning, Swanevelt and Bremen went down the banks of the river, and discovered the body of the hippopotamus, which they dragged on shore, and, returning to the wagons, sent the Caffres to cut it up; but before the Caffres belonging to the caravan could arrive there, they found that the work had been done for them by the natives, and that nothing was left but the bones of the animal; but this is always considered fair in the Caffre-land; every one helps himself when an elephant or other large animal is killed, although he may have had no hand in its destruction. The number of elephant-paths now showed them that they were surrounded by these animals, and the Caffres of the country said that there were large herds close to them.

It was therefore proposed by the Major, that they should have a grand elephant-hunt, at which all the Caffres of their own party and the natives of the country should assist. This proposal was joyfully received by all, especially the natives, who were delighted at such an opportunity of having the assistance of the white men's guns; and the next day was appointed for the sport. By the advice of the natives, the caravan proceeded some miles down to the eastward, to the borders of a very thick forest, where they stated that the elephants were to be found.

They arrived at the spot in the afternoon, and every one was busy in making preparations for the following day. The Hottentots, who had been used to the sport, told long stories to those who had not, and, among the rest, Big Adam spoke much of his prowess and dexterity. Uncommonly large fires were lighted that night, for fear that the elephants should break into the camp. All night their cries were to be heard in the forest, and occasionally the breaking of the branches of the trees proved that they were close to the caravan. Begum, who was particularly alive to danger, crept to Major Henderson's bed, and would remain there all night, although he several times tried to drive her away. Notwithstanding continued alarms, the caravan was, however, unmolested.

CHAPTER XIII

At daylight the following morning, there was a large concourse of Caffres in the camp, all waiting till our travelers were ready for the sport. Having made a hasty breakfast, they, by the advice of the Caffres, did not mount their horses, but started on foot, as the Caffres stated that the elephants were on the side of the hill. Ascending by an elephant-path, in less than half an hour they arrived at the top of the hill, when a grand and magnificent panorama was spread before them. From the crown of the hill they looked down upon a valley studded with clumps of trees, which divided the cleared ground, and the whole face of the valley was covered with elephants. There could not have been less than nine hundred at one time within the scope of their vision.

Every height, every green knoll, was dotted with groups of six or seven, some of their vast bodies partly concealed by the trees upon which they were browsing, others walking in the open plain, bearing in their trunks a long branch of a tree, with which they evidently protected themselves from the flies. The huge bodies of the animals, with the corresponding magnitude of the large timber-trees which surrounded them, gave an idea of nature on her grandest scale.

After a few minutes' survey, they turned to the party who were collected behind them, and gave notice that they were to commence immediately. The head men of the Caffres gave their orders, and the bands of natives moved silently away in every direction, checking any noise from the dogs, which they had brought with them in numerous packs. Our travelers were to leeward of the herd on the hill where they stood, and as it was the intention of the natives to drive the animals toward them, the Caffre warriors as well as the Hottentots all took up positions on the hill ready to attack the animals as they were driven that way.

About an hour passed away, when the signal was given by some of the native Caffres, who had gained the side of the valley to westward of the elephants.

Perched up at various high spots, they shouted with stentorian lungs, and their shouts were answered by the rest of the Caffres on every side of the valley, so that the elephants found themselves encompassed on all sides, except on that where the hill rose from the valley. As the Caffres closed in, their shouts reverberating from the rocks, and mixed up with the savage howlings of the dogs, became tremendous; and the elephants, alarmed, started first to one side of the valley, then to the other, hastily retreating from the clamor immediately raised as they approached, shaking their long ears and trumpeting loudly, as with uplifted trunks they trotted to and fro.

At last, finding no other avenue of escape, the herd commenced the ascent of the hill, cracking the branches and boughs, and rolling the loose stones down into the valleys, as they made their ascent, and now adding their own horrid shrieks to the din which had been previously created. On they came, bearing every thing down before them, carrying havoc in their rage to such an extent, that the forest appeared to bow down before them; while large masses

The Mission

of loose rock leaped and bounded and thundered down into the valley, raising clouds of dust in their passage.

"This is tremendously grand," whispered Alexander to the Major.

"It is most awfully so; I would not have missed the sight for any thing; but here they come – look at that tall tree borne down by the weight of the whole mass."

"See the great bull leader," said Swinton; "let us all fire upon him – what a monster!"

"Look out," said the Major, whose rifle was discharged as he spoke, and was quickly followed by those of Alexander and Swinton.

"He's down; be quick and load again. Omrah, give me the other rifle."

"Take care! take care!" was how cried on all sides, for the fall of the leading elephant and the volleys of musketry from the Hottentots had so frightened the herd, that they had begun to separate and break off two or three together, or singly in every direction.

The shrieks and trumpetings, and the crashing of the boughs so near to them, were now deafening; and the danger was equally great. The Major had but just leveled his other rifle when the dense foliage close to him opened as if by magic, and the head of a large female presented itself within four yards of him.

Fortunately, the Major was a man of great nerve, and his rifle brought her down at his feet, when so near to him that he was compelled to leap away out of the reach of her trunk, for she was not yet dead. Another smaller elephant followed so close, that it tumbled over the carcass of the first, and was shot by Alexander as it was recovering its legs.

"Back, sirs, or you will be killed," cried Bremen, running to them; "this way – the whole herd is coming right upon you." They ran for their lives, following the Hottentot, who brought them to a high rock which the elephants could not climb, and where they were safe.

They had hardly gained it when the mass came forward in a cloud of dust, and with a noise almost inconceivable, scrambling and rolling to and fro as they passed on in a close-wedged body. Many were wounded and tottering, and as they were left behind, the Caffres, naked, with their assaguays in their hands, leaping forward and hiding, as required, running with the greatest activity close up to the rear of the animals, either pierced them with their assaguays, or hamstrung them with their sharp-cutting weapons, crying out in their own tongue to the elephants, "Great captain! don't kill us – don't tread upon us, mighty chief!" – supplicating, strangely enough, the mercy of those to whom they were showing none. As it was almost impossible to fire without a chance of hitting a Caffre, our travelers contented themselves with looking on, till the whole herd had passed by, and had disappeared in the jungle below.

"They have gone right in the direction of the wagons," said Swinton.

"Yes, sir," replied the Hottentot, Bremen; "but we must not interfere with them any more; they are now so scattered in the jungle, that it would be dangerous. We must let them go away as fast as they can."

They remained for a few minutes more, till every elephant and Caffre had disappeared, and then went back cautiously to the spot from whence they had first fired, and where they had such a fine prospect of the valley. Not an elephant was to be seen in it; nothing but the ravages which the herd had committed upon the trees, many of which, of a very large size, had been borne to the ground by the enormous strength of these animals. They then proceeded to the spot where the great bull elephant had fallen by the rifle of Major Henderson.

They found that the ball had entered just under the eye. It was a monster that must have stood sixteen feet high by Bremen's calculation, and it had two very fine tusks. While they were standing by the carcass of the animal, the armed Hottentots returned from the pursuit, and stated that seven elephants had been dispatched, and others were so wounded that they could not live. They now set to work to take the teeth out of the animal, and were very busy, when a Hottentot came running up, and reported that the herd of elephants in their retreat had dashed through the camp, and done a good deal of mischief; that a male elephant had charged the wagon of Major Henderson, and had forced his tusk through the side; that the tusk had pierced one of the casks of liquor, which was running out, although not very fast, and that the wagon must be unloaded to get out the cask and save the rest of the liquor.

Several Hottentots immediately hurried back with him to help in unloading the wagon, and by degrees they all slipped away except Bremen, Swanevelt, who was cutting out the tusks, and Omrah, who remained perched upon the huge carcass of the animal, imitating the trumpeting and motions of the elephant, and playing all sorts of antics. A party of Caffres soon afterward came up and commenced cutting up the carcass, and then our travelers walked away in the direction of the camp, to ascertain what mischief had been done.

On their return, which, as they stopped

occasionally to examine the other animals that had fallen, must have taken an hour, they found that the Hottentots had not commenced unloading the wagon; although they had put tubs to catch the running liquor, of which they had taken so large a quantity that some were staggering about, and the rest lying down in a state of senseless intoxication.

"I thought they were very officious in going back to assist," observed the Major; "a pretty mess we should be in, if we were in an enemy's country, and without our Caffre guard."

"Yes, indeed," replied Alexander, turning over the tub of liquor, and spilling it on the ground, much to the sorrow of the Hottentots who were not yet insensible: "however, we will now let the cask run out, and watch that they get no more."

As the Caffres were busy with the carcasses of the elephants, and most of the Hottentots dead drunk, it was useless to think of proceeding until the following day. Indeed, the oxen and horses were all scattered in every direction by the elephants breaking into the caravan, and it would be necessary to collect them, which would require some time. Our travelers, therefore, gave up the idea of proceeding further that day, and taking their guns, walked on to the forest, in the direction where most of the elephants killed had fallen. They passed by three carcasses, upon which the Caffres were busily employed, and then they came to a fourth, when a sight presented itself which quite moved their sympathy. It was the carcass of a full-grown female, and close to it was an elephant calf, about three feet and a half high, standing by the side of its dead mother.

The poor little animal ran round and round the body with every demonstration of grief, piping sorrowfully, and trying in vain to raise it up with its tiny trunk. When our travelers arrived, it ran up to them, entwining its little proboscis round their legs, and showing its delight at finding somebody. On the trees round the carcass were perched a number of vultures, waiting to make a meal of the remains, as soon as the hunters had cut it up, for their beaks could not penetrate the tough hide. Our travelers remained there for more than an hour, watching the motions and playing with the young elephant, which made several attempts to induce its prostrate mother to take notice of it. Finding, however, that all its efforts were ineffectual, when our travelers quitted the spot to go back, it voluntarily followed them to the caravans, where it remained, probably quite as much astonished to find all the Hottentots lying about as insensible as its mother.

It may be as well here to observe, that the little animal did not live beyond a very few days after, from want of its necessary food.

In the evening, Bremen and Swanevelt returned with tusks of the bull elephant, which were very large, and the Caffre warriors also came in; the other Caffres belonging to the country were too busy eating for the present. The chief of the Caffre warriors brought in the tufts of the other elephant's tails and the teeth, and the men were loaded with the flesh.

As soon as the Caffres found that the oxen and horses had been frightened away, and perceived that the Hottentots were not in a situation to go after them, they threw down their meat and went in pursuit. Before dark the cattle were all brought back; the fires were lighted, and the Caffres did not give over their repast until near midnight.

Our travelers did not think it advisable, as the Hottentots were now no protection, to go to bed; they made up a large fire, and remained by it, talking over the adventures of the day. While they were conversing, Begum, who had been sitting by her master, showed signs of uneasiness, and at last clung round the Major with an evident strong fear.

"Why, what can be the matter with the Princess?" said the Major; "something has frightened her."

"Yes, that is evident; perhaps there is an elephant near; shall we waken Bremen and Swanevelt, who are close to us?"

Begum chattered, and her teeth also chattered with fear, as she clung closer and closer. Little Omrah, who was sitting by, looked very earnestly at the baboon, and at last touching the shoulder of Alexander to attract his attention, he first pointed to the baboon, imitating its fright, and then going on his hands and feet, imitated the motions and growl of an animal.

"I understand," cried the Major, seizing his gun; "the lad means that there is a lion near, and that is what frightens the baboon."

"Lion!" said the Major to Omrah.

But Omrah did not understand him; but pulling out his paper and pencil, in a second almost he drew the form of a lion.

"Clever little fellow! Wake them all, and get your guns ready," said the Major, starting on his legs; "it can't be far off; confound the monkey, she won't let go," continued he, tearing off Begum and throwing her away. Begum immediately scampered to the wagon and hid herself.

They had just awakened up the two Hottentots, when a roar was given so loud and tremendous, that it appeared like thunder, and was reverberated from the rocks opposite for some seconds.

No one but those who have been in the country, and have fallen in with this animal in its wild and savage state, can have any idea of the appalling effect of a lion's roar. What is heard in a menagerie is weak, and can give but a faint conception of it. In the darkness of the night it is almost impossible to tell from what quarter the sound proceeds; this arises from the habit which the animal has of placing his mouth close to the ground when he roars, so that his voice rolls over the earth, as it were like a breaker, and the sound is carried along with all its tremendous force. It is indeed a most awful note of preparation, and so thought Alexander, who had never heard one before.

The Caffres had wakened up at the noise, and our travelers and the Hottentots now fired their guns off in every direction to scare away the animal. Repeated discharges had this effect, and in the course of half an hour every thing was again quiet.

"Well," observed Alexander, "this is the first time that I ever heard the roar of a lion in its wild state; and I can assure you that I shall never forget it as long as I live."

"It is not the first time I have heard it," replied the Major; "but I must say, what with the darkness and stillness of the night, and the reverberation, I never heard it so awful before. But you, Swinton, who have traveled in the Namaqua-land, have, of course."

"Yes, I have, but very seldom."

"But it is rather singular that we have not heard the lion before this, is it not?" said Alexander.

"The lion is often near without giving you notice," replied Swinton; "but I do not think that there are many lions in the country we have traversed; it is too populous. On the other side of the mountains, if we return that way, we shall find them in plenty. Wherever the antelopes are in herds, wherever you find the wild horse, zebra, and giraffe, you will as certainly find the lion, for he preys upon them."

"I know very well, Swinton, that you are closely attentive to the peculiar habits of animals, and that they form a portion of your study. Have you much knowledge of the lion? and if so, suppose you tell us something about them."

"I have certainly studied the habits of the lion, and what I have gathered from my own observation and the information I received from others, I shall be most happy to communicate. The lion undoubtedly does not kill wantonly – of that I have had repeated instances. I recollect one which is rather remarkable, as it showed the sagacity of the noble brute. A man who belonged to one of the Mission stations, on his return home from a visit to his friends, took a circuitous route to pass a pool of water, at which he hoped to kill an antelope. The sun had risen to some height when he arrived there, and as he could not perceive any game, he laid his gun down on a low shelving rock, the back part of which was covered with some brushwood. He went down to the pool and had a hearty drink, returned to the rock, and after smoking his pipe, feeling

The Mission

weary, he lay down and fell fast asleep.

"In a short time, the excessive heat reflected from the rock awoke him, and opening his eyes he perceived a large lion about a yard from his feet, crouched down, with his eyes glaring on his face. For some minutes he remained motionless with fright, expecting every moment that he would be in the jaws of the monster; at last he recovered his presence of mind, and casting his eye toward his gun, moved his hand slowly toward it; upon which the lion raised up his head and gave a tremendous roar which induced him hastily to withdraw his hand. With this the lion appeared satisfied, and crouched with his head between his fore-paws as before. After a little while the man made another attempt to possess himself of his gun. The lion raised his head and gave another roar, and the man desisted; another and another attempt were at intervals made, but always with the same anger shown on the part of the lion."

"Why, the lion must have known what he wanted the gun for."

"Most certainly he did, and therefore would not allow the man to touch it. It is to be presumed that the sagacious creature had been fired at before; but you observe, that he did not wish to harm the man. He appeared to say – You are in my power; you shall not go away: you shall not take your musket to shoot me with, or I will tear you to pieces."

"It certainly was very curious. Pray how did it end?"

"Why the heat of the sun on the rock was so overpowering, that the man was in great agony; his naked feet were so burned, that he was compelled to keep moving them, placing one upon the other and changing them every minute. The day passed, and the night also; the lion never moved from the spot. The sun rose again, and the heat became so intense that the poor man's feet were past all feeling. At noon, on that day, the lion rose and walked to the pool, which was only a few yards distant, looking behind him every moment to see if the man moved; the man once more attempted to reach his gun, and the lion, perceiving it, turned in rage, and was on the point of springing upon him; the man withdrew his hand, and the beast was pacified."

"How very strange!"

"The animal went to the water and drank; it then returned and lay down at the same place as before, about a yard from the man's feet. Another night passed away, and the lion kept at his post. The next day, in the forenoon, the animal again went to the water, and while there looked as if he heard a noise in an opposite quarter, and then disappeared in the bushes.

"Perceiving this, the man made an effort, and seized his gun, but in attempting to rise he found it not in his power, as the strength of his ankles was gone. With his gun in his hand, he crept to the pool and drank, and, looking at his feet, he discovered that his toes had been quite roasted and the skin torn off as he crawled through the grass. He sat at the pool for a few minutes expecting the lion's return, and resolved to send the contents of his gun through his head; but the lion did not return, so the poor fellow tied his gun on his back and crawled away on his hands and knees as well as he could. He was quite exhausted, and could have proceeded no further, when providentially a person fell in with him and assisted him home; but he lost his toes, and was a cripple for life."

"What makes this story more remarkable is," observed the Major, "that the lion, as it is rational to suppose, must have been hungry after watching the man for sixty hours, even admitting that he had taken a meal but a short time before."

"I know many other curious and well-authenticated anecdotes about this noble animal," observed Swinton, "which I shall be happy to give you; but I must look at my memorandum-book, or I may not be quite correct in my story. One fact is very remarkable, and as I had it from Mr.----, the missionary, who stated that he had several times observed it himself, I have no hesitation in vouching for its correctness, the more so, as I did once perceive a similar fact myself; it is, that the fifth commandment is observed by lions – they honor their father and mother.

"If an old lion is in company with his children, as the natives call them, although they are in size equal to himself, or if a number of lions meet together in quest of game, there is always one who is admitted by them to be the oldest and ablest, and who leads. If the game is come up with, it is this one who creeps up to it, and seizes it, while the others lie crouched upon the grass; if the old lion is successful, which he generally is, he retires from his victim, and lies down to breathe himself and rest for perhaps a quarter of an hour. The others in the meantime draw round and lie down at a respectful distance, but never presume to go near the animal which the old lion has killed. As soon as the old lion considers himself sufficiently rested, he goes up to the prey and commences at the breast and stomach, and after eating a considerable portion he will take a second rest, none of the others presuming to move.

"Having made a second repast, he then retires; the other lions watch his motions, and all rush to the remainder of the carcass, which is soon devoured. I said that I witnessed an instance myself in corroboration of this statement, which I will now mention. I was sitting on a rock after collecting some plants, when below me I saw a young lion seize an antelope; he had his paw upon the dead animal, when the old lion came up, – upon which the young one immediately retired till his superior had dined first, and then came in for the remainder. Mercy on us! what is that?"

"I thought it was the lion again," said Alexander, "but it is thunder; we are about to have a storm."

"Yes, and a fierce one too," said the Major; "I am afraid that we must break up our party and retire under cover. We have some large drops of rain already."

A flash of lightning now dazzled them, and was followed by another, and an instantaneous peal of thunder.

"There is no mistake in this," said Swinton; "and I can tell you that we shall have it upon us in less than a minute, so I am for my wagon."

"At all events it will wash these Hottentots sober," observed the Major, as they all walked away to their separate wagons for shelter.

CHAPTER XIV

They had scarcely gained the wagons before the thunder and lightning became incessant, and so loud as to be deafening. It appeared as if they were in the very center of the contending elements, and the wind rose and blew with terrific force, while the rain poured down as if the flood-gates of heaven were indeed opened. The lightning was so vivid, that for the second that it lasted you could see the country round to the horizon almost as clear as day; the next moment all was terrific gloom accompanied by the stunning reports of the thunder, which caused every article in the wagons, and the wagons themselves, to vibrate from the concussion. A large tree, not fifty yards from the caravan, was struck by the lightning, and came down with an appalling crash. The Caffres had all roused up, and had sheltered themselves under the wagons.

The Hottentots had also begun to move, but had not yet recovered their senses – indeed, they were again stupefied by the clamor of the elements. The storm lasted about an hour, and then as suddenly cleared up again; the stars again made their appearance in the sky above, and the red tinge of the horizon announced the approach of daylight. When the storm ceased, our travelers, who had not taken off their clothes, came out from their shelter, and met each other by the side of the extinguished fire.

"Well," said Alexander, "I have been made wise on two points this night; I now know what an African storm is, and also the roar of an African lion. Have you heard if there is any mischief done, Bremen?" continued Alexander to the Hottentot, who stood by.

"No, sir; but I am afraid it will take us a long while to collect the cattle; they will be dispersed in all directions, and we may have lost some of them. It will soon be daylight, and then we must set off after them."

"Are those fellows quite sober now?"

"Yes, sir," replied Bremen, laughing; "water has washed all the liquor out of them."

"Well, you may tell them, as a punishment, I shall stop their tobacco for a week."

"Better not now, sir," said Bremen, thoughtfully; "the men don't like to go further up the country, and they may be troublesome."

"I think so too," said Swinton; "you must recollect that the cask was running out, and the temptation was too strong. I should overlook it this time. Give them a severe reprimand, and let them off."

"I believe it will be the best way," replied Alexander; "not that I fear their refusing to go on, for if they do, I will dismiss them, and go on with the Caffres; they dare not go back by themselves, that is certain."

"Sir," said Bremen, "that is very true; but you must not trust the Caffres too much — Caffres always try to get guns and ammunition: Caffre king, Hinza, very glad to get the wagons and what is in them: make him rich man, and powerful man, with so many guns. Caffre king will not rob in his own country, because he is afraid of the English; but if the wagon's robbed, and you are killed in this country, which is not his, then he make excuses, and say, 'I know nothing about it,' Say that their people do it, not his people."

"Bremen talks very sensibly," said the Major; "we must keep the Hottentots as a check to the Caffres, and the Caffres as a check to the Hottentots."

"That is our policy, depend upon it," replied Swinton.

"You are right, and we will do so; but the day is breaking; so? Bremen, collect the people together to search for the cattle; and, Omrah, tell Mahomed to come here."

"By the by, Swinton," said Major Henderson, "those elephants' tusks lying by the wagon remind me of a question I want to put to you: – In Ceylon, where I have often hunted the elephant, they have no tusks; and in India the tusks are not common, and in general very small. How do you account for this variety?"

"It has been observed before; and it is but a fair surmise, that Providence, ever attentive to the wants of the meanest animals, has furnished such large tusks to the African elephant for the necessity which requires them. In Ceylon there is plenty of grass, and an abundant supply of water all the year round; and further, in Ceylon, the elephant has no enemy to defend himself against. Here, in Africa, the rivers are periodical torrents, which dry up, and the only means which an elephant has of obtaining water during the dry season is to dig with his tusks into the bed of the river, till he finds the water, which he draws up with his trunk. Moreover, he has to defend himself against the rhinoceros, which is a formidable antagonist, and often victorious. He requires tusks also for his food in this country, for the elephant digs up the mimosa here with his tusks, that he may feed upon the succulent roots of the tree. Indeed, an elephant in Africa without his tusks could not well exist."

"Thank you for your explanation, which appears very satisfactory and conclusive; and now let us go to breakfast, for Mahomed, I perceive, is ready, and Omrah has displayed our teacups, and is very busy blowing into the spout of the teapot, a Bushman way of ascertaining if it is stopped up. However, we must not expect to make a London footman out of a 'Child of the Desert.'"

"Where is his adversary and antagonist, the valiant Big Adam?"

"He was among those who indulged in the liquor yesterday afternoon, and I believe was worse than any one of them. The little Bushman did not fail to take advantage of his defenseless state, and has been torturing him in every way he could imagine during the whole night. I saw him pouring water into the Hottentot's mouth as he lay on his back with his mouth wide open, till he nearly choked him. To get it down faster, Omrah had taken the big tin funnel, and had inserted one end into his mouth, which he filled till the water ran out; after that he was trying what he could do with fire, for he began putting hot embers between Big Adam's toes; I dare say the fellow can not walk to-day."

"I fear that some day he will kill Omrah,

or do him some serious injury; the boy must be cautioned," said Alexander.

"I am afraid it will be of no use, and Omrah must take his chance: he is aware of Big Adam's enmity as well as you are, and is always on his guard; but as for persuading him to leave off his tricks, or to reconcile them to each other, it is impossible," said Swinton – "you don't know a Bushman."

"Then pray tell us something about them," said the Major, "as soon as you have finished that elephant-steak, which you appear to approve of. Of what race are the Bushmen?"

"I will tell you when I have finished my breakfast," replied Swinton, "and not before: if I begin to talk, you will eat all the steak, and that won't do."

"I suspect that we shall not leave this to-day," said Alexander. "If, as Bremen says, the cattle have strayed very far, it will be too late to go in the afternoon, and to-morrow you recollect is Sunday, and that, we have agreed, shall be kept as it ought to be."

"Very true," said the Major; "then we must make Swinton entertain us by telling us more about the lions, for he had not finished when the storm came on."

"No," replied Swinton; "I had a great deal more to say, and I shall be very happy at any seasonable time, Major, to tell you what I know – but not just now."

"My dear fellow," said the Major, putting another piece of elephant-steak upon Swinton's plate, "pray don't entertain the idea that I want you to talk on purpose that I may eat your share and my own too; only ascribe my impatience to the true cause – the delight I have in receiving instruction and amusement from you."

"Well, Swinton, you have extorted a compliment from the Major."

"Yes, and an extra allowance of steak, which is a better thing," replied Swinton, laughing. "Now I have finished my breakfast, I will tell what I know about Omrah's people.

"The Bushmen are originally a Hottentot

race — of that I think there is little doubt; but I believe they are a race of people produced by circumstances, if I may use the expression. The Hottentot on the plains lives a nomad life, pasturing and living upon his herds. The Bushman may be considered as the Hottentot driven out of his fertile plains, deprived of his cattle, and compelled to resort to the hills for his safety and subsistence — in short, a Hill Hottentot: impelled by hunger and by injuries, he has committed depredations upon the property of others until he has had a mark set upon him; his hand has been against every man, and he has been hunted like a wild beast, and compelled to hide himself in the caves of almost inaccessible rocks and hills.

"Thus, generation after generation, he has suffered privation and hunger, till the race has dwindled down to the small size which it is at present. Unable to contend against force, his only weapons have been his cunning and his poisoned arrows, and with them he has obtained his livelihood — or rather, it may be said, has contrived to support life, and no more. There are, however, many races mixed up with the Bushmen; for runaway slaves, brought from Madagascar, Malays, and even those of the mixed white breed, when they have committed murder or other penal crimes, have added to the race and incorporated themselves with them; they are called the Children of the Desert, and they are literally such."

"Have you seen much of them?"

"Yes, when I was in the Namaqua-land and in the Bechuana territory I saw a great deal of them. I do not think that they are insensible to kindness, and moreover, I believe that they may often be trusted; but you run a great risk."

"Have they ever shown any gratitude?"

"Yes; when I have killed game for them, they have followed me on purpose to show me the pools of waters without which we should have suffered severely, if we had not perished. We were talking about lions; it is an old-received opinion, that the jackal is the lion's provider; it would be a more correct one to say that the lion is the Bushman's provider."

"Indeed!"

"I once asked a Bushman, 'How do you live?' His reply was, 'I live by the lions.' I asked him to explain to me. He said, 'I will show what I do: I let the lions follow the game and kill it and eat till they have their bellies full, then I go up to where the lion is sitting down by the carcass, and I go pretty near to him; I cry out, What have you got there, can not you spare me some of it? Go away and let me have some meat, or I'll do you some harm. Then I dance and jump about and shake my skin-dress, and the lion looks at me, and he turns round and walks away; he growls very much, but he don't stay, and then I eat the rest.'"

"And is that true?"

"Yes, I believe it, as I have had it confessed by many others. The fact is, the lion is only dangerous when he is hungry – that is, if he is not attacked; and if, as the Bushman said, the lion has eaten sufficiently, probably not wishing to be disturbed, after his repast, by the presence and shouts of the Bushman, the animal retires to some other spot. I was informed that a very short time afterward, this Bushman, who told me what I have detailed to you, was killed by a lioness, when attempting to drive it away from its prey by shouting as he was used to do. The fact was, that he perceived a lioness devouring a wild horse, and went up to her as usual; but he did not observe that she had her whelps with her: he shouted; she growled savagely, and before he had time to retreat, she sprang upon him and tore him to pieces."

"The lion does not prey upon men, then, although he destroys them?"

"Not generally; but the Namaqua people told me that, if a lion once takes a fancy to men's flesh – and they do, after they have in their hunger devoured one or two – they become doubly dangerous, as they will leave all other game and hunt man only; but this I can not vouch for being the truth, although it is very probable."

"If we judge from analogy, it is," replied the Major. "The Bengal tigers in India, it is well known, if they once taste human flesh, prefer it to all other, and they are well known to the natives, who term them man-eaters. Strange to say, it appears that human flesh is not wholesome for them; for their skins become mangy after they have taken to eating that alone. I have shot a 'man-eater' from the back of an elephant, and I found that the skin was not worth taking."

"The Namaquas," replied Swinton, "told me that a lion, once enamored of human flesh, would, in order to obtain it so far overcome his caution, that he would leap through a fire to seize a man. I once went to visit a Namaqua chief, who had been severely wounded by a lion of this description – a man-eater, as the Major terms them, – and he gave me the following dreadful narrative, which certainly corroborates what they assert of the lion who had once taken a fancy to human flesh.

"The chief told me that he had gone out with a party of his men to hunt: they had guns, bows and arrows, and assaguays. On the first day, as they were pursuing an elephant, they came across some lions, who attacked them and they were obliged to save their lives by abandoning a horse, which the lions devoured. They then made hiding-places of thick bushes by a pool, where they knew the elephant and rhinoceros would come to drink.

"As they fired at a rhinoceros, a lion leaped into their inclosure, took up one of the men in his mouth and carried him off, and all that they afterward could find of him the next day was one of the bones of his leg. The next night, as they were sitting by a fire inside of their inclosure of bushes, a lion came, seized one of the men, dragged him through the fire, and tore out his back. One of the party fired, but missed; upon which, the lion, dropping his dying victim, growled at the men across the fire, and they durst not repeat the shot; the lion then took up his prey in his mouth, and went off with it.

"Alarmed at such disasters, the Namaquas collected together in one strong inclosure, and at night sent out one of the slaves for water. He had no sooner reached the pool than he was seized by a lion; he called in vain for help, but was dragged off through the woods, and the next day his skull only was found, clean licked by the rough tongue of the lion.

"Having now lost three men in three days, the chief and his whole party turned out to hunt and destroy lions only. They followed the spoor or track of the one which had taken the slave, and they soon found two lions, one of which, the smallest, they shot; and then, having taken their breakfast, they went after the other, and largest, which was recognized as the one which had devoured the man.

"They followed the animal to a patch of reeds, where it had intrenched itself; they set fire to the reeds and forced it out, and as it was walking off it was severely wounded by one of the party, when it immediately turned back, and, with a loud roar, charged right through the smoke and the burning reeds. The monster dashed in among them and seized the chief's brother by the back, tearing out his ribs and exposing his lungs.

"The chief rushed to the assistance of his expiring brother; his gun burned priming. He dashed it down, and in his desperation seized the lion by the tail. The lion let go the body, and turned upon the chief, and with a stroke of his fore-paw tore a large piece of flesh off the chief's arm; then struck him again and threw him on the ground. The chief rose instantly, but the lion then seized him by the knee, threw him down again, and there held him, mangling his left arm.

"Torn and bleeding, the chief in a feeble voice called to his men to shoot the animal from behind, which was at last done with a ball which passed through the lion's brain. After this destruction of four men in four days, the hunting was given over; the body of the chief's brother was buried, and the party went home, bearing with them their wounded chief."

"Well, that is the most horrible lion-adventure I have yet heard," said the Major. "Heaven preserve us from a man-eating lion!"

"It really has almost taken away my breath," said Alexander.

"Well, then, I will tell you one more amusing, and not so fatal in its results; I was told it by a Bushman," said Swinton. "A Bushman was following a herd of zebras, and had just succeeded in wounding one with his arrow, when he discovered that he had been interfering with a lion, who was also in chase of the same animals. As the lion appeared very angry at this interference with his rights as lord of the manor, and evidently inclined to punish the Bushman as a poacher upon his preserves, the latter, perceiving a tree convenient, climbed up into it as fast as he could. The lion allowed the herd of zebras to go away, and turned his attention to the Bushman. He walked round and round the tree, and every now and then he growled as he looked up at the Bushman.

"At last the lion lay down at the foot of the tree, and there he kept watch all night. The Bushman kept watch also, but toward morning, feeling very tired, he was overcome by sleep, and as he slept, he dreamed, and what do you think that he dreamed? – he dreamed that he fell from the tree into the jaws of the lion. Starting up in horror from the effects of his dream, he lost his hold, and falling from the branch, down he came with all his weight right on the back of the lion. The lion, so unexpectedly saluted, sprang up with a loud roar, tossing off the Bushman, and running away as fast as he could; and the Bushman, recovering his legs and his senses, also took to his heels in a different direction; and thus were the 'sleepers awakened,' and the dream became true."

"Besiegers retreating and fort evacuated both at the same time," cried the Major, laughing.

"Well, I think you have had enough of the lion now," said Swinton.

"No, we had quite enough of him last night, if you choose," replied Alexander. "But your lions are not quite so near as he was."

CHAPTER XV

It was not until the evening that the Caffres and Hottentots returned with the cattle, which they had great difficulty in collecting; two or three of the oxen were not brought back till late at night, so frightened had the animals been by the approach of the lion. In the afternoon, as it was too late to think of proceeding, our travelers, with their guns on their shoulders, and accompanied by Omrah and Begum, who would always follow the Major if she was not tied up, strolled away from the camp to amuse themselves. At first they walked to the hill from which they had such a splendid view of the valley covered with elephants, and, proceeding to where the male elephant had fallen, found that his flesh had, by the Caffres, the wolves, and the vultures, been completely taken off his bones, and it lay there a beautiful skeleton for a museum.

As, however, they had no room for such weighty articles in their wagons, they left it, after Swinton had made some observations upon the structure of the animal. Begum would not go near the skeleton, but appeared to be frightened at it. They then proceeded to the rock which had been their place of refuge when the herd of elephants had charged upon them; and as they stood under it, they were suddenly saluted with a loud noise over their heads, sounding like quah, quah!

As soon as Begum heard it, she ran up to the Major with every sign of trepidation, holding fast to his skin trowsers.

"What was that?" said Alexander; "I see nothing."

"I know what it is," said the Major; "it is a herd of baboons; there they are; don't you see their heads over the rocks?"

"Let them show themselves a little more, and we'll have a shot at them," replied Alexander, cocking his gun.

"Not for your life," cried Swinton; "you will be skinned and torn to pieces, if they are numerous, and you enrage them. You have no idea what savage and powerful creatures they are. Look at them now; they are coming down

The Mission

gradually; we had better be off."

"I think so too," said the Major; "they are very angry; they have seen Begum, and imagine that we have one of their herd in our possession. Pray don't fire, Wilmot, unless it is for your life; we are too few to make them afraid of us. Here they come; there are a hundred of them at least; let us walk away slowly – it won't do to run, for that would make them chase us at once."

The baboons, some of which were of gigantic size, were now descending from the rock, grunting, grinning, springing from stone to stone, protruding their mouths, shaking their heads, drawing back the skin of their foreheads, and showing their formidable tusks, advancing nearer and nearer, and threatening an attack. Some of the largest males advanced so close as to make a snatch at Omrah. As for Begum, she kept behind the Major, hiding herself as much as possible. At last one or two advanced so close, rising on their hind-legs, that the Major was obliged to ward them off with his gun, "Point your guns at them," said Swinton, "if they come too close; but do not fire, I beg you. If we only get from off this rocky ground to the plain below, we shall probably get rid of them."

The ground on which they were formed a portion of the rocky hill upon which they had taken shelter the day of the elephant-hunt; and within twenty-five yards of them there was an abrupt descent of about four feet, which joined it to the plain. They had gained half-way, parrying the animals off as well as they could, as they retreated backward, when some of the baboons came down from the other side of the rock, so as to attempt to cut off their retreat, their object evidently being to gain possession of Begum, whom they considered as belonging to them – and a captive.

Their situation now became more critical; for the whole herd were joining the foremost; and the noise they made, and the anger they expressed, were much greater than before.

"We must fire, I really believe," said the Major, when they heard a deep, hollow growl, followed up by a roar of some animal, apparently not very far off. At this sound the baboons halted, and listened in silence; again the growl was repeated, and followed up by the roar, and the baboons, at a shriek given by one on the rock, turned round and took to their heels, much to the delight of our travelers, who had felt the peculiar difficulty and danger of their situation.

"What animal was that which has frightened them off?" said the Major.

"It was the growl of a leopard," replied Swinton; "we must keep a sharp lookout; it can't be far off. The leopard is the great enemy of the baboons. But where is Omrah?"

They all looked round, but the boy was not to be seen. At last he showed his head above the foot of the rocky hill, where there was a descent of four feet, as we have mentioned, then sprang up the rock, and began capering, and imitating the baboons as they came on to the attack.

As they were laughing at him, all at once he stopped, and putting his hands to his mouth he gave the growl and roar of a leopard, which they had heard, and then set off running away baboon fashion.

"It was the Bushman, then, that frightened them off; he is a clever little fellow."

"And I am not sure that he has not saved our lives," replied Swinton; "but he has been brought up among them, one may say, and knows their habits well. If he had not hid himself below the rocks before he imitated the leopard, it would have been of no use, for they would not have been frightened, hearing the growl proceeding from him. I admire the boy's presence of mind."

"I thought at one time that the baboons had an idea that Omrah was one of them. What a snatch they made at him!"

"It would not have been the first time that these animals have carried off a boy," said Swinton; "I saw one at Latakoo, who had lived two years with the baboons, which had carried him off."

"How did they treat him?"

"Very well indeed; but they kept him a

prisoner. When they found that he would not eat the coarse food which they did, they brought him other things; and they invariably allowed him to drink first at the pools."

"Well, that was homage to our superiority. Confound their quahs, I shall not get them out of my head for a week. What terrible large tusks they have!"

"Yes, their incisors are very strong. They often destroy the leopard when they meet it in numbers; but if one happens to be away from the herd, he has, of course, no chance with such an animal. Begum did not appear at all willing to renew her connection."

"None of the monkey tribe, after they have lived with man, ever are; indeed it is a question, if they had taken possession of her, whether they would not have torn her to pieces immediately, or have worried her to death some way or other."

"Well, at all events, Swinton, you have been rewarded for your kindness to that poor little Bushman, and we have reaped the benefit of it," observed Alexander.

"But here come some of the oxen; I hope we shall be able to start early on Monday. The native Caffres say that the wagons can not proceed much further."

"No, not further than to the banks of the Umtata River: but you will then be not a great way from your destination. Daaka is the chief's name, is it not?"

"Yes, that is his name; and if he is as supposed to be, he is my first cousin. How strange it sounds to me, as I look around me in this savage and wild country, that I should be within forty miles of a blood-relation, who is an inhabitant of it!"

"Well, we shall soon know the truth; but I must say, if it is only to end in a morning call, you have come a long way for the purpose," replied the Major.

"I have come to ascertain a fact, which, from what I now know of the country and its inhabitants, will be the source of any thing but pleasure if it be established. My only hope is that it may prove otherwise than we suppose; and there is little chance of that, I fear."

"At all events, come what may," observed Swinton, "you will have done your duty."

On their return, they found all the men and cattle collected, and that night they increased the number of their fires, and tied the oxen to the wagons, that they might not be scattered by the return of the lion. The latter did not, however, make his appearance, and the night was passed without any disturbance. The following day being Sunday, the Hottentots were assembled, and desired not to start from the camp, as they would be expected to attend to prayers and Divine service; and as no hunting expedition was proposed, the Caffre warriors, as well as the native Caffres, who came in with their baskets of milk and other articles for sale and barter, also remained. Before dinner-time, the bell which had been brought with them from the Cape, to ring in case of any one having strayed from the camp, that he might be guided to return, was tolled by Bremen, and the Hottentots were assembled. Prayers and a portion of the Bible were then read.

The Caffre warriors, who had been told that the white men were going to pray to their God, were very silent and attentive, although they could not understand what was said; and the native Caffres, men, women and children, sat down and listened. As soon as the service was over, the Caffre head man of the warriors asked the interpreter to inquire of our travelers why they struck the bell? was it to let God know that they were about to pray, and did he hear what they said?

Swinton replied, that their God heard all that they said, and listened to the prayers of those who trusted in him.

A great many other questions were put by the Caffres, all of which were replied to with great caution by Mr. Swinton, as he was fearful that they might not otherwise be understood by the Caffres; but they were, as it was proved by the questions which followed in consequence. A great portion of the afternoon was passed away in explaining and replying to the interrogatories of these people, and our travelers felt convinced that by having kept the

Sabbath in that savage land they had done some good by the example; for, as Swinton truly observed –

"The missionaries come into the land to spread the gospel of Christ; they tell the natives that such is the religion and belief of the white men, and that such are the doctrines which are inculcated. Now white men come here as traders, or are occasionally seen here as travelers; and if the natives find, as they have found, that these white men, stated by the missionaries to hold the same belief, not only show no evidence of their belief, but are guilty of sins expressly forbidden by the religion preached, is not the work of the missionary nearly destroyed?

"I have often thought that the behavior of the Dutch boors toward the natives must have had such an effect; indeed, I may say that the colony has been founded upon very opposite principles to those of 'doing unto others as you would they should do unto you.' I believe that there never yet was an intercourse between Christians nominal and savages, in any portion of the globe, but that the savages have with great justice thrown in the Christians' teeth, that they preached one thing but did another. Unfortunately the taunt is but too true. Even those who had left their country for religious persecution have erred in the same way. The conduct of the Puritans who landed at Salem was as barbarous toward the Indians as that of Pizarro and his followers toward the Mexicans. In either case the poor aborigines were hunted to death."

On Monday they started at daylight, and proceeded on the journey; but they made little progress, on account of the difficulty of traveling with the wagons in a country consisting of alternate precipices and ravines, without any roads. The second day proved to be one of greater difficulty; they were obliged to cut down trees, fill up holes, remove large pieces of rock, and with every precaution the wagons were often out of order, and they were obliged to halt for repairs.

At night they were about ten miles from the Umtata River, and it was doubtful, from the accounts received from the natives of the country, if they would be able to go further with the wagons than to its bank. But in the evening, news was brought that the Amaquibi, the nation of warriors which were governed by Quetoo, and which had come from the north, had been attacked by two of the native tribes, aided by some white men with guns; that the white men had all been destroyed, and that the hostile army were marching south.

The native Caffres appeared to be in a panic, and this panic was soon communicated to the Hottentots. At first, murmurings were heard as they sat round the fire, and at last they broke out into open mutiny. Big Adam, with three others, came up to the fire where our travelers were sitting, and intimated that they must return immediately, as they would proceed no further; that if it was decided to go on, the Hottentots would not, as they had no intention of being murdered by the savages who were advancing. Swinton, who could speak the Dutch language, having consulted with Alexander and the Major, replied that it was very true that the army of Quetoo was to the northward;

but that the report of the defeat of the Caffres and of the army advancing was not confirmed. It was only a rumor, and might all be false; that even if true, it did not follow they were advancing in the direction in which they themselves were about to proceed; that it would be sufficient time for them to retreat when they found out what were the real facts, which would be the case in a few days at the furthest. But the Hottentots would not listen to any thing that he said; they declared that they would proceed no further.

By this time all the other Hottentots had joined the first who came up to our travelers, and made the same demand, stating their determination not to proceed a mile further. Only Bremen and Swanevelt opposed the rest, and declared that they would follow their masters wherever they chose to lead them. Alexander now sent for the interpreter and the chief of the Caffre warriors, lent him by Hinza, and desired the interpreter to ask the Caffre whether he and his band would follow them. The Caffre answered that they would; Hinza had given them in charge, and they could not return and say that they had left them because there was an enemy at hand. Hinza would kill them all if they did; they must bring back the travelers safe, or lose their lives in their defense.

"Well, then," said the Major, "now we can do without these cowardly fellows, who are no use to us but to eat and drink; so now let us discharge them at once, all but Bremen and Swanevelt."

"I agree with you, Major," said Alexander; "what do you think, Swinton?"

"Yes, let us discharge them, for then they will be in a precious dilemma. We will discharge them without arms, and desire them to go home; that they dare not do, so they will remain. But let us first secure their muskets, which lie round their fire, before we dismiss them; or they will not, perhaps, surrender them, and we may be in an awkward position. I will slip away, and while I am away, do you keep them in talk until I return, which I shall not do until I have locked up all the guns in the store-wagon."

As Swinton rose, the Major addressed

the Hottentots. "Now, my lads," said he, "here are Bremen and Swanevelt who consent to follow us; all the Caffre warriors agree to follow us; and here are about twenty of you who refuse. Now I can not think that you will leave us; you know that we have treated you well, and have given you plenty of tobacco; you know that you will be punished as soon as you return to the Cape. Why then are you so foolish? Now look you: I am sure that upon reflection you will think better of it. Let me understand clearly your reasons for not proceeding with us; I wish to hear them again, and let each man speak for himself."

The Hottentots immediately began to state over again their reasons for not going on; and thus the Major, who made each give his reason separately, gained their attention, and the time which was required. Before they all had spoken, Swinton came back and took his seat by the fire.

"All's safe," said he; "Bremen and Swanevelt's guns have been locked up with the others." Our travelers had their own lying by them. The Caffre warriors, who were standing behind the Hottentots, had all their assaguays in their hands; but their shields, as usual, were hanging to the sides of the wagons. The Major allowed the whole of the Hottentots to speak, and when they were done, he said, "Now, Wilmot, turn the tables on them."

Alexander then got up with his gun in his hand, the Major and Swinton did the same, and then Alexander told the Hottentots that they were a cowardly set of fellows; that with Bremen and Swanevelt, and the band of Caffre warriors, he could do without them; that since they did not choose to proceed, they might now leave the camp immediately, as they should get neither food nor any thing else from them in future. "So now be off, the whole of you; and if I find one to-morrow morning in sight of the camp, or if one of you dares to follow us, I will order the Caffres to run him through. You are dismissed, and to-morrow we leave without you."

Alexander then called the chief of the Caffre warriors, and desired him, in the presence of the Hottentots, to give particular charge of the cattle, horses, and sheep, to his warriors during the night; and if any one attempted to touch them, to run him through the body. "Do this immediately," said Alexander to the chief, who without delay spoke to his men, and they went off in obedience to his orders.

The Hottentots, who had heard all this, now retreated to their wagon, but were struck with consternation when they found that their guns had been removed; for they trusted to their guns and ammunition to enable them to procure food and protect themselves on their return. They consulted together in a low voice; they looked round and perceived that our three travelers had quitted the fire, and were keeping guard with their guns upon the wagons, to prevent any attempt of breaking them open, on the part of the Hottentots. Moreover, ten of the Caffres, with their spears, had since the breaking up of the conference, been put in charge of the wagons by the chief, at the request of the Major. The Hottentots now perceived their forlorn position.

How could they, without arms and ammunition, and without provisions, return to the Cape, such a number of miles distant? How could they exist, if they remained where they were? When they insisted upon our travelers returning, they had quite overlooked the circumstance that these could protect themselves with the Caffre warriors, and that they were not in a condition to enforce their demand.

After a long conversation, they did what all Hottentots will do under any emergency, – they lay down by the fire, and fell fast asleep. Swinton, having ascertained that they were really asleep, proposed that they themselves should retire to the wagon, and leave the Caffres on guard, which they did; as they well knew that a Hottentot once fast asleep is not easily roused up even to "treason, stratagem, or spoil."

Shortly after break of day, Bremen came to them, stating that he found the wagons could proceed no further, as he had walked on, and discovered that a mile before them there was a ravine so deep that it would be difficult for the cattle to go down, and for the wagons impossible; that at a distance of three miles below he could see the river, which was also so embedded in rocks, as to be impassable by the wagons.

The Major immediately went with Bremen, to satisfy himself of the truth of this, and returned, stating that further progress with wagons was impossible.

"Well, then, we must now hold a council," said Swinton. "Of course, proceed you will, Wilmot, that is decided; the only question is, as we must now proceed on horseback, what force you will take with you, and what shall be left in charge of the wagons?"

"I think we can trust the Caffres, do not you?"

"Yes, I do; but I wish from my heart that the Hottentots had not rebelled; for although in some respects cowardly fellows, yet with their muskets they are brave, and their muskets keep the natives in order."

"To the Caffres, the contents of the

wagons would prove a temptation; but these are not temptations to the Hottentots, whose object is to get back safe, and receive their wages. Thus we play them off against each other."

"Here are all the Hottentots coming up to us," said the Major; "I hope it is to make submission; it is very desirable that they should do so before they know that the wagons proceed no further."

The surmise of the Major was correct: the Hottentots had again canvassed the matter over, and, perceiving the helplessness of their position, had come in a body to beg forgiveness, and to offer to accompany our travelers wherever they pleased to take them.

It was a long while before Alexander would consent to receive them again, and not until they had made promise upon promise, that he seemed at last to be mollified. Swinton then interceded for them, and at last Alexander consented, upon their future good behavior, to overlook their conduct. This matter having been satisfactorily arranged, the former question was resumed.

"One of you, I fear, must remain with the wagons," observed Alexander; "or both of you, if you please. I have no right to ask you to go upon any wild-goose chase, and run into danger for nothing."

"That one should remain with the wagons will be necessary," said Swinton; "and I think that the Major, if he does not object, is the proper person. The party who are left must provide themselves with food by their guns; and it will require more military tact than I possess to arrange that and to defend the wagons. I will accompany you, Wilmot, as I can speak better Dutch, and the interpreter will not get on well without me."

"Will you have the kindness to take charge of the wagons, Major, during our absence?"

"I think, perhaps, it will be as well; although I had rather have gone with you," replied the Major. "I propose that you take thirty of the Caffres, Bremen, and eight Hottentots with you; leave me Swanevelt and the other Hottentots."

"Yes, that will do very well; we will leave the Caffre head man with you."

"No; he must go with the larger portion of his party; he could not well be separated from them. I will find a proper place for the wagons, and stockade myself regularly in; that will be a good job for the Hottentots, and I dare say I shall do very well."

"I shall not leave you Omrah, Major," said Swinton; "for, as we shall take four horses with us, I wish him to ride one, and he can attend upon us, as you have Mahomed."

"You may have Begum to ride the other," replied the Major, "if you please; then you will each have a groom."

"No, no, it would be a pity to part you and her; however, there is no time to be lost, for if this great chief and warrior Quetoo is advancing, it may be as well to be ready for a retreat; the sooner we are off, the sooner we shall be back; so now to pack up."

CHAPTER XVI

The first step taken by Alexander was to send for the Hottentots, and, after again reproving them for their former behavior, he asked who were ready to volunteer to proceed with him, as he had decided to leave the wagons with Major Henderson, and proceed on horseback the short distance of his journey which remained to be accomplished.

Several of the Hottentots immediately came forward; the heads of the mutiny held back, and thus proved to Alexander that the men who had come forward were persuaded into it by the others, and regretted what they had done. He therefore immediately accepted their services, and their muskets were returned to them. Alexander then stated his intentions to the Caffre head man, who selected the thirty warriors that were required, and in the course of three hours every thing was ready for their departure.

It was arranged that in case of danger arising to either party, they should, if possible, fall back to the newly established Mission of Morley, on the sea-coast; but otherwise, the wagons would remain where they were till Alexander's return. Having packed up all they required in small packages, to be carried by the Caffres, they bade farewell to the Major, and set off, having no baggage but what we have mentioned; for Alexander would not be encumbered with a load of heavy articles which must prevent rapid progress, or rapid retreat if necessary.

In two hours they arrived by difficult passes at the banks of the Umtata River, which they crossed, and soon afterward falling in with a Caffre kraal, they were informed that Daaka, the chief whom they sought, did not reside more than twenty miles distant; and they easily procured a guide to show them the way.

The reports of the advance of the Amaquibi army were here fully confirmed, and the natives were preparing to leave the kraal with all their cattle. It appeared, however, that at present the army was stationary; the warriors carousing and enjoying themselves after the victory which they had gained over the Caffres. As these had been assisted by white men and their guns, the spirits of the Amaquibi were raised to an extraordinary degree, and they were intending to carry their arms to the southward, as soon as Quetoo, their chief, had somewhat recovered from his wounds received in the late action. Indeed, it was the wounded state of their chief which was the principal cause of the army not having immediately proceeded to the southward.

Having obtained this information, the travelers resumed their journey along the banks of the Umtata, over a country of surprising beauty, the deep river being full of hippopotami, which were lying on the banks or snorting in the stream. They could not wait to kill one during the daytime, but promised the men they would allow them to make the attempt in the evening, after their day's march was over. Toward sunset, they stopped on the banks of the river on a rising ground, and the Hottentots and some Caffres were then directed to go down to the river in chase of the hippopotami, as it was advisable to save their provisions as much as possible.

Before night they had succeeded, and the carcass of the animal was hauled on shore. As soon as the party had taken as much as they required, the native Caffres carried off the remainder of the flesh. As they were sitting down carousing by the fire which had been lighted, the Caffre head warrior came up to the interpreter, and told Alexander and Swinton not to say that they were Hinza's warriors if asked where they came from. On being asked why, he told them that Hinza had married a daughter of the chief of this country, and after a time had sent her back again to her father, and that this had created ill blood between the tribes, although no war had taken place. Alexander and Swinton, who perceived that the advice was judicious, told him that they would not, and after partaking of the hippopotamus flesh they all lay down to repose under the far-spreading branches of a large tree.

The next morning they set off, and after an hour's journey the guide told them that they were at the kraal of Daaka, the descendant of the Europeans. The bellowing of the cattle and noise of the calves soon directed them to the spot, and they entered a kraal consisting of several very wretched huts. On inquiring for Daaka, a woman pointed out a hut at a little distance, and, as they dismounted and walked up, he came out to meet them. Swinton and Alexander shook hands with the chief, and said that they were very glad to see him, and that they had come far to pay him a visit. The chief ordered a hut to be swept out for their accommodation, which they took possession of.

"You have no idea, Swinton," said Alexander, "how much I am excited already by this interview."

"I can imagine it, my dear Wilmot," said Swinton; "it is but natural, for he is your kinsman by all report, and certainly, although a Caffre in his habits and manners, his countenance and features are strikingly European."

"That I have observed myself, and it has fully convinced me of the truth of the statement. I am most anxious to examine him – we must call the interpreter."

The chief entered the hut soon afterward, and took his seat; the interpreter was sent for, and the conversation was begun by Daaka, who like most of the Caffre chiefs, with the hope of obtaining presents, stated himself to be very poor, his cattle to be dying, and his children without milk. Our travelers allowed him to go on for some time in this manner, and then sent for a present of beads and tobacco, which they gave him. They then commenced their inquiries, and the first question they asked was, why he resided so near the sea.

"Because the sea is my mother," replied he; "I came from the sea, and the sea feeds me when I am hungry."

"In that reply he evidently refers to the wreck of the ship," observed Swinton; "and I presume, from the fish-bones, which we have seen about the kraal, that these Caffres feed on fish, which the other tribes do not, and therefore it is that he says his mother feeds him."

"Was your mother white?" inquired Alexander.

"Yes," replied Daaka, "her skin was white as yours; her hair was just like yours, long and dark; but before she died it was quite white."

"What was your mother's name?"

"Kuma," replied the chief.

"Had you any brothers and sisters?"

"Yes, I had; I have one sister alive now."

"What is her name?" inquired Swinton.

"Bess," replied the chief.

"This is very confirmatory," said Alexander; "my aunt's name was Elizabeth; she must have called her child after herself."

"Whom did your mother marry?"

"She first married my uncle, and had no children; and then she married my father; both were chiefs, and I am a chief; she had five children by my father."

A long conversation took place after this, the substance of which we may as well communicate to our reader in few words. From the children of Kuma, supposed to be Elizabeth, the aunt of Alexander, were produced a numerous race of the European blood, who were celebrated in the Caffre land for their courage; they were continually engaged in war, as their alliance was eagerly sought, and in consequence had nearly all perished. Daaka himself was renowned for warlike exploits, but he was now a very old man. In the evening the chief took his leave, and went to his own hut.

As soon as they were alone, Alexander said to Swinton, "I have now so far fulfilled my promise to my worthy relation that I have seen this descendant of his child; but what am I to do? An old man like him is not very likely to consent to go to England, and as for his sister Bess, he states that she is equally infirm; the progeny of the rest of the family are scattered about, and he himself knows nothing about them; to collect them would be impossible, and if collected, equally impossible to remove them, for they would not leave. My old relative fancies, in his mind's eye, his daughter weeping over her captivity, and longing to be restored to her country and her relations; still retaining European feelings and sympathies, and miserable in her position; her children brought up by her with the same ideas, and some day looking forward to their emancipation from this savage state of existence: I think if he were here, and saw old Daaka, he would soon divest himself of all these romantic ideas."

"I think so too; but there is one thing which has struck me very forcibly, Alexander, which is, if this Daaka is the son of your aunt how comes it that he is so old? When was the *Grosvenor* lost?"

"In the year 1782."

"And we are now in 1829. Your aunt you stated to have been ten or twelve years old at the time of the wreck. Allowing her to marry at the earliest age, Daaka could not well be more than forty-eight years old; and surely he is more than that."

"He looks much older, certainly; but who

can tell the age of a savage, who has been living a life of constant privation, and who has been so often wounded as his scars show that he has been? Wounds and hardship will soon make a man look old."

"That is very true, but still he appears to me to be older than the dates warrant."

"I think his stating that his sister was named Bess is full corroboration."

"It is rather circumstantial evidence, Wilmot: now what do you propose to do?"

"I hardly know; but I wish to be in Daaka's company some time longer, that I may gain more intelligence; and I think of proposing to him that we should go down to visit the remains of the wreck of his mother, as he terms it. I should like to see a spot so celebrated for misfortune, and behold the remains of the ill-fated vessel; I should like to have to tell my good old uncle all I can, and he will wish that I should be able to give him every information."

"Well, I think it is a good plan of yours,

and we will propose it to him to-morrow morning."

"And I should like to visit his sister Bess – indeed, I must do so. He says she is much younger than he is."

"He did, and therefore I think his age does not correspond with our dates, as I observed before," replied Swinton; "but, as you say, you must see his sister."

Daaka had sent an old cow as a present to Alexander, which was a very seasonable supply, as the hippopotamus-flesh had all been eaten. The next morning they proposed that he should accompany them to where the *Grosvenor* had been wrecked.

Daaka did not at first appear to know what they wished, and inquired, through the interpreter, whether they meant the ship that was wrecked on the sea-coast, pointing to the eastward. On receiving an answer in the affirmative, he agreed to set off with them that afternoon, saying that it was about forty miles off, and that they could not get there until the next day.

About noon they set off on their journey, and as they made but slow progress over a rugged although most beautiful country, they stopped at night at a kraal about half-way. Early the next morning they were led by Daaka and some Caffres who accompanied him to the sea-shore, and when they had arrived at the beach, it being then low water, Daaka pointed to a reef, upon which were to be seen the guns, ballast, and a portion of the keelson of a ship – all that remained of the unfortunate *Grosvenor*.

As the sea washed over the reef; now covering and now exposing these mementoes of misery and suffering, Alexander and Swinton remained for some time without speaking; at last Alexander said –

"Swinton, you have read the history of this unfortunate vessel, I know, for you asked me for it to read. What a succession of scenes of horror do these remains, which from their solid weight only have defied the power of the winds and waves, conjure up at this moment in my mind. I think I now behold the brave vessel dashed upon the reefs – the scream of despair from all on board – the heart-rending situation of the women and children – their wonderful escape and landing on shore, only to be subjected to greater suffering. See, Swinton, that must have been the rock which they all gained, and upon which they remained shivering through the night."

"It is, I have no doubt, from its position," said Swinton.

"Yes, it must have been; I think I see them all – men, women, and helpless children – huddled together, half-clothed and suffering, quitting that rock by this only path from it, and setting off upon their mad and perilous journey; the scattering of the parties – their perils and hunger – their conflicts with the natives – their sufferings from heat and from thirst – their sinking down one by one into the welcome arms of death, or torn to pieces by the wolves and hyenas as they lagged behind the others. How much more fortunate those who never gained the shore."

"Yes, indeed," replied Swinton; "except the eight who reached the Cape, and the five that Daaka asserts were saved, all the rest must have perished in that dreadful manner."

Alexander remained for some time in painful thought; at last he turned to Daaka and said, as he pointed to the remains of the wreck, "And this then is your mother?"

Daaka looked at him and shook his head, "No, not my mother this," replied he; "my mother down there," pointing out in a northerly direction.

"What does he mean, Swinton? he says this is not his mother."

"I will speak to him, Wilmot; you are too much agitated," replied Swinton.

"Is not that the vessel which your mother was lost in?" said Swinton, through the interpreter.

"No," replied Daaka; "my mother came on shore in a vessel up the little river out there; I was a boy when this large ship was wrecked; and got some iron from her to make assaguays."

"Merciful heaven! what joy I feel; I trust

it is true what he says."

"I have no doubt of it, Wilmot; I told you he was too old a man," replied Swinton; "but let me question him further."

Our readers may imagine the impatience of Alexander while the questions of Swinton were being answered, and by which it appears that Daaka's mother was lost at the mouth of the Lauwanbaz, a small river some miles to the eastward of the Zemsooboo. An old Caffre, who had come down with Daaka, now gave a particular account of the wreck of the *Grosvenor*, corroborating all Daaka's assertions.

"Were there none of the *Grosvenor's* people left in the country?" inquired Swinton.

"None," replied the old man; "they all went to the southward."

"Did you hear what became of them?"

"Some lay down and died, some fought the natives and were killed; the wolves ate the rest; not one left alive; they all perished."

"Were none of the women and children saved and kept as slaves?"

"No, not one; they had no meat, no milk, and they all died."

After some other inquiries, the old man, who at first did not reply willingly, stated that he had, with other Caffres, followed the last party; had seen them all dead, and had taken off their clothes, and that as they died were buried by those who still survived.

"A better fate, cruel as it was, than living as they must have lived," said Swinton.

"Yes, truly," replied Alexander; "you don't know, Swinton, what a load has been removed from my mind, and how light-hearted I feel, notwithstanding this recital of their sufferings. My poor uncle! God grant that he may live till my return with this distinct intelligence, with the assurance that he has no grandchildren living the life of a heathen, and knowing no God. What a relief will it prove to him; how soothing will it be to his last days! How grateful am I to God, that I have had so happy an issue to my mission! Now, Swinton, we will return as soon as you please; as soon as we arrive at Daaka's kraal, I will take down in writing the statement of these people, and then we will hasten back to the Major."

"And I dare say," said Swinton, as he remounted his horse, "that you will make old Daaka a more handsome present, for proving himself no relation to you, than if he had satisfactorily established himself as your own first cousin."

"You may be sure that my gratitude toward him is much greater than ever could have been my kindred feeling from friendship. I am so light hearted, Swinton, and so grateful to God that I almost wish to dismount in my anxiety to return my thanks; but I do so in my heart of hearts, at all event."

On the following day they arrived at Daaka's kraal, and then Alexander took down very carefully in writing the statements made by Daaka and the other Caffres. They all agreed on the one point, which was, that the European descendants now living in the country were wrecked in another vessel many years before the loss of the *Grosvenor*, and that not one of the *Grosvenor's* people – men, women or children – had survived, except the few who arrived at the Cape.

Having obtained these satisfactory documents, they made a handsome present to Daaka and the other Caffres, and immediately set out upon their return to the wagons. As they journeyed back to the westward, they found the Caffres quitting their huts, and driving away the cattle, that they might not fall into the power of the army of Quetoo, which it was said was now in motion, and scattering the tribes before them. As our travelers were not at all anxious to have any communication with these savage invaders, in two days they crossed the Umtata, and toward the evening were within sight of the wagons. A shout from the Hottentots and Caffres gave notice of their approach. The shout was returned, and in a few minutes they were shaking hands with the Major, who was delighted to see them.

"I did not expect you back so soon," replied the Major; "and as I perceive that you are unaccompanied, I presume that your Caffre relations would not quit their kraals."

"You shall know all about it, Major, very soon; it will be enough at present to let you know that we have nothing but good news."

"That I rejoice to hear; but it was well you came back as you did, for I have been making every preparation, and had you not returned in a few days, I should have retreated; the invaders are close at hand."

"We know it, and, if they are told that there are wagons here well loaded, they will come on quickly, with the hopes of plunder, so we must delay no longer," replied Alexander; "to-morrow we will yoke and set off. We can determine upon our route as we are traveling, but the first point is to retreat from this quarter."

"Exactly; the oxen are in prime order and can make a long day's march, and we know our country for some days, at all events; but enter my fortress, dismount, and let us go into the tent which I have pitched. You shall then tell me your adventures, while Mahomed fries a delicate piece of elephant's flesh for you."

"Have you killed an elephant?"

"Yes, but not without much difficulty and some danger, I assure you; I wanted your help sadly, for these Hottentots are too much alarmed to take good aim, and I had only my own rifle to trust to; but I have done very well considering, and I shall prove to our commander-in-chief that I have supplied the garrison without putting him to any expense during his absence. We have been feeding upon green monkeys for three days, and very good eating they are, if you do not happen upon a very old one."

When they entered the inclosure made by the Major, they were surprised at the state of defense in which he had put it. His hedge of thorns upon rocks piled up was impregnable, and the wagons were in the center, drawn up in a square; the entrance would only admit one person at a time, and was protected by bars at night.

"Why, Major, you might have held out against the whole force of the Amaquibi in this position."

"Yes, provided I had provisions and water," replied the Major; "but I fear they would soon have starved me out; however, it was as well to be prepared against any sudden night-attack, and therefore I fortified my camp: now come in, and welcome back again."

The news which they had to impart to the Major was soon given, and he was highly delighted at the intelligence: – "And now," said he, "what do you mean to do, Wilmot? – go back again, of course, but by what route?"

"Why, Major, you and Swinton have been so kind in coming with me thus far, and I have been so successful in my expedition, that I shall now leave you to decide as you please. I have effected all that I wished, my business is over, and I am ready to meet you in any way you choose; any thing you decide upon I shall agree to willingly and join in heartily, so now speak your wishes."

"Well, I will speak mine very frankly," replied the Major. "We have had some sport in this country, it is true, but not so much as I could have wished; for game is rather scarce, with the exception of elephants and sea-cows. Now I should like to cross the mountains, and get into the Bechuana and Bushman country, where game is as plentiful as I believe water is scarce; we can return that way, if you please, almost as well as we can through the Caffre country – what say you, Swinton?"

"Well, I am of your opinion. As Wilmot says, business is over and we have nothing to do but to amuse ourselves; I am very anxious to pass through this country, as I shall add greatly to my collections, I have no doubt; but it must not be expected that we shall fare as well as we have done in this; it will be the dry season, and we may be in want of water occasionally."

"I am equally desirous of going through that country, where I hope to shoot a giraffe, – that is my great ambition," replied Wilmot; "therefore we may consider that we are all agreed, and the affair is settled; but the question is, how shall we proceed back? We must return to Hinza's territory and send back the Caffres. Shall we return to Butterworth?"

"I think that must depend upon circumstances, and we can talk it over as we go along: the first point to ascertain is, the best passage over the mountains; and it appears to me that we shall be diverging much too far to the eastward if we return to Butterworth; but the Caffres will soon give us the necessary information."

"I wonder if the quarrel between Hinza and Voosani has been made up," said Alexander; "for we must pass through the Tambookie tribe if we cross the mountains, and if there is war between them we may meet with difficulty."

"We shall hear as soon as we have crossed the Bashee river," replied Swinton; "and then we must decide accordingly. All that can be settled now is, that to-morrow we start on our return, and that we will cross the mountains, if we possibly can."

"Yes, that is decided," replied Alexander.

"Well, then, as soon as you have finished your elephant-steak, Wilmot, we will get out a bottle of wine, drink the first half of it to congratulate you upon the success of your mission, and the other half shall be poured out in bumpers to a happy return."

CHAPTER XVII

The Return

The delight of the Hottentots at the announcement of the return of the expedition was not to be concealed; and now that they knew that they were retreating from the danger, as they were further removed they became proportionately brave. We must not include all the Hottentots in this observation, as Bremen, Swanevelt, and one or two more, were really brave men; but we do refer to the principal portion of them, with Big Adam at their head, who now flourished and vapored about, as if he could by himself kill and eat the whole army of the dreaded Quetoo.

As it was the intention of our travelers to pass over the Mambookei chain of mountains, into the Bushman and Koranna territory, they did not return the same route by which they came, but more to the westward through the territory of the Tambookie Caffres, not any one time entering upon the territory of the Amakosas, the tribe of Caffres governed by Hinza, who had lent them his warriors.

Voosani, the chief of the Tambookies, was very friendly, and had offered no opposition to their passage through a portion of his domains on their advance. They now lost no time, but continued their journey as fast as they could, although during the day they saw a great quantity of game, and were almost every night saluted with the roaring of the lions.

In a week they found themselves on the banks of the White Kae River, and not far from the foot of the mountains which they intended to pass. Here they halted, with the intention of remaining some few days, that they might unload and re-arrange the packing of their wagons, repair what was necessary, and provide themselves with more oxen and sheep for their journey in the sterile territory of the Bushmen.

During their route, the rumors relative to the army of Quetoo were incessant. He had attacked and murdered Lieut. Farewell and his people, who were on a

The Mission

trading expedition in the interior, and taken possession of and plundered their wagons. Flushed with success over white people armed with muskets, Quetoo had now resolved to turn his army to the southward, and attack the tribes of the Amaponda Caffres, governed by Fakoo, and the missionary station of Morley, lately established near the coast, between the St. John and the Umtata rivers.

To effect this, Quetoo commenced his ravages upon all the lesser tribes tributary to Fakoo, and having put them to indiscriminate slaughter, driven away their cattle, and burned their kraals, his army advanced to the missionary station, which the missionaries were compelled to desert, and fall back upon the St. John River.

One of the men belonging to the tribe near Morley came to the caravan where our travelers had halted, and, on being questioned as to the loss they had experienced, cried out, "Ask not how many are killed, but how many are saved: our wives, where are they? and our children, do you see any of them?"

But Fakoo, the chief of the Amapondas, had roused himself and collected his army. He resolved upon giving battle to the enemy. He found the Amaquibi encamped in a forest, and he surrounded them with a superior army; he then contrived, by attacking and retreating, to lead them into a position from which there was no escape but by the pass by which they had entered, and which he completely blocked up with his own forces.

The Amaquibi could not retreat, and a furious conflict took place, which ended in the destruction of the whole of Quetoo's army. Quetoo himself was not present, as he still remained confined with the wound he had received in the prior engagement, in which he had been victorious. A portion of Fakoo's army was sent against him, and he fled with the loss of all the cattle and treasures he had collected; and thus was the invading force at last totally dispersed and not heard of any more.

This news was very satisfactory to our travelers, as they did not know whether they would have had time to make their arrangements, if Quetoo's army had been victorious; and it was still more pleasing to the Hottentots, who were now even braver than before, all lamenting that they had not remained on the banks of the Umtata River, where the combat took place, that they might have assisted at the destruction of the invaders.

It was toward the end of August before our travelers had made their preparations and were ready for a start. They had decided to try the pass through the Mambookei chain of mountains, to the eastward of the one named Stormbergen, and as they expected to meet with some difficulties, it was decided that the Caffre warriors should not be dismissed till they had arrived at the Bushman territory; they proposed then to turn to the N.W., so as to fall in with that portion of the Orange River which was known by the name of the Vaal or Yellow River, crossing the Black or Cradock River, which is also another branch of the Orange River.

This arrangement was made, that they might get into the country more abounding with game, and better furnished with water than any other portion of the sterile deserts which they had to pass through.

Having, as usual, kept holy the Lord's day, on the Monday morning they started in high spirits, and with their cattle in excellent order. The passage through the ravine was very difficult; they had to fill up holes, roll away stones, and very often put double teams to drag the wagons.

They made but ten miles on the first day, and found the night cold, after the heat to which they had been subjected. The second day was also one of toil and danger, but on the third they found that they had commenced the descent, and the whole Bushman country was spread before them. But the descent was even more perilous than the ascent, and it was not without great exertion that they saved their wagons from falling over the precipices.

On the fourth evening they had crossed the mountains, and were now at the foot of them on the western side. It was with difficulty that they collected wood enough to make their fires for the night, and the continual roaring told them that they were now in the domain of the lion and his satellites.

At break of day they all rose, that they might view the country which they were about to traverse. It was one wild desert of sand and stones, interspersed with small shrubs, and here and there a patch of bushes; apparently one vast, dry, arid plain, with a haze over it, arising from the heat. Our travelers, however, did not at first notice this change; their eyes were fixed upon the groups of quaggas and various antelopes which were strewed over the whole face of the country; and, as soon as they had taken their breakfast, they mounted their horses in pursuit. It had been their intention to have dismissed the Caffres on that morning, but the chief of the band pointed out that it would be as well that they should kill some game, to provide them with food for their journey back; and our travelers approved of the suggestion, as it would save their sheep.

Alexander and the Major set off with

Bremen, Swanevelt, and Omrah on horseback, while the Caffres on foot kept well up with them. The other Hottentots were ordered to remain with Swinton at the encampment, as they had to repair the damages done to the wagons in crossing the mountains.

Omrah had shown himself so useful, that he had been permitted to practice with a fowling-piece carrying ball, and had proved himself very expert. He now was mounted on the Major's spare horse; that in case the Major's was knocked up, he might change it, for Omrah's weight was a mere nothing.

The plan of the chase was, that the Caffres should spread in a half-circle, and conceal themselves as much as possible, while those on horseback should turn the animals and drive them in their direction. As they advanced on the plain, they discovered what the haze had prevented their seeing at early dawn, that the plain was covered with a variety of beautiful flowers, of the amaryllis and other tribes, and with the hills of ants and ant-eaters' holes, which latter were very dangerous to the horses.

The sun was now up in the heavens, and blazed fiercely; the heat was intense, although still early in the day. When they turned their heads toward the mountains which they had passed, they were struck with astonishment at the grandeur of the scene: rocks and cliffs in wild chaos, barren ridges and towering peaks, worn by time into castellated fortresses and other strange shapes, calling to their fancy the ruins of a former world. With the exception of a pool of water, near to which the caravan had halted, not a vestige of that element was to be seen in any direction; all was one plain, ending only in the horizon, without a tree, the line only broken by the groups of animals and the long necks of the packs of ostriches in the distance.

If, however, the vegetable kingdom was deficient, the animal was proportionably abundant, and Alexander and the Major were soon at their speed after a troop of quaggas and zebras, which they succeeded in turning toward the Caffres. As soon as the animals had entered the radius of the half-circle, and were within distance, they checked their horses and opened their fire upon them; at the same time the Caffres showed themselves, and the animals were for a time confounded by finding themselves so nearly surrounded.

During their hesitation, and while they attempted to break through here and there, and then turned again, several were brought to the ground by the guns of the mounted party, till at last, as if they had summoned up their resolution, the whole herd, led by a splendid male, burst away in a direction close to the horsemen, and made their escape from the circle in a cloud of dust, scattering the stones behind them as they fled.

The Caffres ran up to the animals which lay wounded, and put them out of their misery by inserting the point of their assaguays into the spine, which caused immediate death. Seven animals were killed, three zebras and four quaggas; and as Swinton had requested that they might not be cut up till he had ascertained if he required their skins, Omrah was sent back to bring him to where they were lying.

Swinton soon came, and Alexander said to him, "Now, Swinton, let us know if you want any of the skins of these animals to preserve."

"No," replied Swinton, "I have them already; I just thought it possible that you might have killed a zebra."

"Well, have we not? there are three of them."

"No, my good fellow, they are not of the real zebra species; they belong to a class described by Burchell, the traveler, which is termed the striped quagga. The quagga and striped quagga, as you may see, have the ears of a horse, while the zebra has those of the ass. The true zebra hardly ever descends upon the plains, but lives altogether upon the mountainous regions; occasionally it may be found, it is true, and that is the reason why I came to see."

"Are they good eating, these animals?"

"The quagga is very indifferent food, but the striped quagga is very passable; so if you intend to save any for our dinner, pray let it be some of the latter. Have you done hunting to-day?"

"Yes," replied the Major, "if Wilmot is of my opinion, I think we had better not work our horses any more just now; the plain is so full of large holes, – ant-eaters' holes, Bremen says they are."

"Yes, they are ant-eaters' holes, and very dangerous; I have seen them several feet deep. If we do not start to-day, I will ask the Hottentots to try and procure one for me to-night, as I wish to have a stuffed specimen."

"We do not intend to start till to-morrow morning," replied Alexander; "we must dismiss the Caffres to-night, that they may be also ready to go home to-morrow. They will now have provisions enough."

Our travelers now rode back to the caravan, leaving the Caffres to bring home the flesh. As soon as they had dined, the chief of the warriors was desired to come with all his men, and Alexander then made every man a handsome present, consisting of tobacco, snuff, cloth, knives and beads. To the chief of the band he gave three times as much as the others, and then, having delivered to him a very liberal collection of articles for their king Hinza, Alexander told the chief to acquaint the king that he had been very much pleased with the conduct of the men, and thanked his majesty for the loan of them, and requested that his majesty would accept of the packet of articles which he had selected for him.

He then thanked the men for their good conduct, told them to take all the flesh that they wished for the journey, and stated that they were at liberty to depart that evening or the next morning, as they thought proper. The Caffres were perfectly satisfied with Alexander's liberality, and the chief of the warriors, making a short speech in reply, retired with his men.

"Well, I'm very sorry that these fine fellows are leaving," said the Major.

"And so am I; but I could not well detain them, and they said that they could not go further with us without the king's permission," replied Alexander.

"Of course not," replied the Major; "but

that does not lessen my regret at their departure; they have been both steady and brave, as well as active and willing, and I do not expect that our Hottentots will serve us so well."

"You are right not to expect it, Major," replied Swinton; "if you did, you would be miserably disappointed. If they knew now where we were going, they would desert us. The only hold that we have upon the greater number of them is their fear; they go forward because they are afraid to go back; but if they could get hold of our horses, with their guns and ammunition, they would leave us as soon as we advanced in the desert."

"Very true, I fear; but we have a few stanch fellows among them, and two at least whom we can depend upon – Bremen and Swanevelt."

"How far is it from here to the Black River, Swinton?"

"About forty miles; not so much perhaps to the river's bed, but at least that, if not more, before we shall fall in with any water at this season of the year."

"We must not fail to fill our water-kegs before we leave this."

"No, for we shall have no water to-night, that is certain. We can not travel more than twenty miles over such a country as this; for turning here and there to avoid the holes and ant-hills, the twenty miles will be at least thirty," said Swinton; "but now I must go and tell the Hottentots to find me what I want: a pound of tobacco will procure it, I have no doubt."

"But I have mine," observed the Major, after Swinton was gone; "we are too near the pool, and we shall be surrounded with lions to-night; the Hottentots may pretend that they will go, but they will not."

"One can not well blame them; I'm sure a pound of tobacco would not persuade me to put my head into a lion's mouth; but I agree with you, we are too near the pool, and as we must collect the cattle to secure them during the night, I think we had better fill our water-kegs, and then yoke and take up a position for the night about half a mile further off. But here comes Swinton, who can give us his advice."

As Swinton agreed with them, they yoked the oxen, and drove forward about a mile from the pool; they then secured them to the wagons and lighted large fires round the caravan.

The Major was correct as regarded the Hottentots' procuring an ant-eater for Swinton; they would not leave the fires, and the continual approach of the lions during the night proved that they were wise in so doing. There was no occasion for the lions to roar; the moaning of Begum, and her clinging to the Major, the trembling of the dogs, and the uneasiness of the cattle, invariably gave notice of lions being at hand. Shots were fired off during the night, to keep them at a distance, but otherwise the night passed away undisturbed.

They started the following morning about daybreak, and, at the same time, the Caffres took their departure to their own country. The ground over which the caravan traveled was stony and sandy at intervals, and they had not proceeded

The Mission

far before they again discovered a great variety of game dispersed over the level plain. They did not, however, attempt to pursue them, as they were anxious to go on as far as possible, so as to give the oxen an opportunity of picking up what little food they could during the middle of the day, at which time the Major and Alexander proposed that they should go in pursuit of game. But before they had traveled three hours, they were surprised at a cloud of dust, which obscured the horizon, in the direction they were proceeding.

"What can that be?" said Alexander.

"I think it is springbok," said Bremen the Hottentot.

"Springbok! why, there must be thousands and thousands of them."

"I believe that Bremen is right," said Swinton; "it must be one of the migratory herds of springboks; I have never seen them, but I have often been told of them."

The body of antelopes now advanced toward them, keeping on a straight path;

and to state their numbers would have been impossible: there might have been fifty or a hundred thousand, or more. As far as the eye could see in any direction, it was one moving mass covering the whole plain. As they approached the caravan, those nearest huddled on one side and occasionally bounded away with the remarkable springs made by this animal, and from which it has its name, alighting not upon the earth, but, for want of room, upon the backs of its companions, and then dropping in between the ranks.

A hazy vapor arose from these countless herds as they moved on, and more than once the Hottentots, who were standing on the wagons, which had been stopped as the herd came up to them, pointed out a lion which was journeying with the crowds to feast at his leisure. The animals appeared very tame, and several were killed close to the wheels of the wagons, for the evening's supper. Notwithstanding that the herd moved at a rapid pace, it was more than two hours before the whole had passed by.

"Well," observed Alexander, "I can now

say that I have seen no want of game in Africa. Where will they go to?"

"They will go directly on to the southward," replied Swinton; "the migration of these animals is one of the most remarkable proofs of the fecundity of animal life. Like the ants, they devour every thing before them; and if we journey in the direction they have come from, we shall find no food for the cattle until after the rains. After the rains fall, these animals will return to their former pastures. It is the want of food which has brought them so far to the southward."

"Their track is evidently from the north and eastward," said the Major; "had we not better change our course more to the northward?"

"No, I should think not; they have probably traveled on this side of the Nu Gariep or Black River. We shall have neither water nor food for the cattle to-night, and therefore I think we had better go on as we are going, so as to make sure of water for them to-morrow, at all events. It's useless now stopping to feed the cattle, we had better continue right on till the evening; we shall sooner arrive at the river, and so gain by it."

It was but half an hour before dark that they unyoked the tired oxen. Water or grass there was none; and, what was another misfortune, they could not find sufficient wood of any kind to keep up the necessary fires during the night. All they could collect before dark was but enough for one fire, and they considered it better, therefore, that only one should be lighted.

The wagons were drawn up so as to form a square, inside of which were tied the horses; the sheep were driven underneath, and the oxen were tied up outside. They feasted well themselves upon the delicate meat of the springboks, but the poor animals had neither food nor water after their hard day's journey.

As soon as they had supped they retired to their wagons, and the Hottentots remained by the side of the fire, which was but frugally supplied, that it might last till morning; but that there were lions prowling in the vicinity was evident from the restlessness of the oxen, who tried to break the leathern thongs with which they were fastened.

The moon had just risen, and showed an imperfect light, when they perceived the bodies of some animals between them and the horizon. They appeared very large, as they always do in an imperfect light, and the Hottentots soon made out that they were five or six lions not forty yards distant. The truth of this supposition was confirmed by an angry roar from one of them, which induced most of the Hottentots to seize their guns, and some to creep under the wagons.

The oxen now struggled furiously to escape, for the, roar of the lions had spread consternation.

Our travelers heard it in their wagons, and were out with their guns in a minute. At last one of the oxen broke loose, and, as it was running behind its companions, as if seeking a more secure shelter, being not more than three or four yards from them, another roar was followed by a spring of one of the lions, which bore the animal to the earth.

The Major and Wilmot were advancing before the fire to the attack, when the animal for a moment let go his prey, and was about to spring upon them. Bremen called out for them to retreat, which they did, as the animal advanced step by step toward them.

Satisfied with their retiring, the lion then went to his prey, and dragged it to a distance of about fifty yards, where it commenced its meal; and they distinctly heard, although they could not plainly distinguish, the tearing of the animal's flesh and the breaking of its bones by the lion, while its bellowings were most pitiful.

They all now fired in the direction where they heard the noise; the lion replied to the volley by a tremendous roar, and rushed up within twenty yards of the wagons, so as to be distinctly visible. Bremen begged our travelers not to molest the animal, as it was evidently very hungry and very angry, and would certainly make a spring upon them, which must be attended with disastrous effects.

The other lions were also now moving round and round the camp; they therefore reloaded their guns, and remained still, looking at the lion tearing and devouring his prey.

"We must be quiet here," said Bremen to Alexander; "there are many lions round us, and our fire is not sufficient to scare them away, and they may attack us."

"Would it not be better to fire our guns, – that would frighten them?"

"Yes, sir, it would frighten the other lions, perhaps, but it would enrage this one so near to us, and he would certainly make a charge. We had better throw a little gunpowder upon some ashes now and then, as we have but a small fire: the flash will drive them away for the time."

In the mean time the lion was making his meal upon the poor ox, and when any other of the hungry lions approached him, he would rush at them, and pursue them for some paces with a horrible growl, which made not only the poor oxen, but the men also, to shudder as they heard it.

In this manner was the night passed away, every one with his gun in his hand, expecting an immediate attack; but the morning at last dawned, to the great relief of them all. The lions had disappeared, and they walked out to where the old lion had made his meal, and found that he had devoured nearly the whole of the ox; and such was the enormous strength of his jaws, that the rib-bones were all demolished, and the bones of the legs, which are known as the marrow-bones, were broken as if by a hammer.

"I really," observed the Major, "have more respect for a lion, the more I become intimate with his feline majesty."

"Well, but he is off," observed Swinton, "and I think we had better be off too."

CHAPTER XVIII

The oxen were yoked, and the caravan proceeded at slow pace to gain the wished-for river. As our travelers walked their horses – for the poor animals had been without food or water for twenty-four hours, and all idea of chasing the various herds of animals which were to be seen in their path was abandoned for the present – Swinton remarked, "We are not far from the track of the Mantatees, when they made their irruption upon the Caffres about eighteen months back."

"I was intending to ask you for some information on that point, Swinton. There has been more than one irruption into the country from the natives to the northward. Mr. Fairburn gave me a very fair idea of the history of the Cape colony, but we were both too much engaged after our arrival in Cape Town for me to obtain further information."

"I will, you may be assured, tell you all I know," replied Swinton; "but you must not expect to find in me a Mr. Fairburn. I may as well remark, that Africa appears to be a country not able to afford support to a dense population, like Europe; and the chief cause of this is the great want of water, occasionally rendered more trying by droughts of four or five years' continuance."

"I grant that such is the case at present," observed the Major; "but you well know that it is not that there is not a sufficient quantity of rain, which falls generally once a year, but because the water which falls is carried off so quickly. Rivers become torrents, and in a few weeks pour all their water into the sea, leaving, I may say, none for the remainder of the year."

"That is true," replied Swinton.

"And so it will be until the population is not only dense, but, I may add, sufficiently enlightened and industrious. Then, I presume, they will take the same measures for securing a supply of water throughout the year which have been so long adopted in India, and were formerly in South America by the Mexicans. I mean that of digging large tanks, from which the water can not escape, except by evaporation."

"I believe that it will be the only remedy."

"Not only the remedy, but more than a remedy; for tanks once established, vegetation will flourish, and the vegetation will not only husband the water in the country, but attract more."

"All that is very true," replied Swinton, "and I trust the time will come, when not only this land may be well watered with the dew of heaven, but that the rivers of grace may flow through it in every direction, and the tree of Christ may flourish."

"Amen," replied Alexander.

"But to resume the thread of my discourse," continued Swinton; "I was about to say, that the increase of population, and I may add the increase of riches, – for in these nomadic tribes cattle are the only riches, – is the great cause of these descents from the north; for the continued droughts which I have mentioned of four or five years compel them to seek for pasture elsewhere, after their own is burned up. At all events, it appears that the Caffre nations have been continually sustaining the pressure from without, both from the northward and the southward, for many years.

"When the Dutch settled at the Cape, they took possession of the country belonging to the Hottentot tribes, driving the few that chose to preserve their independence into the Bushman and Namaqua lands, increasing the population in those countries, which are only able to afford subsistence to a very scattered few. Then, again, they encroached upon the Caffres, driving them first beyond the great Fish River, and afterward still more to the northward. The Bushman tribes of hill Hottentots, if we may so term them, have also been increased by various means, notwithstanding the constant massacres of these unhappy people by the Dutch boors; moreover, we have by our injudicious colonial regulations added another and a new race of people, who are already considerable in their numbers."

"Which do you refer to?"

"To the people now known by the name of Griquas, from their having taken possession of the Griqua country. They are the mixed race between the Hottentots and the whites. By the Dutch colonial law, these people could not hold possession of any land in the colony; and this act of injustice and folly has deprived us of a very valuable race of men, who might have added much to the prosperity of the colony. Brave and intelligent, industrious to a great degree, they, finding themselves despised on account of the Hottentot blood in their veins, have migrated from the colony and settled beyond the boundaries. Being tolerably well provided with fire-arms, those who are peaceably inclined can protect themselves, while those who are otherwise commit great depredations upon the poor savages, following the example shown them by the colonists, and sweeping off their cattle and their property, in defiance of law and justice. You now perceive, Alexander, how it is that there has been a pressure from the southward."

"That is very evident," replied the Major.

"Perhaps I had better proceed to the northward by degrees, and make some mention of the Caffre tribes, which are those who have suffered from being, as it were, pressed between encroachments from the north and the south. The Caffre race is very numerous. The origin of the general term Caffre, which means Infidel, and no more, is not known, any more than is that of the term Hottentot."

"A proof of what we found out at school," observed the Major, "that nicknames, as they are termed, stick longer than real ones."

"Precisely," replied Swinton; "our acquaintance is mostly with the more southern Caffres, who occupy the land bordering on the east coast of Africa, from the Cape boundary to Port Natal. These are the Amakosa tribe, whose warriors have just left us; the Tambookies, whose territory we have recently quitted, and to the northward of them by Port Natal, the Hambonas.

These are the Eastern Caffres.

"On the other side of the Mambookei chain of mountains, and in the central portion of Africa, below the tropic, are the Bechuanas, who inhabit an extent of country as yet imperfectly known to us. These may be termed the Central Caffres.

"On the western side of the African coast, and above Namaqua Land, whose inhabitants are probably chiefly of the Hottentot race, we have the Damaras, who may be classed as the Western Caffres; with these we have had little or no communication.

"All these tribes speak the Bechuana or Caffre language, with very slight variations; they are all governed by chiefs or kings, and subdivided into numerous bodies; but they are all Caffres. Of their characters I have only to observe, that as far as we have experienced, the Caffres of the eastern coast, which we have just left, are very superior to the others in courage and in every other good quality. Now, have I made myself intelligible, Alexander?"

"Most clearly so."

"I nevertheless wish we were sitting down in some safe place instead of traveling on horseback over this withered tract, and that I had the map before me to make you understand better."

"I will refer to the map as soon as I can," replied Alexander; "but I have studied the map a great deal, and therefore do not so much require it."

All these Caffre tribes live much the same life; their wealth is in cattle; they are partly husbandmen, partly herdsmen, and partly hunters; and their continual conflicts with the wild beasts of the country prepare them for warriors. The Eastern Caffres, from whom we have lately parted, are the most populous; indeed, now that we have taken from them so much of their country, they have scarcely pasturage for their cattle. I have said that the Eastern Caffres' territory extends as far as the latitude of Port Natal, but it formerly extended much further to the northward, as it did to the southward, before we drove them from their territory; indeed as far north as Delagoa Bay; all the country between Port Natal and Delagoa Bay being formerly inhabited by tribes of Caffres. I believe, Alexander, that Mr. Fairburn gave you a history of the celebrated monarch Chaka, the king of the Zulus?"

"Yes, he did."

"Well, it was Chaka who overran that country I am now speaking of, and drove out all the tribes who occupied it, as well as a large portion of the Bechuana tribes who inhabited lands more to the northward. Now the irruptions we have had into the Caffre and Bechuana country bordering upon the colony have been wholly brought about by the devastations committed by Chaka. Of course I refer to those irruptions which have taken place since our knowledge and possession of the Cape. I have no doubt that such irruptions have been continued, and that they have occurred once in every century for ages. They have been brought about by a population increasing beyond the means of subsistence, and have taken place as soon as the overplus have required it.

"The migration of the springboks, which we witnessed yesterday, may be more frequent, but are not more certain than those of the central population of Africa. The Caffres themselves state that they formerly came from the northward, and won their territory by conquest; and the Hottentots have the same tradition as regards themselves.

"The invasion of the Mantatees, as they are called (and by the Eastern Caffres Ficani), was nothing more than that of a people dispossessed of their property, and driven from the territory by the Zoolus, under Chaka; and, indeed, this last array under Quetoo, which has been destroyed within this month, may be considered as invading from a similar cause. Having separated from Chaka, Quetoo could find no resting-place, and he therefore came to the southward with the intention of wresting the territory from the Caffres, in which he has failed. Had he not failed, and been cut off by the Caffres, he would have destroyed them, and thus made room for his own people."

"Of course; for the end of all these invasions and migrations must be in such a sacrifice of human life as to afford sustenance and the means of subsistence to those who remain," observed the Major.

"Precisely; and such must continue to be the case on this continent, until the arts and civilization have taught men how to increase the means of subsistence. To produce this, Christianity must be introduced; for Christianity and civilization go hand in hand."

"But the Mantatees or Ficani, who are they?"

"I have already said they were northern Caffre tribes, dispossessed of their territory by Chaka. The names of the tribes we do not know. Mantatee, in the Caffre language, signifies an invader, and Ficani also, marauders; both terms applicable to the people, but certainly not the names of the tribes.

"I believe, now, I have said enough on the subject to allow me to enter upon the history of this last invasion; but, to tell the truth, the heat is so overpowering, and I feel my tongue so parched, that you must excuse me for deferring this account till another opportunity. As soon as we are a little more at our ease, I will give you the history of the Mantatees."

"We are much obliged to you for what you have told us, Swinton, and will spare you for the present," replied Alexander. "What animals are those? – look!"

"They are gnoos," replied Swinton. "There are two varieties of them, the common gnoo and the brindled gnoo. They form an intermediate link between the antelope family and the bovine or ox, and they are very good eating."

"Then, I wish we were able to go after them. They do not seem to be afraid of us, but approach nearer at every gallop which they make."

"Yes, although shy, they have a great deal of curiosity," replied Swinton. "Watch them now."

The animals bounded away again, as Swinton spoke, and then returned to gaze upon the caravan, stirring up the dust with their hoofs, tossing their manes, and lashing their sides with their long tails, as they curvetted and shook their heads, sometimes stamping as if in defiance, and then flying away like the wind, as if from fear.

"They are safe this time," observed Major Henderson; "but another day we will try their mettle."

"You will find them fierce and dangerous when wounded, sir," said Bremen, who had ridden up. "We are not many miles from the river, for the cattle begin to sniff."

"I am delighted to hear you say so; for then there must be water near. But the haze and glare together are so great that we can not distinguish above two miles, if so much."

"No, sir," replied the Hottentot; "but I can see well enough to see *them*" continued he, pointing with his finger to a rising ground about a hundred yards off, on the right of them. "One, two, three – there are five of them."

"What are they?" said the Major, looking

in the direction pointed out. "I see; they are lions."

"Yes, sir; but we must take no notice of them, and they will not annoy us. They are not hungry."

"You are right," said Swinton, "we must go right on, neither stopping nor hastening our speed. Let the driver look to the oxen; for, tired as they are, the smell of the lions is sufficient to give them ungovernable strength for the moment."

"Well," said the Major, "bring us our guns, Bremen. I am willing to accept the armed neutrality, if they will consent to it."

The caravan passed on; the lions remaining crouched where they were, eying them, it is true, but not rising from their beds. The oxen, however, either through fear of the lions, or the scent of water near, became more brisk in their motions, and in half an hour they perceived a line of trees before them, which told them that they were near the bed of the Nu Gariep or Cradock River.

The poor animals redoubled their exertions, and soon arrived at the banks. Bremen had ridden forward and reported that there still was water in the river, but only in pools. As the herbage was destroyed on the side where they were, they would have crossed the bed of the river before they unyoked, but that they found impossible. The animals were so impatient for the water, that, had they not been released, they would have broken the wagons.

Horses, oxen and sheep all plunged into the pools together, and for some minutes appeared as though they would never be satisfied. They at last went out, but soon returned again, till their sides were distended with the quantity of the element which they had imbibed.

An hour was allowed for the animals to rest and enjoy themselves, and then they were again yoked to drag the wagons to the other side of the river, where there was a sufficiency of pasturage and of wood to make up their fires.

As it was their intention to remain there

for a day or two, the wagons were drawn up at some distance from the river, so as not to interfere with the path by which the wild animals went down to drink. The spoors or tracks of the lions and buffaloes and other animals were so abundant, as to show that this precaution was necessary.

As soon as the wagons were arranged in the usual manner, the cattle were permitted to graze till the evening, when they were brought in and secured, as usual, inside and round the wagons. They supped off the remainder of the springbok, which was not very sweet; but the horses and men were both too much exhausted with the fatiguing journey to hunt until the following day.

That night they were not disturbed by lions, but the hyenas contrived to crawl under the wagons, and, having severely bitten one of the oxen, succeeded in carrying off one of the sheep. They had been so often annoyed by these animals, that we have never mentioned them; but on the following morning it was found that the ox had been so seriously injured that the leg-bone was broken, and they were obliged to destroy the animal.

"Were the courage of the hyena equal to his strength, it would be a most formidable animal," observed Swinton; "but the fact is, it seldom or never attacks mankind, although there may be twenty in a troop. At the same time, among the Caffres they very often do enter the huts of the natives, and occasionally devour children and infirm people. But this is greatly owing to the encouragement they receive from the custom of the Caffres leaving their dead to be devoured by these animals, which gives them a liking for human flesh, and makes them more bold to obtain it."

"They must have a tremendous power in their jaw," observed Alexander.

"They have, and it is given them for all-wise purposes. The hyena and the vulture are the scavengers of the tropical regions. The hyena devours what the vulture leaves, which is the skin and bones of a dead carcass. Its power of jaw is so great, that it breaks the largest bone with facility."

"Are there many varieties of them?"

"In Africa there are four: – The common spotted hyena, or wolf of the colonists, whose smell is so offensive that dogs leave it with disgust after it is killed; its own fellows will, however, devour it immediately. The striped or ferocious hyena, called the shard-wolf, and another which the colonists call the bay-wolf, and which I believe to be the one known as the laughing hyena. There is another variety, which is a sort of link between the hyena and the dog, called the venatica. It hunts in packs, and the colonists term it the wild honde. It was first classed by Burchell the traveler. This last is smaller, but much fiercer, than the others."

"I know that there are leopards in the country, but we have never yet fallen in with one. Are they dangerous?"

"The leopard shuns any conflict with man, but when driven to desperation it becomes a formidable antagonist. I recollect very well two boors having attacked a leopard, and the animal, being hotly pressed by them and wounded, turned round and sprang upon the one nearest, pulling him to the ground, biting his shoulder, and tearing him with his claws. The other, seeing the danger of his comrade, sprang from his horse and attempted to shoot the animal through the head. He missed, and the leopard left the first man, sprang upon *him*, and, striking him on the face, tore his scalp down over his eyes. The hunter grappled with the animal, and at last they rolled together down a steep cliff. As soon as the first hunter could reload his gun, he rushed after them to save his friend, but it was too late. The animal had seized him by the throat, and mangled him so dreadfully, that death was inevitable and all that the man could do was to avenge his comrade's death by shooting the leopard."

"That proves the leopard is not to be trifled with."

"No animal is, when it stands at bay, or is driven to desperation; and, in confirmation of this, I once witnessed one of these animals – the quaggas – which, being pressed to the edge of a precipice by a mounted hunter, seized the man's foot with its teeth, and actually tore it off, so that, although medical aid was at hand, the man died from loss of blood."

"One would hardly expect such a tragical issue to the chase of a wild jackass," observed the Major.

"No; but 'in the midst of life we are in death,' and we never know from whence the blow may come. Until it occurred, such an event was supposed impossible, and the very idea would have created nothing but ridicule. By the by, one of our good missionaries was very near losing his life by a leopard. He went to save a Hottentot who had been seized, and was attacked by the leopard which, as in the former instance, left his first antagonist to meet his second. Fortunately, Mr. S. was a very powerful man, and assistance was sooner given him than in the former instance. Neither he nor the Hottentot, however, escaped without severe wounds, which confined them for many weeks."

"Is there more than one variety of leopard, Swinton?"

"Yes, there is the common leopard and the hunting leopard; besides, I think, two or three smaller varieties, as the tiger-cat and wild cat. What do you propose doing to-day? Do you stay here, or advance, Wilmot?"

"Why, the Major wishes to have a shot at the gnoos; he has never killed one yet; and as I am of his opinion, that a day's rest will recover the oxen, and we are in no hurry, I think we may as well stop and provision our camp for a few days."

"With all my heart. I am sorry that the hyena has added to our store, by obliging us to kill the poor ox; however, it can not be helped. There is a large body of gnoos and quaggas under that small hill to the westward; but there are better animals for the table when we get a little further to the northward."

"Which are those?"

"The eland, the largest of the antelope species, and sometimes weighing more than a thousand pounds; moreover, they are very fat, and very easy to run down. They are excellent eating. When I was in the Namaquas' land, we preferred them to any other food; but I see another variety of game on the plain there."

"What?"

Omrah pointed them out. "They are either Bushmen (tame Bushmen, as they are called, in contradistinction to the others), or else Korannas; most probably the latter. They are coming right towards us; but Mahomed says breakfast is ready."

By the time that breakfast was finished, a party of twelve Korannas had joined the caravan. They made signs that they were hungry, pointing to the straps which confined their stomachs. The interpreter told them that they were about to hunt, and that they should have some of the game, at which they were much pleased.

"Do you know what those straps are called, round their waists, Wilmot?" said Swinton. "They are called the belts of famine. All the natives wear them when hard pressed by hunger, and they say that they are a great relief. I have no doubt but such is the fact."

"Well," said the Major, "I hope soon to

enable the poor fellows to loosen their belts, and fill their stomachs till they are as tight as a drum. Saddle the horses, Bremen. Omrah, you ride my spare horse and carry my spare rifle."

Omrah, who now understood English, although he spoke but few words, gave a nod of the head and went off to the wagon for the Major's rifle.

CHAPTER XIX

As soon as the horses were ready, our travelers set out in chase of the gnoos and quaggas, which were collected to the westward of the caravan. Bremen, Swanevelt, and Omrah were mounted, and ten of the Hottentots followed with their guns, and the Korannas on foot; among the others, Big Adam, who had been explaining to those who had never seen the gnoos the manner in which he used to kill them.

The herd permitted them to approach within two hundred yards of them, and then, after curvetting and prancing, and galloping in small circles, they stood still at about the same distance, looking, with curiosity and anger mixed, at the horsemen. After a time, they took to their heels and scoured the plain for about two miles, when they again stopped, tossing their heads and manes, and stamping as if in defiance.

The mounted party remained quiet till those on foot had again drawn near, and the Hottentots, firing their guns, drove the herd within shot of our travelers' guns, and three of the gnoos fell, while the others bounded off to a greater distance; but as they neared the caravan, they again started back, and were again closed in by the whole party.

The Hottentots now advanced cautiously, creeping as near as they could to the animals, whose attention was directed to the horsemen. The Hottentots were nearly within range, when Omrah, who was mounted on the Major's spare horse, fastened to the ramrod of the Major's rifle a red bandanna handkerchief, which he usually wore round his head, and separating quickly from the rest of the horsemen, walked his horse to where Big Adam was creeping along to gain a shot, and stationed himself behind him, waving the red handkerchief at the animals. Omrah was well aware that a gnoo is as much irritated at a red handkerchief as a bull, and as soon as he commenced waving it, one of the largest males stepped out in that direction, pawing the ground and preparing for a charge.

The Mission

Big Adam, who had no idea that Omrah was so occupied behind him, now rose to have a shot, and just as he rose the gnoo made his charge, and Big Adam, being between the gnoo and the horse which Omrah rode, was of course the party against whom the animal's choler was raised.

Omrah, as soon as the animal charged, had wheeled round and galloped away, while in the meantime Big Adam, perceiving the animal rushing at him, lost all presence of mind, his gun went off without effect, and he turned tail; the horns of the gnoo were close upon him, when of a sudden, to the surprise of those who were looking on, Big Adam disappeared, and the gnoo passed over where he had been.

"Why, what has become of him?" said Alexander, laughing.

"I don't know, but I think he has had a wonderful escape," replied the Major: "he has disappeared like a ghost through a trap-door."

"But I see his heels," cried Swinton, laughing; "he has fallen into an ant-eater's hole, depend upon it; that mischievous little urchin might have caused his death."

"It was only to make him prove his steady aim which he was boasting so much about," replied the Major; "but stop a moment; I will bring down that gallant little animal, and then we will look for big Adam."

But before the Major could get near enough to the gnoo, which was still tearing up the ground and looking for his adversary, Omrah, who had put by the handkerchief, advanced with the Major's rifle, and brought the animal down. A volley was at the same time discharged at the herd by the Hottentots, and three more fell, after which the remainder scampered away, and were soon out of sight.

They then rode up to where Big Adam had disappeared, and found him, as Swinton had supposed, in a deep ant-eater's hole, head downward, and bellowing for help. His feet were just above the surface, and that was all; the Hottentots helped him out, and Big

Adam threw himself on his back, and seemed exhausted with fright and having been so long in a reversed position, and was more vexed at the laugh which was raised against him.

The gnoos were soon cut up, and when the Hottentots had taken away as much as they required, the rest of the carcasses were made over to the hungry Korannas. Swinton shook his head at Omrah, who pretended that he did not understand why, until the laughter of Alexander and the Major was joined in by Swinton himself.

As they had pretty well fatigued their horses in the chase, they resolved to return to the caravan, and keep them as fresh as they could for future service. They dined and supped on the flesh of the gnoos, which was approved of, and after supper Alexander said – "And now, Swinton, if you feel inclined, the Major and I will be very glad to hear your history of the Mantatees."

"With pleasure," replied Swinton. "The assemblage of tribes known as the Mantatees or Invaders, according to the best authorities we can collect, inhabited the countries to the westward of the Zoolu territory, in the same latitude, which is that of Delagoa Bay. As all these tribes subsist almost entirely upon the flesh and the milk of their cattle, if deprived of them, they are driven to desperation, and must either become robbers in their turn, or perish by hunger. Such was the case of the Mantatees. Unable to withstand the attacks of the Zoolus, they were driven from their country, and joined their forces with others who had shared the same fate.

"Such was the origin of the Mantatees, who, although they had not courage to withstand the attacks of the Zoolus, were stimulated by desperation and famine to a most extraordinary courage in the attacks which they made upon others.

"Forming an immense body, now that they were collected together, accompanied by their wives and children, and unable to procure the necessary subsistence, it is certain that their habits were so far changed that they at last became cannibals, and were driven to prey upon the dead bodies of their enemies, or the flesh of their comrades who fell in the combats.

"The Bechuana tribes, who are the Caffres of the interior, were the first assailed, their towns sacked and burned, and their cattle seized and devoured. They proceeded on to the Wankeets, one of the Damara tribes, who inhabit the western coast to the northward of the Namaqua Land; but the Wankeets were a brave people, and prepared for them, and the Mantatees were driven back with great slaughter. Astounded at their defeat, they turned to the southward, and invaded the Bechuana country.

"At that time our missionaries had established themselves at Koranna, and when the report of the Mantatees advancing was brought to them, the Bechuanas were in a great consternation; for although finer-looking men than the eastern Caffres, they are not by any means so brave and warlike.

"As the advance of these people would have been the ruin of the mission, as well as the destruction of the tribe, who were afraid to encounter them, Mr. M., the missionary, determined upon sending for the assistance of the Griquas, the people whom I have before mentioned, and who had not only horses, but were well armed. The Griquas came under their chief, Waterboer, and marched against the enemy, accompanied by a large army of Bechuanas, who, encouraged by the presence of the Griquas, now went forth to the combat.

"The Mantatees had at that time advanced as far, and had taken possession of, Litakoo, a Bechuana town, containing 16,000 inhabitants; and I will now give, as nearly as I can recollect it, the account of Mr. M., the missionary at Kuruman, who accompanied the Griquas to propose and effect, if it were possible, an amicable arrangement with the invaders.

"He told me that as they proceeded with a small party, ahead of the Griqua force, to effect their purpose, they passed by numbers of the enemy, who had advanced to the pools to drink, and had there sunk down and expired from famine. As they neared the mass of the enemy, they found that all the cattle which they had captured were inclosed in the center of a vast multitude. They attempted a parley, but the enemy started forward, and hurled their spears with the most savage fury, and they were compelled to retreat, finding no hopes of obtaining a parley.

"The next day it was decided that the Griquas should advance. They numbered about one hundred well-mounted and well-armed men. The enemy flew at them with terrible howls, hurling their javelins and clubs; their black dismal appearance, their savage fury, and their hoarse loud voices producing a strange effect. The Griquas, to prevent their being surrounded, very wisely retreated.

"It was at last decided that the Griquas should fire, and it was hoped that as the Mantatees had never seen the effects of fire-arms they would be humbled and alarmed, and thus further bloodshed might be prevented. Many of the Mantatees fell; but, although the survivors looked with astonishment upon the dead and their wounded warriors writhing in the dust, they flew with lion-like vengeance at the horsemen, wrenching the weapons from the hands of their dying companions, to replace those which they had already discharged at their antagonists.

"As those who thus stepped out from the main body to attack the Griquas were the chiefs of the Mantatees, and many of them were killed, their deaths, one after the other, disheartened the whole body.

"After the Griquas had commenced the attack, the Bechuana army came up and assisted with their poisoned arrows, with which they plied the enemy; but a small body of the fierce Mantatees, sallying out, put the whole of the Bechuanas to flight.

"After a combat of two hours and a half, the Griquas, finding their ammunition failing, determined, at great risk, to charge the whole body. They did so, and the Mantatees gave way, and fled in a westerly direction; but they were intercepted by the Griquas, and another charge being made, the whole was pell-mell and confusion.

"Mr. M. says that the scene which now presented itself was most awful, and the state of suspense most cruel. The undulating country around was covered with warriors – Griquas, Mantatees, and Bechuanas, all in motion – so that it was impossible to say who were enemies and who were friends. Clouds of dust rose from the immense masses, some flying, others pursuing; and to their screams and yells were added the bellowing of the oxen, the shouts of the yet unvanquished warriors, the groans of the dying, and the wails of women and of children. At last the enemy retreated to the town, which they set in flames, to add to the horror of the scene.

"Then another desperate struggle ensued, the Mantatees attempted to inclose the Griquas in the burning town; but not succeeding, they fled precipitately. Strange to say, the Mantatee forces were divided into two parts, and during the time that the Griquas engaged the one, the other remained in the town, having such confidence in the former that they did not come to their assistance.

"When the town was set on fire, both armies united, and retreated together to the northward, in a body of not less than 40,000 warriors. As soon as the Mantatees retreated, the Bechuanas commenced the work of slaughter. Women and children were butchered without mercy; but as for the wounded Mantatees, it appeared as if nothing would make them yield. There were many instances of an individual being surrounded by fifty Bechuanas, but as long as life remained he fought.

"Mr. M. says that he saw more than one instance of a Mantatee fighting wildly against numbers, with ten or twelve arrows and spears pierced in his body. Struggling with death, the men would rally, raise themselves from the ground, discharge their weapons, and fall dead, their revengeful and hostile spirit only ceasing when life was extinct."

"And yet these same people permitted their own country to be taken from them by the Zoolus."

"Yes, it was so; but want and necessity had turned them into desperate warriors."

"I wonder they never thought of going back and recovering their own country. They would have been a match for the Zoolus. Is that the end of their history, Swinton?"

"No, not quite. But perhaps you are tired?"

"Oh, no. Pray go on."

"The Mantatees, although defeated by the Griquas, soon recovered their courage, and intelligence came that they were about to make a descent upon Kuruman, where the missionaries had their station. The Mantatees, having been informed that the Griquas had gone home, now determined to revenge themselves upon the Bechuanas, whom they considered but as the dust under their feet.

"On this information, Mr. M. wrote to Waterboer, who commanded the Griquas, requesting his immediate return; but Waterboer replied that an immense body of Mantatees were coming down upon the Griquas by the Val or Yellow River, and that they were forced to remain, to defend their own property, advising Mr. M. to retreat with his family to the Griqua town, and put themselves under their protection.

"As they could no longer remain, the mission station was abandoned, and the missionaries, with their wives and families, retreated to Griqua town. They had not, however, been long at Griqua town before news arrived that both the bodies of Mantatees had altered their routes. One portion of them went eastward, toward the country from which they had been driven by the Zoolus, and another, it appears, took possession of the country near the sources of the Orange River, where for many years they carried on a predatory warfare with the tribes in that district. At last a portion of them were incorporated, and settled down on that part which is now known as the Mantatee new country; the remainder made an irruption into the eastern Caffre country, where they were known as the Ficani."

"And what became of them?"

"They defeated one or two of the Caffre chiefs, and the Caffres implored the assistance of the English colonists, which was granted, and a large armed force was sent out against the invaders. They were found located – for they had built a town – near the sources of the Umtata River. The Caffres joined with all their forces, and the Ficani were surprised. A horrid slaughter took place; muskets, artillery and Congreve rockets were poured upon the unfortunate wretches, who were hemmed in on all sides by the Caffres, and the unfortunate Ficani may be said to have been exterminated, for the Caffres spared neither man, woman nor child. Such is the history of the Mantatees; their destruction was horrible, but perhaps unavoidable."

"Very true," observed Alexander; "I can not help thinking that desolating contests like these are permitted by a controlling Providence as chastisements, yet with a gracious end; for, surely it was better that they should meet with immediate death, than linger till famine put an end to their misery. This is certain, that they must have been destroyed, or others destroyed to make room for them. In either case a great sacrifice of life was to be incurred. War, dreadful as it is in detail, appears to be one of the necessary evils of human existence, and a means by which we do not increase so rapidly as to devour each other.

"I don't know whether you have made the observation, but it appears to me the plague and cholera are almost necessary in the countries where they break out; and it is very remarkable that the latter disease never made its appearance in Europe (at least not for centuries, I may say) until after peace had been established, and the increase of population was so rapid.

"During the many years that Europe was devastated and the population thinned by war, we had no cholera, and but little of one or two other epidemics which have since been very fatal. What I mean to infer is, that the hand of Providence may be seen in all this. Thus sanguinary wars and the desolating ravages of disease, which are in themselves afflictive visitations, and probably chastisements for national sins, may nevertheless have the effect, in some cases, of preventing the miseries which result from an undue increase of population."

"You may be quite right, Alexander," observed Swinton; "the ways of Heaven are inscrutably mysterious, and when we offer up prayers for the removal of what may appear to be a heavy calamity, we may be deprecating that which in the end may prove a mercy."

"One thing I could not help remarking in your narrative, Swinton," observed the Major, "which is the position of the missionaries during this scene of terror. You passed it slightly over, but it must have been most trying."

"Most surely it was."

"And yet I have not only read but heard much said against them, and strong opposition made to subscriptions for their support."

"I grant it, but it is because people know

that a great deal of money has been subscribed, and do not know the uses to which it is applied. They hear reports read, and find perhaps that the light of the Gospel has but as yet glimmered in one place or another; that in other places all labor has hitherto been thrown away. They forget that it is the grain of mustard-seed which is to become a great tree, and spread its branches; they wish for immoderate returns, and are therefore disappointed. Of course I can not give an opinion as to the manner in which the missions are conducted in other countries; but as I have visited most of the missions in these parts, I can honestly assert, and I think you have already yourself seen enough to agree with me, that the money intrusted to the societies is not thrown away or lavishly expended; the missionaries labor with their own hands, and almost provide for their own support."

"There I agree with you, Swinton," replied Alexander; "but what are the objections raised against them? for now that I have seen them with my own eyes, I can not imagine what they can be."

"The objections which I have heard, and have so often attempted to refute, are, that the generality of missionaries are a fanatical class of men, who are more anxious to inculcate the peculiar tenets of their own sects and denominations than the religion of our Saviour; that most of them are uneducated and vulgar men – many of them very intemperate and very injudicious – some few of them of bad moral character; and that their exertions, if they have used them – whether to civilize or to Christianize the people among whom they are sent – have not been followed by any commensurate results."

"And now let us have your replies to these many objections."

"It is no doubt true that the missionaries who are laboring among the savages of the interior are, many, if not most of them, people of limited education. Indeed, the major portion of them have been brought up as mechanics. But I much question whether men of higher attainments and more cultivated minds would be better adapted to meet the capacities of unintellectual barbarians. A highly-educated man may be appreciated among those who are educated themselves; but how can he be appreciated by the savage? On the contrary, the savage looks with much more respect upon a man who can forge iron, repair his weapons, and excite his astonishment by his cunning workmanship; for then the savage perceives and acknowledges his superiority, which in the man of intellect he would never discover.

"Besides, admitting that it would be preferable to employ persons of higher mental attainments, where are they to be found? Could you expect, when so many laborers are required in the vineyard, a sufficient number of volunteers among the young men brought up at the universities? Would they be able to submit to those privations, and incur those hardships, to which the African missionaries are exposed? Would they be able to work hard and labor for their daily bread, or be willing to encounter such toil and such danger as must be encountered by those who are sent here? I fear not. And allow me here to remark, that at the first preaching of Christianity it was not talented and educated men who were selected by our Saviour; out of the twelve, the Apostle Paul was the only one who had such claims.

"If we had beheld the Galilean fishermen mending their nets, should we have ever imagined that those humble laborers were to be the people who should afterward regenerate the world? – should overthrow the idolatries and crumble the superstitions of ancient empires and kingdoms? – and that what they – uneducated, but, we admit, divinely inspired and supported – had taught should be joyfully received, as it is now, we may say, from the rising to the setting of the sun, to the utmost boundaries of the earth?"

"Most truly and most admirably argued, Swinton," replied Alexander. "The Almighty, as if to prove how insignificant in his sight is all human power, has often made use of the meanest instruments to accomplish the greatest ends. Who knows but that even our keeping holy the Sabbath-day in the desert may be productive of some good, and be the humble means of advancing the Divine cause? We must ever bear in mind the counsel, 'In the morning sow thy seed, and in the evening withhold not thy hand; for thou knowest not whether shall prosper, either this or that, or whether they both shall be alike good.'"

"Surely so," replied Swinton; "the natives consider us as a superior race; they see our worship, and they are led to think that must be right which they perceive is done by those to whom they look up as their superiors. It may induce them to inquire and to receive information – eventually to be enrolled among the followers of our Saviour. It is, however, not to be denied that in some few instances persons have been chosen for the office of missionaries who have proved themselves unworthy; but that must and will ever be the case where human agents are employed. But it argues no more against the general respectability and utility of the missionaries as a body, than the admission of the traitor Judas among the apostles. To the efficacy of their works, and their zeal in the cause, I myself, having visited the station, have no hesitation in bearing testimony. Indeed I can not but admire the exemplary fortitude, the wonderful patience and perseverance, which the missionaries have displayed.

"These devoted men are to be found in the remotest deserts, accompanying the wild and wandering savages from place to place, suffering from hunger and from thirst, destitute of almost every comfort, and at times without even the necessaries of life. Some of them have without murmuring spent their whole lives in such service; and yet their zeal is set down as fanaticism by those who remain at home, and assert that the money raised for their equipment is thrown away. Happily, they have not looked for their reward in this world, but have built their hopes upon that which is to come."

"That the people who joined the Mission stations have become more civilized, and that they are very superior to their countrymen, is certain," observed the Major; "but have you seen any proof of Christianity having produced any remarkably good effect among the natives? – I mean one that might be brought forward as convincing evidence to those who have shown themselves inimical or lukewarm in the cause."

"Yes," replied Swinton, "the history of Africaner is one; and there are others, although not so prominent as that of the party to whom I refer."

"Well, Swinton, you must now be again taxed. You must give us the history of Africaner."

"That I will, with pleasure, that you may be able to narrate it, when required, in support of the missions. Africaner was a chief, and a descendant of chiefs of the Hottentot nation, who once pastured their own flocks and herds on their own native hills, within a hundred miles of Cape Town. As the Dutch colonists at the Cape increased, so did they, as Mr. Fairburn has stated to Alexander, dispossess the Hottentots of their lands, and the Hottentots, unable to oppose their invaders, gradually found themselves more and more remote from the possessions of their forefathers.

"After a time, Africaner and his

diminished clan found themselves compelled to join and take service under a Dutch boor, and for some time proved himself a most faithful shepherd in looking after and securing the herds of his employer. Had the Dutch boor behaved with common humanity, not to say gratitude, toward those who served him so well, he might now have been alive; but, like all the rest of his countrymen, he considered the Hottentots as mere beasts of burden, and at any momentary anger they were murdered and hunted down as if they were wild animals.

"Africaner saw his clan daily diminished by the barbarity of his feudal master, and at last resolved upon no further submission. As the Bushmen were continually making attempts upon the cattle of the boor, Africaner and his people had not only been well trained to fire-arms, but had them constantly in their possession. His assumed master, having an idea that there would be a revolt, resolved upon sending a portion of Africaner's people to a distant spot, where he intended to secure them, and by their destruction weaken the power of the clan.

"This, as he was a sort of magistrate, he had the power to enforce; but Africaner, suspecting his views, resolved to defeat them. Order after order was sent to the huts of Africaner and his people. They positively refused to comply. They requested to be paid for their long services, and be permitted to retire further into the interior. This was sternly denied, and they were ordered to appear at the house of the boor. Fearful of violence, yet accustomed to obey his order, Africaner and his brothers went up; but one of his brothers concealed his gun under his cloak. On their arrival, the boor came out and felled Africaner to the ground. His brother immediately shot the boor with his gun, and thus did the miscreant meet with the just reward of his villainies and murder.

"The wife, who had witnessed the murder of her husband, shrieked and implored mercy; they told her that she need not be alarmed, but requested that the guns and ammunition in the house should be delivered up to them, which was immediately done. Africaner then hastened back to his people, collected them and all his cattle, with what effects they could take with them, and directed his course to the Orange River.

"He was soon out of the reach of his pursuers, for it required time in so scattered a district to collect a sufficient force. Africaner fixed his abode upon the banks of the Orange River, and afterward a chief ceding to him his dominion in Great Namaqua land, the territory became his by right as well as by conquest. I think I had better leave off now; it is getting late, and we must to bed, if we are to start early to-morrow morning."

"We will have mercy upon you, Swinton, and defer our impatience," said the Major. "Good-night to you, and may you not have a lion's serenade."

"No, I hope not; their music is too loud to be agreeable; – good-night."

CHAPTER XX

Having filled their water-kegs, the next morning at day-light they yoked the oxen and left the banks of the Cradock or Black River, to proceed more to the northward, through the Bushmen's country; but as they were aware that there was no water to be procured, if they quitted the stream altogether, till they arrived at the Val or Yellow River, they decided upon following the course of the Black River to the westward for some time, before they struck off for the Val or Yellow River, near to which they expected to fall in with plenty of game, and particularly the giraffe and rhinoceros.

Although at that season of the year the river was nearly dry, still there was a scanty herbage on and near its bank, intermixed with beds of rushes and high reeds; this was sufficient for the pasture of the cattle, but it was infested with lions and other animals, which at the dry season of the year kept near the river-bank for a supply of water.

By noon they had proceeded about fifteen miles to the westward, and as they advanced they found that the supply of water in the river was more abundant; they then unyoked the cattle to allow them to feed till the evening, for it was too dangerous to turn them loose at night. As they were in no hurry, they resolved that they would only travel for the future from daylight till noon; the afternoon and evening were to be spent in hunting, and at night they were to halt the caravan and secure every thing as before, by inclosing the horses and sheep, and tying up the oxen.

By this arrangement the cattle would not be exhausted with their labor, and they would have time to follow the object of their journey – that of hunting the wild animals with which the country abounded, and also of procuring a constant supply of food for themselves and their attendants.

Having now traveled as far as they wished, they stopped at the foot of a rising ground, about a quarter of a mile from the river's bank, and which was on the outskirts of a large clump of mimosa and other trees. As soon as the cattle were unyoked and had gone down to the river to drink, our travelers ordered their horses to be saddled, and as the banks of the river on that side were low, they rode up to the rising ground to view the country beyond, and to ascertain what game might be in sight.

When they arrived at the summit, and were threading their way through the trees, Omrah pointed to a broken branch, and said, "Elephant here not long ago."

Bremen said that Omrah was right, and that the animals could not have left more than a week, and that probably they had followed the course of the stream. The print of another foot was observed by Omrah, and he pointed it out; but not knowing the name to give the animal in English or Dutch, he imitated its motions.

"Does he mean a gnoo?" said Alexander.

Omrah shook his head, and, raising his hands up, motioned that the animal was twice as big.

The Mission

"Come here, Bremen; what print of a hoof is this?" said Swinton.

"Buffalo, sir, – fresh print – was here last night."

"That's an animal that I am anxious to slay," said the Major.

"You must be very careful that he does not slay *you*," replied Swinton; "for it is a most dangerous beast, almost as much so as a lion."

"Well, we must not return without one, at all events," said Alexander; "nor without a lion also, as soon as we can find one alone; but those we have seen in the daytime have always been in threes and fours, and I think the odds too great with our party; but the first single lion we fall in with, I vote we try for his skin."

"Agreed," replied the Major; "what do you say, Swinton?"

"Why, I say agreed also; but as I came here to look for other things rather than lions, I should say, as far as I am concerned, that the best part of valor would be discretion. However, depend upon it, if you go after a lion I shall be with you: I have often been at the destruction of them when with Dutch boors; but then recollect we have no horses to spare, and therefore we must not exactly follow their method."

"How do they hunt the lions, then?" inquired Alexander.

"They hunt them more for self-defense than for pleasure," replied Swinton; "but on the outskirts of the colony the lions are so destructive to the herds, that the colonists must destroy them. They generally go out, ten or twelve of them, with their long guns, not fewer if possible; and you must recollect that these boors are not only very cool, brave men, but most excellent shots. I fear you will not find that number among our present party, as, with the exception of our three selves and Breman and Swanevelt, I do not believe that there is one man here who would face a lion; so that when we do attack one, it will be at a disadvantage.

"The Dutch boors, as soon as they have

ascertained where the lion lies, approach the bushes to within a moderate distance, and then alighting, they make all their horses fast together with their bridles and halters. In this there is danger, as sometimes the lion will spring out upon them at once, and, if so, probably not only horses but men are sacrificed. If the lion remains quiet, which is usually the case, they advance toward him within thirty paces or thereabouts, as they know that he generally makes a spring at half that distance; but as they advance, they back their horses toward him, as a shield in front of them, knowing that the lion will spring upon the horses.

"As they move forward, the lion at first looks at them very calmly, and very often wags his tail as if in a playful humor; but when they approach nearer, he growls, as if to warn them off. Then, as they continue to approach, he gradually draws up his hind legs under his body, ready for a spring at them as soon as they are within distance, and you see nothing of him except his bristling mane and his eyes glaring like fire; for he is then fully enraged, and in the act of springing the next moment.

"This is the critical moment, and the signal is given for half the party to fire. If they are not successful in laying him dead on the spot with this first volley, he springs like a thunderbolt upon the horses. The remainder of the party then fire, and seldom fail to put an end to him; but generally one or more of the horses are either killed or so wounded as to be destroyed in consequence; and sometimes, although rarely, one or more of the hunters share the same fate. So you observe that, with every advantage, it is a service of danger, and therefore should not be undertaken without due precaution."

"Very true, Swinton; but it will never do to return to the Cape without having killed a lion."

"As you please; but even that would be better than being killed yourself by a lion, and not returning at all. However, my opinion is that you will have to kill a lion before you have traveled much further, without going in quest of him. There are hundreds of them here; as many as there are in Namaqua-land."

"Look, master!" said Bremen, pointing to seven or eight splendid antelopes about a mile distant.

"I see," replied the Major. "What are they?"

"Gemsbok," said Swinton. "Now I will thank you for a specimen of that beautiful creature, if you can get it for me. We must dismount, leave our horses here, and crawl along from tree to tree, and bush to bush, till we get within shot."

"They are, indeed, noble animals. Look at that large male, which appears to be the leader and master of the herd. What splendid horns!" cried Alexander.

"Give the horses to Omrah and Swanevelt. Bremen shall go with us. Hist; not a word; they are looking in this direction." said the Major.

"Recollect to try for the large male. I want him most particularly," said Swinton.

"Master," said Bremen, "We must creep

till we get those bushes between us and the game. Then we can crawl through the bushes and get a good shot."

"Yes, that will be the best plan," said Swinton. "As softly as we can, for they are very shy animals."

They followed one another for two or three hundred yards, creeping from one covert to another, till they had placed the bushes on the plain between them and the herd. They then stopped a little and reconnoitered. The herd of antelopes had left off feeding, and now had all their heads turned toward the bushes, and in the direction where they were concealed; the large male rather in advance of the others, with his long horns pointing forward, and his nose close to the ground. Our party kept silence for some time, watching the animals; but none of them moved much from their positions; and as for the male, he remained as if he were a statue.

"They must have scented us," whispered Alexander.

"No, sir," said Bremen; "the wind blows

from them to us. I can't think what they are about. But perhaps they may have seen us."

"At all events, we shall gain nothing by remaining here; we shall be more concealed as we descend and approach them," observed the Major.

"That is true; so come along. Creep like mice," said Swinton.

They did so, and at last arrived at the patch of brushwood which was between them and the antelopes, and were now peeping and creeping to find out an opening to fire through, when they heard a rustling within. Bremen touched the sleeve of the Major and beckoned a retreat, and motioned to the others; but before they could decide, as they did not know why the Hottentot proposed it, for he did not speak himself, and put his hand to his mouth as a hint to them to be silent, a roar like thunder came from the bushes, within three yards of them, accompanied with a rushing noise which could not be mistaken. It was the roar and spring of the lion; and they looked round amazed and stunned, to ascertain

The Mission

who was the victim.

"Merciful Heaven!" exclaimed Alexander, "and no one hurt!"

"No, master; lion spring at antelope. Now we shall find him on other side of the bush, and kill him easy, when his eyes are shut."

Bremen led the way round the copse, followed by our travelers; they soon arrived on the other side of it, with their guns all ready; but on their arrival, to their astonishment they perceived the lion and the male gemsbok lying together. The antelope was dead, but the lion still alive; though the horns of the gemsbok had passed through his body. At the sight of the hunters, the lion, pierced through as he was, raised his head with a loud roar, and struck out with his paw, as he twisted toward them, his eyes glowing like hot coals, and showing his tremendous fangs. Alexander was the first who fired, and the ball penetrating the brain of the noble animal, it fell down dead upon the body of the antelope.

"This is the finest sight I ever

witnessed," observed Swinton. "I have heard that the gemsboks' horns are sometimes fatal to the lion, but I could hardly credit it. They have passed nearly through his body; the points are under the skin."

"Now we know, master, why gemsbok have his nose to the ground and his horn pointed," said Bremen; "he saw the lion, and fought him to save his herd."

"I am quite stunned yet," observed Alexander. "What a noble animal it is! Well, at all events I can say that I have shot a lion, which is more than you can, Major."

"I only wish that when I shoot one I may have no more danger to incur," replied the Major. "What a different idea does one have of a lion in a menagerie and one in its free and native state. Why, the menagerie lions can't roar at all; they are nothing but overgrown cats, compared to the lion of the desert."

"That is very true," observed Swinton; "however, I am delighted, for now I have not only my gemsbok, which is a gem above price, but also as fine a lion as I have ever seen. I should like to have them stuffed and set up just as they were before Alexander killed them. His rage and agony combined were most magnificent. After all, the lion is the king of the beasts. Bremen, send Swanevelt to the caravan for some of the men. I must have both skin and skeleton of the antelope, and the skin of the lion."

Our travelers were quite satisfied with the sport of the day, and after waiting for some time, while the Hottentots disentangled the animals and took off the skins, they returned to the caravan, Omrah having secured a portion of the flesh of the gemsbok for their supper.

As they were returning, they observed a herd of buffaloes at a great distance, and proposed to themselves the hunting of them after they had halted on the following day, if the animals were at any reasonable distance from them. At supper the flesh of the antelope was pronounced better than that of the gnoo; and after supper, as soon as the cattle had been all secured, and the fires lighted, Alexander proposed that

Swinton should finish his history of Africaner.

"If I remember right, I left off where Africaner and his people had escaped to Namaqua-land, where he became a chief. Attempts were made to take him prisoner and bring him to the colony, but without success. Expedition after expedition failed, and Africaner dared them to approach his territories. At last, the colonists had recourse to the Griquas, and offered them a large reward if they would bring Africaner in.

"The Griquas, commanded by a celebrated chief of the name of Berend, made several attempts, and in consequence a cruel war was carried on between Berend and Africaner, in which neither party gained the advantage. Africaner, discovering that the colonists had bribed Berend to make war against him, now turned his wrath against them. A Dutch boor fell a victim to his fury, and he carried off large quantities of their cattle, and eventually Africaner became the terror of the colony. The natives also who resided in Namaqua-land commenced depredations upon

The Mission

Africaner, but he repaid them with such interest that at last every tribe fled at his approach, and his name carried dismay into their solitary wastes. The courage and intrepidity shown by Africaner and his brothers in their various combats were most remarkable; but to narrate all his adventures would occupy too much time. It is certain that he not only became dreaded, but in consequence of his forbearance on several occasions he was respected.

"It was in 1810 that the missionaries came into the Namaqua-land, and it unfortunately happened that a dispute arose about some of Africaner's property which was seized, and at the same time Africaner lost some cattle. The parties who were at variance with Africaner lived near to the Mission station, and very unwisely the people at the Mission station were permitted to go to their assistance.

"This roused the anger of Africaner, who vowed vengeance on the Mission and the people collected around it or connected with it. As Africaner had commenced his attacks upon the Namaquas, and was advancing toward the mission, the missionaries were compelled to abandon the station and return to the colony. The Mission station was soon afterward taken possession of by Africaner, and the houses burned to the ground.

"A curious circumstance occurred during this affair: his followers were seeking everywhere for plunder, when some of them entered the burial ground, and one of them, treading on an apparently new made grave, was astonished by soft notes of music proceeding from the ground beneath.

"Superstitious as the natives are, and having most of them, in former days, heard something of the Christian doctrines, they started and stood transfixed with astonishment, expecting the dead to arise, as they had been once told. One of them mustered courage to put his foot again upon the spot, and the reply was soft and musical as before. Away they all started to Africaner, to inform him that there was life and music in the grave.

"The chief, who feared neither the living

nor the dead, went to the burial-ground with his men, and jumped upon the spot, which immediately gave out the soft note as before. Africaner ordered an immediate exhumation, when the source of the mystery proved to be the pianoforte of the missionary's wife, which being too cumbrous an article to take away, had been buried there, with the hope of being one day able to recover it. Never having seen such an instrument before, Africaner had it dissected for the sake of the brass wires; and thus the piano was destroyed."

"I doubt if it would ever have been dug up in Caffreland," observed Alexander.

"I am convinced it never would have been, but have remained as a wonder and object of fear as long as it held together," replied Swinton; "but to proceed –

"The Mission station having been for some time broken up by this attack of Africaner, Mr. C., a missionary, anxious to restore it, wrote a letter to Africaner on the subject, and received a favorable reply, and a Mr. E. was sent to the residence of Africaner himself. After a short time, Africaner and his two brothers, with a number of others, were baptized.

"At first it must be admitted that their profession of Christianity did not greatly improve their conduct; but this was very much to be ascribed to the circumstance that the duties of the station had devolved upon one who ought not to have been selected for the task. Upon his removal, and a more fitting minister of the Gospel taking his place, a great change was soon observable in Africaner; and, from having been one of the most remorseless pursuers of his vengeance – a firebrand spreading discord, war and animosity among the neighboring tribes – he would now make every concession and any sacrifice to prevent collision and bloodshed between contending parties.

"Although his power was so great that he might have raised his arm and dared them to lift a spear or draw a bow, he would entreat them as a suppliant to be reconciled.

The Mission

"'Look at me,' he would say, 'how many battles have I fought; how much cattle have I taken; but what has it done for me, but make me full of shame and sorrow?'

"In short, from that time till he died, he became a peacemaker and a Christian, both in word and deed. His whole life was devoted to acts of kindness and charity – to instructing and exhorting, and following the precepts of Him in whose faith eventually he lived and died."

"Well, Swinton, you have indeed given us a remarkable proof that the missionary labors are not always thrown away, and we thank you for your compliance with our request."

"It is a remarkable instance, if you only consider how many hundreds of lives might have been sacrificed, if Africaner had continued his career of slaughter and of plunder; and how many lives, I may add, have been also saved by his interference as a peacemaker, instead of being, as he formerly was, a promoter of war and bloodshed."

"Swinton," said Alexander, "I wanted to ask you a question which I had nearly forgotten. Do you recollect what Bremen said to us, that the lion had seized the gemsbok, and that now the lion would shut his eyes, and that he would shoot him?"

"Yes, I do; and he was correct in what he stated, for I have witnessed it myself. When a lion seizes a large animal like an ox or horse, or the animal he fell a martyr to this afternoon, he springs upon it, seizes it by the throat with his terrible fangs, and holds it down with his paws till it expires. From the moment the lion seizes his prey, he shuts his eyes, and never opens them again until the life of his prey is extinct. I remember a Hottentot, when a lion had seized an ox in this way, running up to him with his gun and firing within a few yards' distance. The lion, however, did not deign to notice the report of the gun, but continued to hold fast his prey. The Hottentot loaded again, fired, and again missed; reloaded again, and then shot the lion through the head."

"How very strange!"

"It is, and I can not give any reason for it; but that it is so, I well know to be a fact. Perhaps it may be that the animal, after long fasting, is quite absorbed with the grateful taste of the blood flowing into his mouth, while the animal is writhing under his clutches. But there are many singular points about the lion, which is a much more noble and intelligent animal than most people have any idea of; I have collected a number of facts relative to his majesty which would surprise you. The Bushmen know the animal and his habits so well, that they seldom come to any accident from their inhabiting a country in which I really believe the population of lions exceeds that of Bushmen."

"Is it true that the lion, as well as other animals, is afraid of the eye of man?" said the Major; "can you reply to that question?"

"Yes, I can," answered Swinton; "I was about to say that he is and is not, but a better answer will be to give you what has come to my knowledge: I consider that the lion is a much more dangerous animal in this country, and indeed in any other where there are no firearms, than where the occupants are possessed of them.

"It may appear strange, but it is my fixed opinion, that the lion has an idea of the deadly nature of firearms, and that he becomes in consequence more afraid of man. You remember a story I told you of a lion watching a man for two days without destroying him, but never permitting him to lay hold of his gun. Now it is satisfactorily proved that a lion will pass a man who has a gun in his hand without attacking him, provided that he does not attempt to level the gun; but the moment that he does he will spring upon him.

"An instance of that occurred to the great lion-hunter Diedrich Muller, who mentioned it to me. He had been alone hunting in the wilds, when he came suddenly upon a large lion, which, instead of giving way as they usually do, seemed disposed, from the angry attitude which he assumed, to dispute his progress.

"Muller instantly alighted, and, confident

of his unerring aim, leveled his gun at the forehead of the lion, which had crouched in the act to spring, within sixteen paces of him; but as he fired, his horse, whose bridle was round his arm, started back, and, jerking him aside, caused him to miss; the lion bounded forward, but stopped within a few paces, confronting Muller, who stood defenseless, as his gun was discharged, and his horse had galloped off.

"The man and the beast stood looking each other in the face for a short time. At length the lion moved backward, as if to go away. Muller began loading his gun; the lion looked over his shoulder, growled, and immediately returned to his former position within a few paces of Muller. Muller stood still, with his eyes fixed on the animal. The lion again moved cautiously off; when he was at a certain distance, Muller proceeded to ram down his bullet. The lion again looked back and growled angrily. Muller again was quiet, and the animal continued turning and growling as it moved off, till at last it bounded away."

"You imagine then, that the lion is

aware of the fatal effects of fire-arms?" said the Major.

"It would appear so, not only on account of their being so angry if presented at them, or being touched even when they are close to them, but also from the greater respect the lion pays to man where fire-arms are in use. The respect that he pays to men in the colony is not a general custom of the animal.

"As I said before, the lion is more dangerous in this Bushman country; because, in the first place, his awe of man has been removed, from his invariably successful encounters with those who have no weapons of force with which to oppose him; and, secondly, because he has but too often tasted human flesh, after which a lion becomes more partial to it than any other food.

"It is asserted, that when a lion has once succeeded in snatching some unfortunate Bushman from his cave, he never fails to return regularly every night, in hopes of another meal, until the horde is so harassed that they are compelled to seek some other shelter.

From apprehension of such attacks, it is also asserted that the Bushmen are in the habit of placing their aged and infirm people at the entrance of the cave during the night, that, should the lion come, the least valuable and most useless of their community may first fall a prey to the animal."

"Of course, if permitted to help himself in that way, the lion can not have much fear of man," observed Wilmot; "and his lurking abroad in the night takes away much from the nobleness of disposition which you are inclined to attribute to him."

"By no means," continued Swinton. "That a lion generally lurks and lies in wait to seize his prey is certain, but this is the general characteristic of the feline tribe, of which he may be considered as the head; and it is for this mode of hunting that nature has fitted him.

"The wolf, the hound, and others, are furnished with an acute scent, and are enabled to tire down their prey by a long chase. The feline tribe are capable of very extraordinary efforts of activity and speed for a very short time; if they fail to seize their prey at the first spring, or after a few tremendous bounds, they generally abandon the pursuit.

"The lion can spring from nine to twelve yards at a leap, and for a few seconds can repeat these bounds with such activity and velocity as to outstrip the movements of the quickest horse; but he can not continue these amazing efforts and does not attempt it. In fact, the lion is no more than a gigantic cat, and he must live by obtaining his prey in the same manner as a cat.

"In these countries, his prey is chiefly of the antelope species, the swiftest animals on earth; and what chance would he have, if he were to give one of his magnanimous roars to announce his approach? He knows his business better; he crouches in the rank grass and reeds by the sides of the paths made by the animals to descend to the rivers and pools to drink, and as they pass he makes his spring upon them.

"Now I do not consider that his obtaining his food as nature has pointed out to him is any argument against what I consider the really noble disposition of the lion, which is, that he does not kill for mere cruelty, and that he is really generous, unless compelled by hunger to destroy, as I have already shown by one or two examples."

"We are convinced, my dear Swinton," said Alexander; "but now let us have your opinion as to his being afraid to meet the eye of man."

"I consider that the lion will generally retreat before the presence of man; but he does not retreat cowardly, like the leopard or hyena, and others. He never slinks away, he appears calmly to survey his opponent, as apparently measuring his prowess. I should say that the lion seems to have a secret impression that man is not his natural prey, and although he will not always give place to him, he will not attack him, if, in the first place, the man shows no sign of fear, and in the second, no signs of hostility.

"But this instinctive deference to man is not to be reckoned upon. He may be very angry, he may be very hungry, he may have been just disappointed in taking his prey, or he may be accompanied by the female and cubs; in short, the animal's temper may have been ruffled, and in this case he becomes dangerous.

"An old Namaqua chief with whom I was conversing, and who had been accustomed to lions from childhood, fully corroborated these opinions, and also that there is that in the eye of man before which the lion quails. He assured me that the lion very seldom attacks a man, if not provoked; but he will approach him within a few paces and survey him steadily. Sometimes he attempts to get behind him, as if he could not stand his look, but was desirous of springing upon him unawares. He said, that if a man in such a case attempted to fly, he would run the greatest danger, but that if he had presence of mind to confront the animal, it would in almost every instance after a short time retire.

"Now I have already brought forward the instance of Muller and the lion, as a proof of the effect of a man's eye upon the lion. I will now give another, still more convincing, as the contact was still closer, and the lion had even tasted blood.

"A boor of the name of Gyt was out with one of his neighbors hunting. Coming to a fountain, surrounded as usual with tall reeds and rushes, Gyt gave his gun to his comrade, and alighted to see if there was any water remaining in it; but as he approached the fountain, an enormous lion started up close at his side, and seized him by the left arm. Gyt, although thus taken by surprise, stood motionless and without struggling, for he was aware that the least attempt to escape would occasion his immediate destruction. The animal also remained motionless, holding Gyt fast by the arm with his fangs, but without biting it severely, at the same time shutting his eyes, as if he could not withstand the eyes of his victim fixed upon him."

"What a terrible position!"

"Yes; but I may here observe that the lion was induced to seize the man in consequence of their coming so

The Mission

completely in contact, and, as it were, for self-defense. Had they been further apart, the lion would, as usually is the case, have walked away; and, moreover, the eye of the man being so close to him had, at the same time, more power over the lion, so as to induce him to shut his own. But to continue –

"As they stood in this position, Gyt recovered his presence of mind, and beckoned to his comrade to advance with his gun and shoot the lion through the head. This might easily have been done, as the animal continued still with his eyes closed, and Gyt's body concealed any object approaching. But his comrade was a cowardly scoundrel, and, instead of coming to Gyt's assistance, he cautiously crawled up a rock to secure himself from any danger. For a long while Gyt continued earnestly to entreat his comrade by signs to come to his assistance – the lion continuing all this while perfectly quiet – but in vain."

"How my blood boils at the conduct of this scoundrel," said the Major; "admitting his first impulse to have been fear, yet to allow his comrade to remain in that position so long a while covers him with infamy."

"I think if Gyt escaped, he must have felt very much inclined to shoot the wretch himself."

"The lion-hunters affirm that, if Gyt had but persevered a little longer, the animal would have at last released his hold and left Gyt uninjured; that the grip of the lion was more from fear that the man would hurt him, than from any wish to hurt the man; and such is my opinion. But Gyt, indignant at the cowardice of his comrade, and losing patience with the lion, at last drew his hunting-knife, which all the boors invariably carry at their side, and with all the power of his right arm thrust it into the lion's breast.

"The thrust was a deadly one, for it was aimed with judgment, and Gyt was a bold and powerful man; but it did not prove effectual so as to save Gyt's life, for the enraged lion, striving in his death agonies to grapple with Gyt, – held at arm's length by the strength of desperation on the part of the boor, – so dreadfully lacerated with his talons the breast and arms of poor Gyt, that his bones were left bare.

"At last the lion fell dead, and Gyt fell with him. His cowardly companion, who had witnessed this fearful struggle from the rock, now took courage to advance, and carried the mangled body of Gyt to the nearest house. Medical aid was at hand, but vainly applied, as on the third day, he died of a locked jaw. Such was the tragical end of this rencounter, from the sheer cowardice of Gyt's companion.

"I could mention many other instances in which lions have had men in their power and have not injured them, if they have neither attempted to escape nor to assault; but I think I have given enough already, not only to prove the fact of his general forbearance toward man, but also that there is something in the eye of man at which the lion and other animals, I believe, will quail."

"I can myself give an instance that this fascinating effect, or whatever it may be, of the human eye, is not confined wholly to the lion," said the Major.

"One of our officers in India, having once

rambled into a jungle adjoining the British encampment, suddenly encountered a Bengal tiger. The meeting was evidently most unexpected on both sides, and both parties made a dead halt, earnestly gazing at each other. The officer had no fire-arms with him, although he had his regulation sword by his side; but that he knew would be of no defense if he had to struggle for life with such a fearful antagonist. He was, however, a man of undaunted courage, and he had heard that even a Bengal tiger might be checked by looking him steadily in the face.

"His only artillery being, like a lady's, that of his eyes, he directed them point blank at the tiger. He would have infinitely preferred a rifle, as he was not at all sure but that his eyes might miss fire. However, after a few minutes, during which the tiger had been crouched ready for his spring, the animal appeared disturbed and irresolute, slunk on one side, and then attempted to crawl round behind the officer.

"This, of course, the officer would not permit, and he turned to the tiger as the tiger turned, with the same constancy that, Tom Moore says, the 'sunflower turns to the sun.'

"The tiger then darted into the thicket, and tried to catch him by coming suddenly upon him from another quarter, and taking him by surprise; but our officer was wide awake, as you may suppose, and the tiger, finding that it was no go, at last went off himself, and the officer immediately went off too, as fast as he could, to the encampment."

"I am glad to have heard your narrative, Major," replied Swinton; "for many doubts have been thrown upon the question of the power of the human eye, and your opinion is a very corroborative one."

"Do not you imagine that the lion-tamers who exhibit in Europe have taken advantage of this peculiar fact?"

"I have no doubt but that it is one of their great helps; but I think that they resort to other means, which have increased the instinctive fear that the animals have of them. I have witnessed these exhibitions, and always observed that the man never for a moment took his eyes off the animal which he was playing with or commanding.

"I have observed that also; but what are the other means to which you allude?"

"I can not positively say, but I can only express an opinion. The most painful and most stunning effects of a blow upon any part of the body, not only of man but of brutes, is a blow on the nose. Many animals, such as the seal and others, are killed by it immediately, and there is no doubt but a severe blow on that tender part will paralyze almost any beast for the time and give him a dread for the future. I believe that repeated blows upon the nose will go further than any other means to break the courage of any beast, and I imagine that these are resorted to: but it is only my opinion, recollect, and it must be taken for just as much as it is worth."

"Do not you think that animals may be tamed by kindness, if you can produce in them the necessary proportion of love and fear?"

"Yes, I was about to say every animal, but I believe some must be excepted;

and this is from their having so great a fear of man, rather than from any other cause. If their fear could be overcome, they might be tamed. Of course there are some animals which have not sufficient reasoning power to admit of their being tamed; for instance, who would ever think of taming a scorpion?"

"I believe that there is one animal which, although taken as a cub, has resisted every attempt to tame it in the slightest degree, – this is the grizzly bear of North America."

"I have heard so too," replied Swinton; "at all events, up to the present time they have been unsuccessful. It is an animal of most unamiable disposition, that is certain; and I would rather encounter ten lions, if all that they say of it is true. But it is time for us to go to bed. Those fires are getting rather low. Who has the watch?"

The Major rose and walked round to find the Hottentot who was on that duty, and found him fast asleep. After sundry kicks in the ribs, the fellow at last woke up.

"Is it your watch?"

"Yaw, Mynher," replied Big Adam, rolling out of his kaross.

"Well, then, you keep it so well, that you will have no tobacco next time it is served out."

"Gentlemen all awake and keep watch, so I go to sleep a little," replied Adam, getting up on his legs.

"Look to your fires, sir," replied the Major, walking to his wagon.

CHAPTER XXI

As they fully expected to fall in with a herd of buffaloes as they proceeded, they started very early on the following morning. They had now the satisfaction of finding that the water was plentiful in the river, and, in some of the large holes which they passed, they heard the snorting and blowing of the hippopotami, to the great delight of the Hottentots, who were very anxious to procure one, being very partial to its flesh.

As they traveled that day, they fell in with a small party of Bushmen; they were shy at first, but one or two of the women at last approached, and receiving some presents of snuff and tobacco, the others soon joined; and as they understood from Omrah and the Hottentots that they were to hunt in the afternoon, they followed the caravan, with the hopes of obtaining food.

They were a very diminutive race, the women, although very well formed, not being more than four feet high. Their countenances were pleasing, – that is, the young ones; and one or two of them would have been pretty, had they not been so disfigured with grease and dirt. Indeed the effluvia from them was so unpleasant, that our travelers were glad that they should keep at a distance; and Alexander said to Swinton, "Is it true that the lion and other animals prefer a black man to a white, as being of a higher flavor, Swinton, or is it only a joke?"

"I should think there must be some truth in the idea," observed the Major; "for they say that the Bengal tiger will always take a native in preference to a European."

"It is, I believe, not to be disputed," replied Swinton, "that for one European devoured by the lion or other animals, he feasts upon ten Hottentots or Bushmen, perhaps more; but I ascribe the cause of his so doing, not exactly to his perceiving any difference in the flesh of a black and white man, and indulging his preference. The lion, like many other beasts of prey, is directed to his game by his scent as well as by his eye; that is certain. Now I appeal to you, who have got rid of these Bushmen, and who know so well how odoriferous is the skin of a Hottentot, whether a lion's nose is not much more likely to be attracted by one of either of these tribes of people, than it would by either you or me. How often, in traveling, have we changed our position, when the wind has borne down upon us the effluvia of the Hottentot who was driving? – why that effluvia is borne down with the wind for miles, and is as savory to the lion, I have no doubt, as a beefsteak is to us."

"There can, I think, be no doubt of that," said Alexander; "but it is said that they will select a Hottentot from white men."

"No doubt of it, because they follow up the scent right to the party from whence it emanates. I can give you an instance of it. I was once traveling with a Dutch farmer, with his wagon and Hottentots. We unyoked and lay down on the sand for the night; there were the farmer and I, two Hottentot men and a woman – by the by, a very fat one, and who consequently was more heated by the journey. During the night a lion came and carried away the woman from among us all, and by his tracks, as we found on the following morning, he had passed close to the farmer and myself."

"Was the woman killed?"

"The night was so dark that we could see nothing; we were roused by her shrieks, and seized our guns, but it was of no use. I recollect another instance which was not so tragical. A Hottentot was carried off by a lion during the night, wrapped up in his sheep-skin kaross, sleeping, as they usually do, with his face to the ground. As the lion trotted away with him, the fellow contrived to wriggle out of his kaross, and the lion went off only his mantle."

"Well, I should think one of the karosses must be a very savory morsel for a hungry lion," said the Major; – "but I imagine it is almost time to unyoke; we must have traveled nearly twenty miles, and these forests promise well for the game we are in search of."

"I suspect that they contain not only buffaloes, but elephants; however, we shall soon find out by examining the paths down to the river, which they make in going for water."

"I think that yonder knoll would be a good place to fix our encampment, Swinton," said the Major; "it is well shaded with mimosas, and yet clear of the main forest."

"Well, you are quartermaster-general, and must decide."

The Major ordered Bremen to arrange the wagons as usual, and turn the cattle out to feed. As soon as this had been accomplished, they saddled their horses, and awaited the return of Swanevelt, who had gone to reconnoiter. Shortly afterward he returned, with the report that there were the tracks of elephants, buffaloes, and lions, in every direction by the river's banks; and as the dogs would now be of use, they were ordered to be let loose, which they seldom were, unless the game was large and to be regularly hunted down. Our travelers mounted and proceeded into the forest, accompanied by all the Hottentots except the cattle-keepers and the Bushmen; Bremen, Swanevelt, and

Omrah only being on horseback, as well as themselves. As they rode forward slowly and cautiously at the outset, Swinton asked the Major whether he had ever shot buffaloes.

"Yes, in India," replied the Major; "and desperate animals they are in that country."

"I was about to say that you will find them such here; and, Alexander, you must be very careful. In the first place, a leaden bullet is of little use against their tough hides, and, I may almost say, impenetrable foreheads. The best shot is under the fore-shoulder."

"Our balls are hardened with tin," observed Alexander.

"I know that," replied Swinton; "but still they are most dangerous animals, especially if you fall in with a single buffalo. It is much safer to attack a herd; but we have no time to talk over the matter now, only, as I say, be very careful, and whatever you do, do not approach one which is wounded, even if he be down on his knees. But here comes Bremen with news."

The Hottentot came up and announced that there was a large herd of buffaloes on the other side of the hill, and proposed that they should take a sweep round them, so as to drive them toward the river.

This proposal was considered good, and was acted upon; and, after riding about a mile, they gained the position which seemed the most desirable. The dogs were then let loose, and the Hottentots on foot, spread themselves on every side, shouting so as to drive the animals before them. The herd collected together and for a short while stood at bay with the large bulls in front, and then set off through the forest toward the river, followed by all the hunters on horse and on foot. In a quarter of an hour the whole herd had taken refuge in a large pool in the river, which, with the reeds and rushes, and small islands in the center, occupied a long slip of ground.

The Major, with Swanevelt and two other Hottentots, proceeded further up the river, that they might cross it before the attack commenced, and the others agreed to wait until the signal was given by the Major's firing. As soon as they heard the report of the Major's rifle, Swinton and Alexander, with their party, advanced to the banks of the river. They plunged in, and were soon up to the horses' girths, with the reeds far above their heads. They could hear the animals forcing their way through the reeds, but could not see them; and after some severe labor, Swinton said – "Alexander, it will be prudent for us to go back; we can do nothing here, and we shall stand a chance of being shot by our own people, who can not see us. We must leave the dogs to drive them out, or the Hottentots and Bushmen; but we must regain the banks."

Just as Swinton said this, a loud rushing was heard through the reeds. "Look out!" cried he; but he could say no more before the reeds opened and a large hippopotamus rushed upon them, throwing over Alexander's horse on his side, and treading Alexander and his horse both deep under the water as he passed over them and disappeared. Although the water was not more than four feet in depth, it was with difficulty that the horse and rider could extricate themselves from the reeds, among which they had been jammed and entangled; and Alexander's breath was quite gone when he at last emerged. Bremen and Swinton hastened to give what assistance they could, and the horse was once more on his legs. "My rifle," cried Alexander; "it is in the water." "We will find it," said Swinton: "haste up to the banks as fast as you can, for you are defenseless."

Alexander thought it advisable to follow Swinton's advice, and with some difficulty regained the bank, where he was soon afterward followed by Swinton and Bremen, who had secured his rifle. Alexander called Omrah, and sent him to the caravan for another rifle, and then for the first time he exclaimed, "Oh, what a brute! It was lucky the water was deep, or he would have jammed me on the head, so that I never should have risen up again."

"You have indeed had a providential escape, Alexander," replied Swinton; "is your horse hurt!"

"He must be, I should think," said Alexander, "for the animal trod upon him; but he does not appear to show it at present."

In the mean time several shots were fired from the opposite side of the river by the Major and his party, and occasionally the head or horns of the buffalo were seen above the reeds by the Hottentots, who remained with Swinton and Alexander: but the animals still adhered to their cover. Omrah having brought another rifle, Bremen then proposed that the Hottentots, Bushmen, and dogs should force their way through the reeds and attempt to drive the animals out; in which there would be no danger, as the animals could not charge with any effect in the deep water and thick rushes.

"Provided they don't meet with a hippopotamus," said Alexander, laughing.

"Won't say a word about him, sir," replied Bremen, who then went and gave the directions.

The Hottentots and Bushmen, accompanied

by the dogs, then went into the reeds, and their shouting and barking soon drove out some of the buffaloes on the opposite side, and the reports of the guns were heard.

At last one came out on that side of the river where Alexander and Swinton were watching; Swinton fired, and the animal fell on its knees; a shot from Alexander brought it down dead and turned on its side. One of the Bushmen ran up to the carcass, and was about to use his knife, when another buffalo charged from the reeds, caught the Bushman on his horns, and threw him many yards in the air. The Bushman fell among the reeds behind the buffalo, which in vain looked about for his enemy, when a shot from Bremen brought him to the ground.

Shortly afterward the Bushman made his appearance from the reeds; he was not at all hurt, with the exception of a graze from the horns of the animal, and a contusion of the ribs.

The chase now became warm; the shouting of the Hottentots, the barking of the dogs, and the bellowing of the herd, which were forcing their way through the reeds before them, were very exciting. By the advice of Swinton, they took up their position on a higher ground, where the horses had good footing, in case the buffaloes should charge.

As soon as they arrived there, they beheld a scene on the other side of the river, about one hundred yards from them, which filled them with anxiety and terror; the Major's horse was galloping away, and the Major not to be seen. Under a large tree, Swanevelt was in a sitting posture, holding his hands to his body as if severely wounded, his horse lying by his side, and right before him an enormous bull buffalo, standing motionless; the blood was streaming from the animal's nostrils, and it was evidently tottering from weakness and loss of blood; at last it fell.

"I fear there is mischief done," cried Swinton; "where can the Major be, and the two Hottentots who were with him! Swanevelt is hurt and his horse killed, that is evident. We had better call them off, and let the buffaloes remain quiet, or escape as they please."

"There is the Major," said Alexander, "and the Hottentots too; they are not hurt, don't you see them? – they were up the trees; thank God."

They now observed the Major run up to Swanevelt, and presently the two Hottentots went in pursuit of the Major's horse. Shortly afterward, Swanevelt, with the assistance of the Major, got upon his legs, and, taking up his gun, walked slowly away.

"No great harm done, after all," said Alexander; "God be praised: but here come the whole herd, Swinton."

"Let them go, my good fellow," replied Swinton, "we have had enough of buffalo-hunting for the present."

The whole herd had now broken from the reeds about fifty paces from where they were stationed, and with their tails raised, tossing with their horns, and bellowing with rage and fear, darted out of the reeds, dripping with slime and mud, and rushed off toward the forest. In a few seconds they were out of sight.

"A good riddance," said Swinton; "I hope the Major is now satisfied with buffalo-hunting."

"I am, at all events," replied Alexander. "I feel very sore and stiff. What a narrow escape that Bushman had."

"Yes, he had indeed; but, Alexander, your horse is not well: he can hardly breathe. You had better dismount."

Alexander did so, and unloosed his girths. Bremen got off his horse, and, offering it to Alexander, took the bridle of the other and examined him.

"He has his ribs broken, sir," said the Hottentot, – "two of them, if not more."

"No wonder, poor fellow; lead him gently, Bremen. Oh, here comes the Major. Now we shall know what has occurred; and there is Swanevelt and the two men."

"Well, Major, pray tell us your adventures, for you have frightened us dreadfully."

"Not half so much as I have been frightened myself," replied the Major;

"we have all had a narrow escape. I can assure you, and Swanevelt's horse is dead."

"Is Swanevelt hurt?"

"No, he was most miraculously preserved; the horn of the buffalo has grazed the whole length of the body, and yet not injured him. But let us go to the caravan and have something to drink, and then I will tell you all about it – I am quite done up, and my tongue cleaves to the roof of my mouth."

As soon as they had arrived at the caravan and dismounted, the Major drank some water, and then gave his narrative. "We had several shots on our side of the river, for the buffaloes had evidently an intention of crossing over, had we not turned them. We had killed two, when a bull buffalo charged from the reeds upon Swanevelt, and before he could turn his horse and put him to his speed, the horns of the buffalo had ripped up the poor animal, and he fell with Swanevelt under him. The enraged brute disengaged himself from the horse, and made a second charge upon

Swanevelt; but he twisted on one side, and the horn only grazed him, as I have mentioned. I then fired and wounded the animal. He charged immediately, and I turned my horse, but from fright he wheeled so suddenly that I lost my stirrups, and my saddle turned round.

"I found that I could not recover my seat, and that I was gradually sliding under the horse's belly, when he passed under a tree, and I caught a branch and swung myself on to it, just as the buffalo, which was close behind us, came up to me. As he passed under, his back hit my leg; so you may imagine it was 'touch and go.' The animal, perceiving that the horse left him, and I was not on it, quitted his pursuit, and came back bellowing and roaring, and looking everywhere for me.

"At last it perceived Swanevelt, who had disengaged himself from the dead horse, and was sitting under the tree, apparently much hurt, as he is, poor fellow, although not seriously. It immediately turned back to him, and would certainly have gored him to death, had not Kloet, who was up in a tree, fired at the animal and wounded him mortally – for his career was stopped as he charged toward Swanevelt, and was not ten yards from him. The animal could proceed no further, and there he stood until he fell dead."

"We saw that portion of the adventure ourselves, Major," said Swinton; "and now we will tell you our own, which has been equally full of incident and danger." Swinton having related what had passed on his side of the river, the Major observed:

"You may talk about lions, but I'd rather go to ten lion-hunts than one more buffalo-hunt. I have had enough of buffaloes for all my life."

"I am glad to hear you say so," replied Swinton, "for they are most ferocious and dangerous animals, as you may now acknowledge, and the difficulty of giving them a mortal wound renders the attack of them very hazardous. I have seen and heard enough of buffalo-hunting to tell you that you have been fortunate, although you have lost one horse and have another very much hurt; – but here come the spoils of the chase; at all events, we will benefit by the day's sport, and have a good meal."

"I can't eat now," said Alexander; "I am very stiff. I shall go and lie down for an hour or two."

"And so shall I," said the Major; "I have no appetite."

"Well, then, we will all meet at supper," said Swinton. "In the mean time I shall see if I can be of any use to Swanevelt. Where's Omrah?"

"I saw him and Begum going out together just now," said the Major. "What for, I do not know."

"Oh! I told him to get some of the Bushman roots," said Alexander; "they are as good as potatoes when boiled; and he has taken the monkey to find them."

The Major and Alexander remained on their beds till supper-time, when Mahomed woke them up. They found themselves much refreshed by their sleep, and also found that their appetites had returned. Buffalo-steaks and fried Bushman roots were declared to be a very good substitute for beefsteaks and fried potatoes; and after they had made a hearty meal, Alexander inquired of Swinton what he had seen of buffalo-hunting when he had been at the Cape before.

"I have only been once or twice engaged in a buffalo-hunt; but I can tell you what I have heard, and what I have collected from my own knowledge, as to the nature of the animal, of which indeed to-day you have had a very good proof. I told you this morning, that a single buffalo was more dangerous than a herd; and the reason is this: – At the breeding season, the fiercest bulls drive the others away from the herd, in the same manner as the elephants do; and these solitary buffaloes are extremely dangerous, as they do not wait to be attacked, but will attack a man without any provocation. They generally conceal themselves, and rush out upon you unawares, which makes it more difficult to escape from them. They are so bold, that they do not fear the lion himself; and I have been told by the Dutch boors, that when a buffalo has killed one of their comrades by goring and tossing him, it will not leave its victim for hours, but continue to trample on him with his hoofs, crushing the body with its knees as an elephant does, and with its rough tongue stripping off the skin as far as it can. It does not do all this at one time, but it leaves the body, and returns again, as if to glut its vengeance."

"What a malicious brute!"

"Such is certainly its character. I recollect a history of a buffalo-hunting adventure, told me by a Dutch farmer, who was himself an eye-witness to the scene. He had gone out with a party to hunt a herd of buffaloes which were grazing on a piece of marshy ground, sprinkled with a few mimosa-trees. As they could not get within shot of the herd, without crossing a portion of the marsh, which was not safe for horses, they agreed to leave their steeds in charge of two Hottentots, and to advance on foot; thinking that, in case any of the buffaloes should charge them, it would be easy to escape by running back to the marsh, which would bear the weight of a man, but not of a horse, much less that of a buffalo.

"They advanced accordingly over the marsh, and being concealed by some bushes, they had the good fortune to bring down, with the first volley, three of the fattest of the herd; and also so severely wounded the great bull, which was the leader of the herd, that he dropped down on his knees, bellowing most furiously. Thinking that the animal was mortally wounded, the foremost of the huntsmen walked out in front of the bushes from which they had fired, and began to reload his musket as he advanced, in order to give the animal a finishing shot. But no sooner did the enraged animal see the man advancing, than he sprang up and charged headlong at him. The man threw down his gun, and ran toward the marsh; but the beast was so close upon him, that he despaired of escaping by that direction, and turning suddenly round a clump of copsewood, began to climb an old mimosa tree which stood close to it.

"The buffalo was, however, too quick for him. Bounding forward with a roar, which the farmer told me was one of the most hideous and appalling sounds that he ever heard, he caught the poor fellow with his terrible horns, just as he had nearly got out of reach, and tossed him in the air with such force, that after whirling round and round to a great height, the body fell into the fork of the branches of the tree. The buffalo went round the tree roaring, and looking for the man, until, exhausted by wounds and loss of blood, it again fell down on its knees. The other hunters then attacked and killed him; but they found their comrade, who was still hanging in the tree, quite dead."

"Well; I have no doubt but that such would have been the fate of Swanevelt or of me, had the brute got hold of us," said the Major; "I never saw such a malignant, diabolical expression in any animal's countenance as there was upon that buffalo's. A lion is, I should say, a gentleman and a man of honor compared to such an evil-disposed ruffian."

"Well, Major, you have only to let them alone; recollect, you were the aggressor," said Swinton, laughing.

"Very true; I never wish to see one again."

"And I never wish to be in the way of a hippopotamus again, I can assure you," said Alexander, "for a greater want of politeness I never met with."

During this conversation the Hottentots and Bushmen at the other fires had not been idle. The Hottentots had fried and eaten, and fried and eaten, till they could hold no more; and the Bushmen, who in the morning looked as thin and meager as if they had not had a meal for a month, were now so stuffed that they could hardly walk, and their lean stomachs were distended as round as balls. The Bushman who had been tossed by the buffalo came up and asked for a little tobacco, at the same time smiling and patting his stomach, which was distended to a most extraordinary size.

"Yes, let us give them some," said Alexander; "it will complete their day's happiness. Did you ever see a fellow so stuffed? I wonder he does not burst."

"It is their custom. They starve for days,

and then gorge in this way when an opportunity offers, which is but seldom. Their calendar, such as it is, is mainly from recollections of feasting; and I will answer for it, that if one Bushman were on some future day to ask another when such a thing took place, he would reply, just before or just after the white men killed the buffaloes."

"How do they live in general?"

"They live upon roots at certain seasons of the year; upon locusts when a flight takes place; upon lizards, beetles – any thing. Occasionally they procure game, but not very often. They are obliged to lie in wait for it, and wound it with their poisoned arrows, and then they follow its track and look for it the next day. Subtle as the poison is they only cut out the part near the wound, and eat the rest of the animal. They dig pit-holes for the hippopotamus and rhinoceros and occasionally take them. They poison the pools for the game also; but their living is very precarious, and they often suffer the extremities of hunger."

"Is that the cause, do you imagine, of

their being so diminutive a race, Swinton?"

"No doubt of it. Continual privation and hardships from generation to generation have, I have no doubt, dwindled them down to what you see."

"How is it that these Bushmen are so familiar? I thought that they were savage and irreclaimable."

"They are what are termed tame Bushmen; that is, they have lived near the farmers, and have, by degrees, become less afraid of the Europeans. Treated kindly, they have done good in return to the farmers by watching their sheep, and performing other little services, and have been rewarded with tobacco. This has given them confidence to a certain degree. But we must expect to meet with others that are equally wild, and who will be very mischievous; attempting to drive off our cattle, and watching in ambush all round our caravan, ready for any pilfering that they can successfully accomplish; and then we shall discover that we are in their haunts without even seeing them."

"How so?"

"Because it will only be by their thefts that we shall find it out. But it is time for bed, and as to-morrow is Sunday you will have a day of rest, which I think you both require."

"I do," replied Alexander, "so good-night to you both."

CHAPTER XXII

As arranged, they did not travel on the Sunday. Early in the morning the oxen and horses and sheep were turned out to pasture; all except the horse which had been ridden by Alexander on the preceding day, and which was found to be suffering so much that they took away a large quantity of blood from him before he was relieved.

The Bushmen still remained with them, and were likely to do so as long as there was any prospect of food. The four buffaloes which had been killed, as well as the horse which had been gored to death, were found picked clean to the bones on the following day, by the hyenas and other animals which were heard prowling during the whole night. But as large quantities of the buffalo-flesh had been cut off, and hung upon the trees near the caravan, there was more than sufficient for a second feast for the Bushmen and Hottentots, and there was nothing but frying and roasting during the whole of the day.

The sun was intensely hot, and Alexander and the Major both felt so fatigued from the exertions of the day before, that after breakfast they retired to their wagons, and Swinton did not attempt to disturb them, as they were in a sound sleep till the evening, when they were much refreshed and very hungry. Swinton said he had thought it better that they should not be awakened, as the heat was so overpowering, and they could perform Divine service in the evening, if they thought proper, when it would be cooler. This was agreed to, and, after an early supper, they summoned all the Hottentots, who, although gorged, were still unwilling to leave their fires; as they said the Bushmen would devour all the flesh that was left, in their absence.

This remonstrance was not listened to, and they all assembled. The prayers were read and the service gone through by the light of a large fire, for it was very dark before the service was finished. The Bushmen, as the Hottentots prophesied, had taken advantage of their absence, to help themselves very liberally; and as

Swinton read the prayers, the eyes of the Hottentots were continually turning round to their own fires, where the Bushmen were throwing on large pieces of buffalo-flesh, and, before they were even heated through, were chewing them and tearing them to pieces with their teeth.

Never perhaps was there a congregation whose attention was so divided, and who were more anxious for the conclusion of the service. This uneasiness shown by the Hottentots appeared at last to be communicated to the oxen, which were tied up round the wagons. The fire required replenishing, but none of the Hottentots moved to perform the office; perhaps they thought that if Swinton could no longer see, the service must conclude: but Swinton knew it by heart, and continued reading the Commandments, which was the last portion which he read, and Alexander and the Major repeated the responses. The Major, whose face was toward the cattle, had observed their uneasiness, and guessed the cause, but did not like to interrupt the service, as it was just over. Begum began clinging to him in

The Mission

the way she always did when she was afraid; Swinton had just finished, and the Major was saying, "Swinton, depend upon it," when a roar like thunder was heard, and a dark mass passed over their heads.

The bellowing and struggling of the oxen was almost instantaneously succeeded by a lion, with an ox borne on his shoulder, passing right through the whole congregation, sweeping away the remnants of the fire and the Hottentots right and left, and vanishing in a moment from their sight. As may be imagined, all was confusion and alarm. Some screamed, some shouted and ran for their guns; but it was too late. On examination, it was found that the lion had seized the ox which had been tied up near to where they were sitting; their fire being nearly extinguished, and the one which should have been kept alight next to it altogether neglected by the Hottentots, in their anxiety to keep up those on which they had been broiling their buffalo-steaks.

The leather thongs by which the ox had been tied up were snapped like threads, and many of the other oxen had, in their agony of fear, broken their fastenings and escaped. As the lion bounded away through the assembled party, it appeared as if the ox was not a feather's weight to him. He had, however, stepped rather roughly upon two of the Hottentots, who lay groaning, as if they had been severely hurt; but upon examination it was found that they had only been well scratched and covered with ashes. The Bushmen, however, had left their meal, and with their bows and small poisoned arrows had gone in pursuit. Bremen and one or two of the Hottentots proposed also to go, but our travelers would not permit them. About an hour afterward the Bushmen returned, and Omrah had communication with them; and through Bremen they learned that the Bushmen had come up with the lion about a mile distant, and had discharged many of their arrows at him, and, they were convinced, with effect, as a heavy growl or an angry roar was the announcement when he was hit; but, although he was irritated, he continued his repast. Omrah then said, "Lion dead to-morrow, – Bushmen find him."

"Well," said Alexander, as they went to their wagons, which, in consequence of this event, and their having to make up large fires before they went to bed, they did not do till late, "I believe this is the first time that Divine service was ever wound up by such intrusion."

"Perhaps so," replied Swinton; "but I think it proves that we have more cause for prayer, surrounded as we are by such danger. The lion might have taken one of us, and by this time we should have suffered a horrid death."

"I never felt the full force of the many similes and comparisons in the Scriptures, where the lion is so often introduced, till now," observed Alexander.

"It was indeed a most awful sermon after the prayers," said the Major: "I trust never to hear such a one again: but is it not our own fault? This is the second time that one of our oxen has been carried off by a lion, from the circle of fires not being properly attended to. It is the neglect of the Hottentots, certainly; but if they are so neglectful, we should attend to them ourselves."

"It will be as well to punish them for their neglect," said Swinton, "by stopping their tobacco for the week; for if they find that we attend to the fires ourselves, they will not keep one in, that you may depend upon. However, we will discuss that point to-morrow, so good-night."

Omrah came to the Major the next morning, before the oxen were yoked, to say that the Bushmen had found the lion, and that he was not yet dead, but nearly so; that the animal had dragged away that portion of the ox that he did not eat, about half a mile further; that there he had lain down, and he was so sick that he could not move.

At this intelligence they mounted their horses, and, guided by the Bushmen, arrived at the bush where the lion lay. The Bushmen entered at once, for they had previously reconnoitered, and were saluted with a low snarl, very different from the roar of the preceding night. Our travelers followed, and found the noble creature in his last agonies, his strength paralyzed, and his eyes closed. One or two of the small arrows of the Bushmen were still sticking in his hide, and did not appear to have entered more than half an inch; but the poison was so subtle, that it had rapidly circulated through his whole frame; and while they were looking down upon the noble beast, it dropped its jaws and expired.

As our travelers turned back to join the caravan, Alexander observed: "Those Bushmen, diminutive as they are in size, and contemptible as their weapons appear, must be dangerous enemies, when the mere prick of one of their small arrows is certain death. What is their poison composed of?"

"Of the venom extracted from snakes, which is mixed up with the juice of the euphorbia, and boiled down till it becomes of the consistency of glue. They then dip the heads of the arrows into it, and let it dry on."

"Is then the venom of snakes so active after it has been taken away from the animal?"

"Yes, for a considerable time after. I remember a story, which is, I believe, well authenticated, of a man who had been bitten through his boot by a rattlesnake in America. The man died, and shortly afterward his two sons died one after the other, with just the same symptoms as their father, although they had not been bitten by snakes. It was afterward discovered that upon the father's death the sons had one after the other taken possession of and put on his boots, and the boots being examined, the fang of the rattlesnake was discovered to have passed through the leather and remained there. The fang had merely grazed the skin of the two sons when they put on the boots, and had thus caused their death."

"Are the snakes here as deadly in their poison as the rattlesnake of America?"

"Equally so, – that is, two or three of them; some are harmless. The most formidable is the cobra capella (not the same as the Indian snake of the same name). It is very large, being usually five feet long; but it has been found six and even seven feet. This snake has been known to dart at a man on horseback, and with such force as to overshoot his aim. His bite is certain death, I believe, as I never heard of a man recovering from the wound."

"Well, that is as bad as can be. What is the next?"

"The next is what they call the puff adder. It is a very heavy, sluggish animal, and very thick in proportion to its length, and when attacked in front, it can not make any spring. It has, however, another power, which, if you are not prepared for it, is perhaps equally dangerous – that of throwing itself backward in a most surprising manner. This is, however, only when trod upon or provoked; but its bite is very deadly. Then two of the mountain adders are among the most dangerous snakes here. The mountain adder is small, and, from its not being so easily seen and so easily avoided, is very dangerous, and its bite as fatal as the others."

"I trust that is the end of your catalogue?"

"Not exactly; there is another, which I have specimens of, but whose faculties I have never seen put to the test, which is called the spirting snake. It is about three feet long, and its bite, although poisonous, is not fatal. But it has a faculty, from which its name is derived, of spirting its venom into the face of its assailant, and if the venom enters the eye, at which the animal darts it, immediate blindness ensues. There are a great many other varieties, some of which we have obtained possession of during our journey. Many of them are venomous, but not so fatal as the first three I have mentioned.

"Indeed, it is a great blessing that the Almighty has not made the varieties of snakes aggressive or fierce, – which they are not. Provided, as they are, with such dreadful powers, if they were so, they would indeed be formidable; but they only act in self-defense, or when provoked. I may as well here observe, that the Hottentots, when they kill any of the dangerous snakes, invariably cut off the head and bury it; and this they do, that no one may by chance tread upon it, as they assert that the poison of the fangs is as potent as ever, not only for weeks but months afterward."

"That certainly is a corroboration of the story that you told us of the rattlesnake's fang in the boot."

"It is so; but although there are so many venomous snakes in this country, it is remarkable how very few accidents or deaths occur from them. I made an inquiry at the Moravian Mission, where these venomous snakes are very plentiful, how many people they had lost by their bites, and the missionaries told me, that out of 800 Hottentots belonging to the Mission, they had only lost two men by the bites of snakes during a space of seven years; and in other places where I made the same inquiry, the casualties were much less in proportion to the numbers."

"Is the boa constrictor found in this part of Africa?"

"Not so far south as we now are, but it is a few degrees more to the northward. I have never seen it, but I believe there is no doubt of its existence."

"The South American Indians have a very subtle poison with which they kill their game. Are you aware, Swinton, of its nature? Is it like the Bushmen's poison?"

"I know the poison well; it was brought over by Mr. Waterton, whose amusing works you may have read. It is called the wourali poison, and is said to be extracted from a sort of creeping vine, which grows in the country. The natives, however, add the poison of snakes to the extract; and the preparation is certainly very fatal, as I can bear witness to."

"Have you ever seen it tried?"

"Yes, I have tried it myself. When I was in Italy I became acquainted with Mr. W., and he gave two or three of us, who were living together, a small quantity, not much more than two grains of mustard-seed in size. We purchased a young mule to make the experiment upon; an incision was made in its shoulder, and the poison inserted under the skin. I think in about six or seven minutes the animal was dead. Mr. W. said that the effects would have been instantaneous, if the virtue of the poison had not somewhat deteriorated from its having been kept so long."

"The wourali poison only acts upon the nerves, I believe?" said the Major.

"Only upon the nerves; and although so fatal, if immediate means are resorted to, a person who is apparently dead from it may be brought to life again by the same process as is usual in the recovery of drowned or suffocated people. A donkey upon which the poison had acted was restored in this manner, and for the remainder of his days permitted to run in Sir Joseph Banks's park. But the poison of snakes acts upon the blood, and therefore occasions death without remedy."

"But there are remedies, I believe, for even the most fatal poisons?"

"Yes, in His provident mercy God has been pleased to furnish remedies at hand, and where the snake exists the remedy is to be found. The rattlesnake root is a cure, if taken and applied immediately; and it is well known that the ichneumon when bitten by the cobra capella, in his attack upon it, will hasten to a particular herb and eat it immediately, to prevent the fatal effect of the animal's bite."

"I once saw a native of India," said the Major, "who for a small sum would allow himself to be bitten by a cobra capella. He was well provided with the same plant used by the ichneumon, which he swallowed plentifully, and also rubbed on the wound. It is impossible to say, but, so far as I could judge, there was no deception."

"I think it very possible; if the plant will cure the ichneumon, why not a man? I have no doubt but that there are many plants which possess virtues of which we have no knowledge. Some few, and perhaps some of the most valuable, we have discovered; but our knowledge of the vegetable kingdom, as far as its medicinal properties are known, is very slight; and perhaps many which were formerly known have, since the introduction of mineral antidotes, been lost sight of."

"Why, yes; long before chemistry had made any advances, we do hear in old romances of balsams of most sovereign virtues," said Alexander, laughing.

"Which, I may observe, is almost a proof that they did in reality exist; and the more so, because you will find that the knowledge of these sovereign remedies was chiefly in the hands of the Jews, the oldest nation upon the earth; and from their constant communication with each other, most likely to have transmitted their knowledge from generation to generation."

"We have also reason to believe that not only they had peculiar *remedies* in their times, but also – if we are to credit what has been handed down to us – that the art of *poisoning* was much better understood," said the Major.

"At all events, they had not the knowledge of chemistry which now leads to its immediate detection," replied Swinton. "But, Alexander, there are three hippopotami lying asleep on the side of the river. Have you a mind to try your skill?"

"No, not particularly," replied Alexander; "I have had enough of hippopotami. By the by, the river is much wider than it was."

"Yes, by my calculation we ought to travel no more to the westward after to-day. We must now cut across to the Yellow or Val River. We shall certainly be two days without water or pasturage for the cattle, but they are in such good condition that they will not much feel it. There is a river which we shall cross near its head, but the chance of water is very small; indeed, I believe we shall find it nowhere, except in these great arteries, if I may so call them."

"Well; I was thinking so myself, Swinton, as I looked at the map yesterday, when I lay in my wagon," said the Major; "so then to-morrow for a little variety; that is, a desert."

"Which it will most certainly be," replied Swinton; "for, except on the banks of the large rivers, there are no hopes of vegetation in this country at this season of the year; but in another month we may expect heavy falls of rain."

"The Bushmen have left us, I perceive," said Alexander.

"Yes, they have probably remained behind to eat the lion."

"What, will they eat it now that it has been poisoned?"

"That makes no difference to them; they merely cut out the parts wounded, and invariably eat all the carcasses of the animals which they kill, and apparently without any injury. There is nothing which a Bushman will not eat. A flight of locusts is a great feast to him."

"I can not imagine them to be very palatable food."

"I have never tasted them," replied Swinton; "but I should think not. They do not, however, eat them raw; they pull off their wings and legs, and dry their bodies; they then beat them into a powder."

"Do you suppose that St. John's fare of locusts and wild honey was the locust which we are now referring to?"

"I do not know, but I should rather think not, and for one reason, which is, that although a person in the wilderness might subsist upon these animals, if always to be procured, yet the flights of locusts are very uncertain. Now there is a tree in the country where St. John retired, which is called the locust-tree, and produces a large sweet bean, shaped like the common French bean, but nearly a foot long, which is very palatable and nutritious. It is even now given to cattle in large quantities; and I imagine that this was the locust referred to; and I believe many of the commentators on the holy writings have been of the same opinion. I think we have now gone far enough for to-day; we may as well halt there. Do you intend to hunt, Major? I see some animals there at a distance."

"I should say not," said Alexander; "if we are to cross a desert tract to-morrow, we had better not fatigue our horses."

"Certainly not. No, Swinton, we will remain quiet, unless game comes to us."

"Yes, and look after our water-kegs being filled, and the fires lighted to-night," said Alexander; "and I trust we may have no more sermons from lions, although Shakespeare does say, 'sermons from stones, and good in everything.'"

They halted their caravan upon a rising ground, and having taken the precaution to see the water-kegs filled and the wood collected, they sat down to dinner upon fried ham and cheese; for the Hottentots had devoured all the buffalo-flesh, and demanded a sheep to be killed for supper. This was consented to although they did not deserve it; but as their tobacco had been stopped for their neglect of providing fuel and keeping up the fires, it was considered politic not to make them too discontented.

Alexander had been walking by the side of the river with the Major, while the Hottentots were arranging the camp, and Swinton was putting away some new specimens in natural history which he had collected, when Omrah, who was with them, put his finger to his lips and stopped them. As they perfectly understood what he required, they stood still and silent. Omrah then pointed to something which was lying on the low bank, under a tuft of rushes; but they could not distinguish it, and Omrah asked by signs for the Major's rifle, took aim, and fired. A loud splashing was heard in the water, and they pushed their way through the high grass and reeds, until they arrived at the spot, where they perceived an animal floundering in the agonies of death."

"An alligator!" exclaimed the Major; "well, I had no idea that there were any here inland. They said that there were plenty at the mouths of the rivers, on the coast of the Eastern Caffres, but I am astonished to find one here."

"What did you fire at?" asked Swinton, who now joined them.

"An alligator, and he is dead. I am afraid that he won't be very good eating," replied the Major.

"That's not an alligator, Major," said Swinton, "and it is very good eating. It is a large lizard of the guana species, which is found about these rivers; it is amphibious, but perfectly harmless, subsisting upon vegetables and insects. I tell you it is a great delicacy, ugly as it looks. It is quite dead, so let us drag it out of the water, and send it up to

Mahomed by Omrah."

The animal, which was about four feet long, was dragged out of the water by the tail, and Omrah took it to the camp.

"Well, I really thought it was a small alligator," said the Major; "but now I perceive my mistake. What a variety of lizards there appears to be in this country."

"A great many from the chameleon upward," replied Swinton. "By the by, there is one which is said to be very venomous. I have heard many well-authenticated stories of the bite being not only very dangerous, but in some instances fatal. I have specimens of the animal in my collection. It is called here the geitje."

"Well, it is rather remarkable, but we have in India a small lizard, called the gecko by the natives, which is said to be equally venomous. I presume it must be the same animal, and it is singular that the names should vary so little. I have never seen an instance of its poisonous powers, but I have seen a whole company of sepoys run out of their quarters because they have heard the animal make its usual cry in the thatch of the building; they say that it drops down upon people from the roof."

"Probably the same animal; and a strong corroboration that the report of its being venomous is with good foundation."

"And yet if we were to make the assertion in England, we should in all probability not be believed."

"Not by many, I grant – not by those who only know a little; but by those who are well informed, you probably would be. The fact is, from a too ready credulity, we have now turned to almost a total skepticism, unless we have ocular demonstration. In the times of Marco Polo, Sir John Mandeville, and others, – say in the fifteenth century, when there were but few travelers and but little education, a traveler might assert almost any thing, and gain credence; latterly a traveler hardly dare assert any thing. Le Vaillant and Bruce, who traveled in the South and North of Africa, were both stigmatized as liars, when they published their accounts of what they had seen, and yet every tittle has since been proved to be correct. However, as people are now better informed, they do not reject so positively; for they have certain rules to guide them between the possible and the impossible."

"How do you mean?"

"I mean, for instance, that if a person was to tell me that he had seen a mermaid, with the body of a woman and the scaly tail of a fish, I should at once say that I could not believe him. And why? because it is contrary to the laws of nature. The two component parts of the animal could not be combined, as the upper portion would belong to the mammalia, and be a hot-blooded animal, the lower to a cold-blooded class of natural history. Such a junction would, therefore, be impossible. But there are, I have no doubt, many animals still undiscovered, or rather still unknown to Europeans, the description of which may at first excite suspicion, if not doubt. But as I have before observed, the account would, in all probability, not be rejected by a naturalist, although it might be by people without much knowledge of the animal kingdom, who would not be able to judge by comparison whether the existence of such an animal was credible. Even fabulous animals have had their origin from existing ones. The unicorn is, no doubt, the gemsbok antelope; for when you look at the animal at a distance, its two horns appear as if they were only one, and the Bushmen have so portrayed the animal in their caves. The dragon is also not exactly imaginary; for, the *Lacerta volans*, or flying lizard of Northern Africa, is very like a small dragon in miniature. So that even what has been considered as fabulous has arisen from exaggeration or mistake."

"You think, then, Swinton, that we are bound to believe all that travelers tell us?"

"Not so; but not to reject what they assert, merely because it does not correspond with our own ideas on the subject. The most remarkable instance of unbelief was relative to the aerolites or meteoric stones formed during a thunder-storm in the air, and falling to the earth. Of course you have heard that such have occurred?"

"I have," replied the Major, "and I have seen several in India."

"This was treated as a mere fable not a century back; and when it was reported (and not the first time) that such a stone had fallen in France, the *savans* were sent in deputation to the spot. They heard the testimony of the witnesses that a loud noise was heard in the air; that they looked up and beheld an opaque body descending; that it fell on the earth with a force which nearly buried it in the ground, and was so hot at the time that it could not be touched with the hand. It afterward became cold. Now the *savans* heard all this, and pronounced that it could not be; and for a long while every report of the kind was treated with contempt. Now every one knows, and every one is fully satisfied of the fact, and not the least surprise is expressed when they are told of the circumstance. As Shakespeare makes Hamlet observe very truly — 'There are more things in heaven and earth, Horatio, than are dreamt of in your philosophy.'"

CHAPTER XXIII

There was no alarm during the night, and the next morning they yoked the oxen and changed their course to the northward. The whole of the cattle had been led down to the river to drink, and allowed two hours to feed before they started; for they were about to pass through a sterile country of more than sixty miles, where they did not expect to find either pasturage or water. They had not left the river more than three miles behind them, when the landscape changed its appearance. As far as the eye could scan the horizon, all vestiges of trees had disappeared, and now the ground was covered with low stunted bushes and large stones. Here and there were to be seen small groups of animals, the most common of which were the quaggas. As our travelers were in the advance, they started six or seven ostriches which had been sitting, and a ball from the Major's rifle brought one to the ground, the others running off at a velocity that the fastest horse could scarcely have surpassed.

The Mission

"That was a good shot, Major," said Alexander.

"Yes," replied Swinton; "but take care how you go too near the bird; you have broken his thigh, and he may be dangerous. They are very fierce. As I thought, here is the nest. Let Bremen kill the bird, – he understands them, Major. It is the male, and those which have escaped are all females."

"What a quantity of eggs!" said Alexander. "Is the nest a joint concern?"

"Yes," replied Swinton. "All those which are in the center of the nest with their points upward are the eggs for hatching. There are, let me see, twenty-six of them, and you observe that there are as many more round about the nest. Those are for the food of the young ostriches as soon as they are born. However, we will save them that trouble. Bremen must take the eggs outside the nest for us, and the others the people may have. They are not very particular whether they are fresh or not."

"This is a noble bird," said the Major, "and has some beautiful feathers. I suppose we may let Bremen take the feathers out and leave the body!"

"Yes; I do not want it; but Bremen will take the skin, I dare say. It is worth something at the Cape."

As soon as the Hottentots had secured the eggs, and Bremen had skinned the ostrich, which did not occupy many minutes, they rode on, and Swinton then said –

"The male ostrich generally associates with from three to seven females, which all lay in the same nest. He sits as well as the females, and generally at night, that he may defend the eggs from the attacks of the hyenas and other animals."

"You do not mean to say that he can fight these animals!"

"And kill them also. The ostrich has two powerful weapons; its wing, with which it has often been known to break a hunter's leg, the blow from it is so violent; and what is more fatal, its foot, with the toe of which it strikes and kills both animals and men. I once myself, in

Namaqua-land, saw a Bushman who had been struck on the chest by the foot of the ostrich, and it had torn open his chest and stomach, so that his entrails were lying on the ground. I hardly need say that the poor wretch was dead."

"I could hardly have credited it," observed Alexander.

"The Bushmen skin the ostrich, and spread the skin upon a frame of wicker-work; the head and neck are supported by a skin thrust through them. The skin they fix on one of their sides, and carry the head and neck in one of their hands, while the other holds the bow and arrows. In this disguise – of course with the feathered side of him presented to the bird or beast he would get near to – he walks along, pecking with the head at the bushes, and imitating the motions of the ostrich. By this stratagem he very often is enabled to get within shot of the other ostriches, or the quaggas and gnoos which consort with these birds."

"I should like to see that very much," said the Major.

"You would be surprised at the close

imitation, as I have been. I ought to have said that the Bushman whitens his legs with clay. It is, however, a service of danger, for I have, as I told you, known a man killed by the male ostrich; and the natives say that it is by no means uncommon for them to receive very serious injury."

"Hold hard," said the Major, "there is a lion; what a terrible black mane he has got! What do you say, Swinton? He is by himself."

Swinton looked at the animal, which was crossing about three hundred yards ahead of them; he was on a low hill, with his head close to the ground.

"I certainly say not. Let him pass, by all means; and I only hope he will take no notice of us. I must give you the advice which an old Namaqua chief gave me. He said – 'Whenever you see a lion moving in the middle of the day, you may be certain that he is in great want of food and very angry. Never attack one then, for they are very dangerous and most desperate,' If, therefore, Major, you wish a very serious affair, and one or two lives lost you will attack that animal. But you must expect that what I say will happen."

"Indeed, my dear Swinton, I neither wish to lose my own life, nor to risk those of others, and therefore we will remain here till his majesty has had time to get out of our way; and I hope he may soon find a dinner."

By this time the caravan had come up with them, and they then proceeded. The face of the country became even more sterile, and at last not an animal of any description was to be seen. As there was nothing for the oxen to feed upon they continued their route during the whole of the day, and at night they halted and secured the cattle to the wagons. Wood for fires they were not able to procure, and therefore they made one half of the Hottentots watch during the night with their muskets to scare off wild beasts. But, as Swinton observed, there was little chance of their being disturbed by lions or other animals, as they were so distant from water, and there was no game near them upon which the wild beasts prey; and so it proved, for during the whole night they did not even hear the cry of a hyena or a jackal.

At the first gleaming of light the oxen were again yoked, with the hopes of their being able to gain the Val River by night. The relay oxen were now put to, to relieve those which appeared to suffer most. At noon the heat was dreadful, and the horses, which could not support the want of water as the oxen could, were greatly distressed. They continued for about two hours more, and then perceived a few low trees. Begum, who had been kept without water, that she might exert herself to find it, started off as fast as she could, followed by Omrah. After running to the trees, they altered their course to the eastward, toward some ragged rocks. The caravan arrived at the trees, which they found were growing on the banks of the river Alexandria, which they knew they should pass; but not a drop of water was to be discovered; even the pools were quite dry. As they searched about, all of a sudden Begum came running back screaming, and with every mark of terror, and clung, as usual, to the Major when frightened.

"Where is the Bushboy?" said Bremen.

"Something has happened," cried Swinton; "come all of you with your guns."

The whole party, Hottentots and all, hastened toward the rocks where Omrah and Begum had been in search of water. As soon as they reached within fifty paces, quite out of breath with their haste, they were saluted with the quah, quah, of a herd of baboons, which were perched at the edge of the rocks, and which threatened them in their usual way, standing on their fore-legs, and making as if they would fly at them.

"Now, then, what is to be done?" said the Major. "Shall we fire? Do you think that they have possession of the boy?"

"If they have, they will let him go. Yes, we are too numerous for them now, and they will not show fight, depend upon it. Let us all take good aim and fire a volley right into them."

"Well, then, I'll take that venerable old chap that appears to be the leader, and the great-grandfather of them all," said the Major. "Are you all ready? – then fire."

The volley had its effect; three or four of the animals were killed, many were wounded, and the whole herd went scampering off with loud shrieks and cries, the wounded trailing themselves after the others as well as they could.

The whole party then ascended the crags to look after Omrah – all but Begum, who would not venture. They had hardly gained the summit when they heard Omrah's voice below, but could not see him. "There he is, sir," said Swanevelt, "down below there." Swinton and the Major went down again, and at last, guided by the shouts of the boy, they came to a narrow cleft in the rock, about twenty feet deep, at the bottom of which they heard, but could not see, the boy. The cleft was so narrow that none of the men could squeeze down it. Swinton sent one of them back for some leathern thongs or a piece of rope to let down to him.

During the delay, Bremen inquired of Omrah if he was hurt, and received an answer in the negative. When the rope came, and was lowered down to him, Omrah seized it, and was hauled up by the Hottentots. He appeared to have suffered a little, as his hair was torn out in large handfuls, and his shirt was in ribbons; but with the exception of some severe scratches from the nails of the baboons, he had no serious injury. Omrah explained to the Hottentots, who could talk his language, that Begum and he had come to the cleft, and had discovered that there was water at the bottom of it; that Begum had gone down, and that he was following, when the baboons, which drank in the chasm, had come upon them. Begum had sprung up and escaped, but he could not; and that the animals had followed him down, until he was so jammed in the cleft that he could descend no further; and that there they had pulled out his hair and torn his shirt, as they saw. Having heard Omrah's story, and satisfied themselves that he had received no serious injury, they then went to where the baboons had been shot. Two were dead; but the old one, which the Major had fired at, was alive, although severely wounded, having received two shots, one in his arm and the other in his leg, which was broken by the ball. All the poor old creature's fierceness appeared to have left him. It was evidently very weak from the loss of blood, and sat down leaning against the rock. Every now and then it would raise itself, and look down upon the wound in its leg, examining the hole where the bullet had passed through; then it would hold up its wounded arm with its other hand, and look them in the face inquiringly, as much as to say, "What have you done this for?"

"Poor creature," said Alexander; "how much its motions are those of a human being. Its mute expostulation is quite painful to witness."

"Very true," said the Major; "but still, if it had not those wounds, it would tear you to pieces if it could."

"That it certainly would," said Swinton; "but still it is an object of pity. It can not recover, and we had better put it out of its misery."

Desiring Bremen to shoot the animal

through the head, our travelers then walked back to the caravan. As they returned by the banks of the river, they perceived Begum very busy, scraping up the baked mud at the bottom of a pool.

"What is the princess about?" said Alexander.

"I know," cried Omrah, who immediately ran to the assistance of the baboon; and after a little more scraping, he pulled out a live tortoise about a foot long.

"I have heard that when the pools dry up, the tortoises remain in the mud till the pools are filled up again," said Swinton.

"Are they good eating, Swinton?"

"Excellent."

"Turtle soup in the desert, that's something unexpected."

The Hottentots now set to work and discovered five or six more, which they brought out. They then tried in vain to get at the water in the deep cleft, but finding it impossible, the caravan continued its course.

The Mission

"How much more of this desert have we to traverse," said Alexander, "before we come to the river?"

"I fear that we shall not arrive there before to-morrow night," said Swinton, "unless we travel on during the night, which I think will be the best plan; for fatiguing as it will be to the animals, they will be even more exhausted if they pass another day under the sun without water, and at night they will bear their work better. We gain nothing by stopping, as the longer they are on the journey, the more they will be exhausted."

"I am really fearful for the horses, they suffer so much."

"At night we will wash their mouths with a sponge full of water; we can spare so much for the poor creatures."

"In the deserts of Africa you have always one of three dangers to encounter," said Swinton; "wild men, wild beasts, and want of water."

"And the last is the worst of the three," replied the Major. "We shall have a

The Mission

moon to-night for a few hours."

"Yes, and if we had not, it would be of no consequence; the stars give light enough, and we have little chance of wild beasts here. We now want water; as soon as we get rid of that danger, we shall then have the other to encounter."

The sun went down at last; the poor oxen toiled on with their tongues hanging out of their mouths. At sunset, the relay oxen were yoked, and they continued their course by the stars. The horses had been refreshed, as Swinton had proposed; but they were too much exhausted to be ridden, and our travelers, with their guns on their shoulders, and the dogs loose, to give notice of any danger, now walked by the sides of the wagons over the sandy ground. The stars shone out brilliantly, and even the tired cattle felt relief, from the comparative coolness of the night air. All was silent, except the creaking of the wheels of the wagons, and the occasional sighs of the exhausted oxen, as they thus passed through the desert.

"Well," observed the Major, after they

had walked about an hour without speaking, "I don't know what your thoughts may have been all this while, but it has occurred to me that a party of pleasure may be carried to too great lengths; and I think that I have been very selfish, in persuading Wilmot to undergo all that we have undergone and are likely to undergo, merely because I wished to shoot a giraffe."

"I presume that I must plead guilty also," replied Swinton, "in having assisted to induce him; but you know a naturalist is so ardent in his pursuit that he thinks of nothing else."

"I do not think that you have either of you much to answer for," replied Alexander; "I was just as anxious to go as you were; and as far as I am concerned, have not the slightest wish to turn back again, till we have executed our proposed plans. We none of us undertook this journey with the expectation of meeting with no difficulties or no privations; and I fully anticipate more than we have yet encountered, or are encountering now. If I get back on foot, and without a sole left to my shoe, I shall be quite content; at the same time, I will not continue it if you both wish to return."

"Indeed, my dear fellow, I have no wish but to go on; but I was afraid that we were running you into dangers which we have no right to do."

"You have a right, allowing that I did not myself wish to proceed," replied Alexander. "You escorted me safe through the country to ascertain a point in which you had not the slightest interest, and it would indeed be rewarding you very ill, if I were now to refuse to gratify you: but the fact is, I am gratifying myself at the same time."

"Well, I am very glad to hear you say so," replied the Major, "as it makes my mind at ease; what time do you think it is, Swinton?"

"It is about three o'clock; we shall soon have daylight, and I hope with daylight we shall have some sight to cheer us. We have traveled well, and can not by my reckoning be far from the Val River. Since yesterday morning we have made sixty miles or thereabouts; and if we

The Mission

have not diverged from our course, the poor animals will soon be relieved."

They traveled on another weary hour, when Begum gave a cry, and started off ahead of the wagons; the oxen raised their heads to the wind, and those which were not in the yokes after a short while broke from the keepers, and galloped off, followed by the horses, sheep, and dogs. The oxen in the yokes also became quite unruly, trying to disengage themselves from the traces.

"They have smelt the water; it is not far off, sir," said Bremen; "we had better unyoke them all, and let them go."

"Yes, by all means," said Alexander.

So impatient were the poor beasts, that it was very difficult to disengage them, and many broke loose before it could be effected; as soon as they were freed, they followed their companions at the same rapid pace.

"At all events, we shall know where to find them," said the Major, laughing: "well, I really so felt for the poor animals that I am as happy as if I was as thirsty as they are, and was now quenching my thirst. It's almost daylight."

As the day dawned, they continued to advance in the direction that the animals had taken, and they then distinguished the trees that bordered the river, which was about two miles distant. As soon as it was broad daylight, they perceived that the whole landscape had changed in appearance. Even where they were walking there was herbage, and near to the river it appeared most luxuriant. Tall mimosa-trees were to be seen in every direction, and in the distance large forests of timber. All was verdant and green, and appeared to them as a paradise after the desert in which they had been wandering on the evening before. As they arrived at the river's banks, they were saluted with the lively notes of the birds hymning forth their morning praise, and found the cattle, after slaking their thirst, were now quietly feeding upon the luxuriant grass which surrounded them.

"Well may the Psalmist and prophets talk of the beauty of flowing rivers," said Alexander; "now we feel the truth and beauty of the language; one would almost imagine that the sacred writings were indited in these wilds."

"If not in these, they certainly were in the Eastern countries, which assimilate strongly with them," said Swinton; "but, as you truly say, it is only by having passed through the country that you can fully appreciate their beauties. We never know the real value of any thing till we have felt what it is to be deprived of it; and in a temperate climate, with a pump in every house, people can not truly estimate the value of 'flowing rivers.'"

The Hottentots having now arrived, the cattle were driven back to the wagons and yoked, that they might be brought up to a spot which had been selected for their encampment. In the mean time our travelers, who were tired with their night's walk, lay down under a large mimosa-tree, close to the banks of the river.

"We shall stay here a day or two, of course," said the Major.

"Yes, for the sake of the cattle; the poor

creatures deserve a couple of days' rest."

"Do you observe how the mimosas are torn up on the other side of the river?" said Swinton; "the elephants have been very numerous there lately."

"Why do they tear the trees up?" said Alexander.

"To feed upon the long roots, which are very sweet; they destroy an immense number of the smaller trees in that manner."

"Well, we must have another elephant-hunt," said the Major.

"We may have hunts of every kind, I expect, here," replied Swinton; "we are now in the very paradise of wild animals, and the further we go the more we shall find."

"What a difference there is in one day's journey in this country," observed Alexander; "yesterday morning there was not a creature to be seen, and all was silent as death. Now listen to the noise of the birds, and as for beasts, I suspect we shall not have far to look for them."

"No, for there is a hippopotamus just risen; and now he's down again – there's food for a fortnight at one glance," cried the Major.

"How the horses and sheep are enjoying themselves – they are making up for lost time; but here come the wagons."

"Well, then, I must get up and attend to my department," said the Major. "I presume that we must expect our friends the lions again now."

"Where there is food for lions, you must expect lions, Major," said Swinton.

"Very true, and fuel to keep them off; by the by, turtle soup for dinner, recollect; tell Mahomed."

"I'll see to it," said Alexander; "but we must have something for breakfast, as soon as I have had a wash at the river's side. I would have a bath, only I have such a respect for the hippopotami."

"Yes, you will not forget them in a hurry," said Swinton, laughing.

"Not as long as I have breath in my body, for they took all the breath out of it. Come, Swinton, will you go with me, and make your toilet at the river's banks?"

"Yes, and glad to do so; for I am covered with the sand of the desert."

CHAPTER XXIV

Our travelers remained very quiet that day and the next. The horses had suffered so much, that they required two days of rest, and they themselves were not sorry to be inactive after their fatiguing journey over the desert. The cattle enjoyed the luxuriant pasture, and although the tracks of the lions were discovered very near to them, yet, as they had plenty of fuel and attended themselves to the fires, they had not any visits from them during the night. The Hottentots had been out to reconnoiter, and found a profusion of game, in a large plain, about two miles distant; and it was decided that they would rest where they were for a day or two, if the game were not frightened away. The river had been crossed by Swanevelt, who stated that there was a large herd of elephants on the other side, and the tracks of the rhinoceros were to be seen on both sides of the river.

On the third morning after their arrival at the Val, they set off, accompanied by the Hottentots, to the plain which they had spoken of; riding through magnificent groups of acacia or camelthorn trees, many of which were covered with the enormous nests of the social grosbeaks. As they descended to the plain they perceived large herds of brindled gnoos, quaggas, and antelopes, covering the whole face of the country as far as the eye could reach, moving about in masses to and fro, joining each other and separating, so that the whole plain seemed alive with them.

"Is not this splendid?" cried the Major. "Such a sight is worth all the trouble and labor which we have undergone. What would they say in England, if they could but behold this scene?"

"There must be thousands and thousands," said Alexander. "Tell me, Swinton, what beautiful animals are those of a purple color?"

"They are called the purple sassabys," replied Swinton; "one of the most elegant of the antelope tribe."

"And those red and yellow out there?"

"They are the harte beests. I wish to have male and female specimens of both, if I can."

"See!" said the Major, "there is a fine flock of ostriches. We are puzzled where to begin. Come, we have surveyed the scene long enough; now forward, – to change it."

They rode down, and were soon within shot of the animals, and the rifles began their work. The Hottentots commenced firing from various points, and, alarmed by the report of the guns, the animals now fled away in every direction, and the whole place was one cloud of dust. Our travelers put their horses to their speed, and soon came up with them again, as their numbers impeded the animals in their flight. Every shot told, for it was hardly possible to miss; and the Hottentots who followed on foot, put those who were wounded out of their misery. At last the horses were too fatigued and too much out of wind to continue the pursuit, and they reined up.

"Well, Alexander, this has been sport, has it not?" said the Major.

"Yes, a grand battue, on a grand scale, indeed."

"There were three animals which you did not observe," said Swinton; "but it was impossible to get at them, they were so far off; but we must try for them another time."

"What were they?"

"The elands, the largest of the antelope tribe," replied Swinton, "and the best eating of them all. Sometimes they are nineteen hands high at the chest, and will weigh nearly 2,000 lbs. It has the head of an antelope, but the body is more like that of an ox. It has magnificent straight horns, but they are not dangerous. They are easily run down, for, generally speaking, they are very fat and incapable of much exertion."

"We will look out for them to-morrow," said the Major. "See how the vultures are hovering over us; they know there will be bones for them to pick this night."

"More than bones," replied Alexander;

"for what can we do with so many carcasses? There is provision for a month, if it would keep. What a prodigious variety of animals there appears to be in this country."

"Yes, they are congregated here, because the country, from want of rain, may be considered as barren. But within eight or nine degrees of latitude from the Cape, we find the largest and most minute of creation. We have the ostrich and the little creeper among the birds. Among the beasts we have the elephant, weighing 4,000 lbs., and the black specked mouse, weighing a quarter of an ounce. We have the giraffe, seventeen feet high, and the little viverra, a sort of weasel, of three inches. I believe there are thirty varieties of antelopes known and described; eighteen of them are found in this country, and there are the largest and smallest of the species; for we have the eland, and we have the pigmy antelope, which is not above six inches high. We see here also the intermediate links of many genera, such as the eland and the gnoo; and as we find the elephant, the rhinoceros, and Wilmot's friend, the hippopotamus, we certainly have the bulkiest animals in existence."

Bremen now came up to say that they had discovered a rhinoceros close to the river-side, concealed in the bushes underneath a clump of acacia. The Major and Alexander having declared their intention of immediately going in pursuit, Swinton advised them to be cautious, as the charge of a rhinoceros was a very awkward affair, if they did not get out of the way. They rode down to the clump of trees and bushes where the animal was said to be hid, and, by the advice of Bremen, sent for the dogs to worry the animal out. Bremen, who was on foot, was desired by the Major to take the horse which Omrah rode, that he might be more expeditious, and our travelers remained with a clear space of two hundred yards between them and the bushes where the animal was concealed. The Hottentots had also followed them, and were ordered on no account to fire till they had taken their positions, and the dogs were sent in to drive the animal out.

When Bremen was but a short distance

from them with the dogs, Swinton advised that they should dismount and take possession of a small clump of trees which grew very close together, as they would be concealed from the animal. They called Omrah to take the horses, but he was not to be seen; so they gave them to one of the Hottentots, to lead them to some distance out of harm's way.

"The vision of the rhinoceros is so limited," observed Swinton, "that it is not difficult to get out of his way on his first charge; but at his second he is generally prepared for your maneuver. A ball in the shoulder is the most fatal. Look out, Bremen has turned in the dogs." The barking of the dogs, which commenced as soon as they entered the bushes, did not continue more than a minute, when a female rhinoceros of the black variety burst out of the thicket in pursuit of the retreating dogs. Several shots were fired by the Hottentots, who were concealed in different quarters without effect; the animal rushing along and tearing up the ground with its horns, looking out for its enemies. At last it perceived a Hottentot, who showed himself from a bush near to where our travelers were concealed. The animal charged immediately, and in charging was brought down on its knees by a shot from Alexander. The Hottentots rushed out, regardless of Swinton's calling out to them to be careful, as the animal was not dead, and had surrounded it within a few yards, when it rose again and fiercely charged Swanevelt, who narrowly escaped. A shot from the Major put an end to its career, and they then walked to where the animal lay, when a cry from Omrah, who was standing near the river, attracted their notice, and they perceived that the male rhinoceros, of whose presence they were not aware, had just burst out of the same covert, and was charging toward them.

Every one immediately took to his heels; many of the Hottentots in their fear dropping their muskets, and fortunately the distance they were from the covert gave them time to conceal themselves in the thickets before the animal had time to come up with them. A shot from Swinton turned the assailant, who now tore up the earth in his rage, looking everywhere round with its sharp flashing eye for a victim. At this moment, while it seemed hesitating and peering about, to the astonishment of the whole party, Omrah showed himself openly on the other side of the rhinoceros, waving his red handkerchief, which he had taken off his head. The rhinoceros, the moment that the boy caught his eye, rushed furiously toward him. "The boy's lost," cried Swinton; but hardly had the words gone from his mouth, when to their astonishment, the rhinoceros disappeared, and Omrah stood capering and shouting with delight. The fact was that Omrah, when he had left our travelers, had gone down toward the river, and as he went along had with his light weight passed over what he knew full well to be one of the deep pits dug by the Bushmen to catch those animals. Having fully satisfied himself that it was so, he had remained by the side of it, and when the rhinoceros rushed at him, had kept the pit between himself and the animal. His object was to induce the animal to charge at him, which it did, and when within four yards of the lad, had plunged into the pit dug for him. The success of Omrah's plan explained the whole matter at once, and our travelers hastened up to where the rhinoceros was impounded, and found that a large stake, fixed upright in the center of the pit, had impaled the animal. A shot from the Major put an end to the fury and agony of the animal.

"I never was more excited in my life; I thought the boy was mad and wanted to lose his life," said Alexander.

"And so did I," replied Swinton; "and yet I ought to have known him better. It was admirably done; here we have an instance of the superiority of man endowed with reasoning power over brutes. A rhinoceros will destroy the elephant; the lion can make no impression on him, and flies before him like a cat. He is, in fact, the most powerful of all animals; he fears no enemy, not even man, when he is provoked or wounded; and yet he has fallen by the cleverness of that little monkey of a Bushboy. I think, Major, we have done enough now, and may go back to the caravan."

"Yes, I am well satisfied with our day's

sport, and am not a little hungry. We may now let the Hottentots bring home as much game as they can. You have taken care to give directions about your specimens, Swinton?"

"Yes, Bremen knows the animals I require, and is now after them. Omrah, run and tell that fellow to bring our horses here."

"Swinton, can birds and beasts talk, or can they not?" said the Major. "I ask that question because I am now looking at the enormous nests of the grosbeaks. It is a regular town, with some hundreds of houses. These birds, as well as those sagacious animals, the beaver, the ant, and the bee, not to mention a variety of others, must have some way of communicating their ideas."

"That there is no doubt of," replied Swinton, laughing; "but still I believe that man only is endowed with speech."

"Well, we know that; but if not with speech, they must have some means of communication which answers as well"

"As far as their wants require it, no

doubt," replied Swinton, "but to what extent is hidden from us. Animals have instinct and reasoning powers, but not reason."

"Where is the difference?"

"The reasoning powers are generally limited to their necessities; but with animals who are the companions of man, they appear to be more extended."

"We have a grand supper to-night," said Alexander; "what shall I help you to – harte-beest, sassaby, or rhinoceros?"

"Thank you," replied the Major, laughing; "I'll trouble you for a small piece of that rhinoceros steak – underdone, if you please."

"How curious that would sound in Grosvenor Square."

"Not if you shot the animals in Richmond Park," said Swinton.

"Those rascally Hottentots will collect no fuel to-night if we do not make them do it now," said the Major. "If they once begin to stuff it will be all over with them."

"Very true; we had better set them about it before the feast begins. Call Bremen, Omrah."

"Having given their directions, our party finished their supper, and then Alexander asked Swinton whether he had ever known any serious accidents resulting from the hunting of the rhinoceros.

"Yes," replied Swinton; "I once was witness to the death of a native chief."

"Then pray tell us the story," said the Major. "By hearing how other people have suffered, we learn how to take care of ourselves."

"Before I do so, I will mention what was told me by a Namaqua chief about a lion; I am reminded of it by the Major's observations as to the means animals have of communicating with each other. Once when I was traveling in Namaqualand, I observed a spot which was imprinted with at least twenty spoors or marks of a lion's paw; and as I pointed them out a Namaqua chief told me that a lion had been practicing his leap. On demanding an explanation, he said that if a lion sprang at an animal, and missed it by leaping short, he would always go back to where he sprang from, and practice the leap so as to be successful on another occasion; and he then related to me the following anecdote, stating that he was an eye-witness to the incident:

"'I was passing near the end of a craggy hill from which jutted out a smooth rock of from ten to twelve feet high, when I perceived a number of zebras galloping round it, which they were obliged to do, as the rock beyond was quite steep. A lion was creeping toward the rock to catch the male zebra, which brought up the rear of the herd. The lion sprang and missed his mark; he fell short, with only his head over the edge of the rock, and the zebra galloped away, switching his tail in the air. Although the object of his pursuit was gone, the lion tried the leap on the rock a second and a third time, till he succeeded. During this two more lions came up and joined the first lion. They seemed to be talking, for they roared a great deal to each other; and then the first lion led them round the rock again and again. Then he made another grand leap, to show them what he and they must do another time.' The chief added, 'They evidently were talking to each other, but I could not understand a word of what they said, although they talked loud enough; but I thought it was as well to be off, or they might have some talk about me.'"

"Well, they certainly do not whisper," said the Major, laughing. "Thank you for that story, Swinton, and now for the rhinoceros hunt."

"I was once out hunting with a Griqua, of the name of Henrick, and two or three other men; we had wounded a springbok, and were following its track, when we came upon the footing of a rhinoceros, and shortly afterward we saw a large black male in the bush."

"You mention a black rhinoceros. Is there any other?"

"Yes, there is a white rhinoceros, as it is called, larger than the black, but not so dangerous. It is, in fact, a stupid sort of animal. The black rhinoceros, as you are aware, is very fierce. Well, to continue: Henrick slipped down behind a bush, fired, and wounded the animal severely in the foreleg. The rhinoceros charged, we all fled, and the animal, singling out one of our men, closely pursued him; but the man, stopping short, while the horn of the rhinoceros plowed up the ground at his heels, dexterously jumped on one side. The rhinoceros missed him and passed on in full speed, and before the brute could recover himself and change his course, the whole of us had climbed up into trees. The rhinoceros, limping with his wound, went round and round, trying to find us out by the scent, but he tried in vain. At last, one of the men, who had only an assaguay, said, 'Well, how long are we going to stay here? Why don't you shoot?'

"'Well,' said Henrick, 'if you are so anxious to shoot, you may if you please. Here is my powder-and-shot belt, and my gun lies under the tree. The man immediately descended from the tree, loaded the gun, and approaching the rhinoceros he fired and wounded it severely in the jaw. The animal was stunned, and dropped on the spot. Thinking that it was dead, we all descended fearlessly and collected round it; and the man who had fired was very proud, and was giving directions to the others, when of a sudden the animal began to recover, and kicked with his hind legs. Henrick told us all to run for our lives, and set us the example. The rhinoceros started up again, and singling out the unfortunate man who had got down and fired at it, roaring and snorting with rage, thundered after him.

"The man, perceiving that he could not outrun the beast, tried the same plan as the other hunter did when the rhinoceros charged him: stopping short, he jumped on one side, that the animal might pass him; but the brute was not to be balked a second time; he caught the man on his horn under the left thigh, and cutting it open as if it had been done with an ax, tossed him a dozen yards up in the air. The poor fellow fell facing the rhinoceros, with his legs spread; the beast rushed at him again, and ripped up his body from his stomach to almost his throat, and again tossed him in the air. Again he fell heavily to the ground. The rhinoceros watched his fall, and running up to him trod upon him and pounded him to a mummy. After this horrible tragedy, the beast limped off into a bush. Henrick then crept up to the bush; the animal dashed out again, and would certainly have killed another man if a dog had not turned it. In turning short round upon the dog, the bone of its fore-leg, which had been half broken through by Henrick's first shot, snapped in two, and it fell, unable to recover itself, and was then shot dead."

"A very awkward customer, at all events," observed the Major. "I presume a leaden bullet would not enter?"

"No, it would flatten against most parts of his body. By the by, I saw an instance of a rhinoceros having been destroyed by that cowardly brute the hyena."

"Indeed!"

"Yes, patience and perseverance on the hyena's part effected the work. The rhinoceros takes a long while to turn round, and the hyena attacked him behind, biting him with his powerful jaws above the joint of the hind leg, and continued so to do, till he had severed all the muscles, and the animal, forced from pain to lie down, was devoured as you may say alive from behind; the hyena still tearing at the same quarter, until he arrived at the vital parts. By the track which was marked by the blood of the rhinoceros, the hyena must have followed the animal for many miles, until the rhinoceros was in such pain that it could proceed no further. – But if you are to hunt to-morrow at daybreak, it is time to go to sleep; so good-night."

At daybreak the next morning, they took a hasty meal, and started again for the plain. Swinton, having to prepare his specimens, did not accompany them. There was a heavy fog on the plain when they arrived at it, and they waited for a short time, skirting the south side of it, with the view of drawing the animals toward the encampment. At last the fog vanished, and discovered the whole country, as before, covered with every variety of wild animals. But as their object was to obtain the eland antelope, they remained stationary for some time, seeking for those animals among the varieties which were scattered in all directions. At last Omrah, whose eyes were far keener than even the Hottentots', pointed out three at a distance, under a large acacia thorn. They immediately rode at a trot in that direction, and the various herds of quaggas, gnoos, and antelopes scoured away before them; and so numerous were they, and such was the clattering of hoofs, that you might have imagined that it was a heavy charge of cavalry. The objects of their pursuit remained quiet until they were within three hundred yards of them, and then they set off at a speed, notwithstanding their heavy and unwieldy appearance, which for a short time completely distanced the horses. But this speed could not be continued, and the Major and Alexander soon found themselves rapidly coming up. The poor animals exerted themselves in vain; their sleek coats first turned to a blue color, and then white with foam and perspiration, and at last they were beaten to a stand-still, and were brought down by the rifles of our travelers, who then dismounted their horses, and walked up to the quarry.

"What magnificent animals!" exclaimed Alexander.

"They are enormous, certainly," said the Major.

"Look at the beautiful dying eye of that noble beast. Is it not speaking?"

"Yes, imploring for mercy, as it were, poor creature."

"Well, these three beasts, that they say are such good eating, weigh more than fifty antelopes."

"More than fifty springboks, I grant. Well, what shall we do now?"

"Let our horses get their wind again, and then we will see if we can fall in with some new game."

"I saw two or three antelopes, of a very different sort from the sassabys and harte-beests, toward that rising ground. We will go that way as soon as the Hottentots come up and take charge of our game."

"Does Swinton want to preserve one of these creatures?"

"I believe not, they are so very bulky. He says we shall find plenty as we go on, and that he will not encumber the wagons with a skin until we leave the Val River, and turn homeward. Now, Bremen and Omrah, come with us."

The Major and Alexander then turned their horses' heads, and rode slowly toward the hill which they had noticed, and the antelopes which the Major had observed were now seen among the bushes which crowned the hill. Bremen said that he did not know the animals, and the Major was most anxious to obtain one to surprise Swinton with. As soon as they came within two hundred yards of the bushes on the other side of which the antelopes were seen, the Major gave his horse to Omrah and advanced alone very cautiously, that he might bring one down with his rifle. He gained the bushes without alarming the animals, and the party left behind were anxiously watching his motions, expecting him every moment to fire, when the Major suddenly turned round and came back at a hurried pace.

"What is the matter?" said Alexander.

"Matter enough to stop my growth for

all my life," replied the Major. "If ever my heart was in my mouth, it was just now. I was advancing softly, and step by step, toward the antelopes, and was just raising my rifle to fire, when I heard something flapping the ground three or four yards before me. I looked down, and it was the tail of a lioness, which fortunately was so busy watching the antelopes with her head the other way, that she did not perceive my being near her; whereupon I beat a retreat, as you have witnessed."

"Well, what shall we do now?"

"Wait a little till I have recovered my nerves," said the Major, "and then I'll be revenged upon her. Swinton is not here to preach prudence, and have a lion-hunt I will."

"With all my heart," replied Alexander. "Bremen, we are going to attack the lioness."

"Yes, sir," said Bremen; "then we had better follow Cape fashion. We will back the horses toward her, and Omrah will hold them while we will attack her. I think one only had better fire, so we keep two guns in reserve."

"You are right, Bremen," said Alexander. "Then you and I will reserve our fire, and the Major shall try his rifle upon her."

With some difficulty the horses were backed toward the bush, until the Major could again distinguish where the lioness lay, at about sixty paces' distance. The animal appeared still occupied with the game in front of her, watching her opportunity to spring, for her tail and hind-quarters were toward them. The Major fired, and the animal bounded off with a loud roar; while the antelopes flew away like the wind. The roar of the lioness was answered by a deep growl from another part of the bush, and immediately afterward a lion bolted out, and bounded from the bushes across the plain, to a small mimosa grove about a quarter of a mile off.

"What a splendid animal!" said Alexander; "look at his black mane, it almost sweeps the ground."

"We must have him," cried the Major, jumping on his horse.

Alexander, Bremen, and Omrah did the same, and they followed the lion, which stood at bay under the mimosas, measuring the strength of the party, and facing them in a most noble and imposing manner. It appeared, however, that he did not like their appearance, or was not satisfied with his own position, for as they advanced he retreated at a slow pace, and took up his position on the summit of a stony hill close by, the front of which was thickly dotted with low thorn-bushes. The thorn-bushes extended about 200 yards from where the lion stood, disdainfully surveying the party as they approached toward him, and appearing, with a conscious pride in his own powers, to dare them to approach him.

They dismounted from their horses as soon as they arrived at the thorn-bushes, and the Major fired. The rifle-ball struck the rock close to the lion, who replied with an angry growl. The Major then took the gun from Omrah and fired, and again the ball struck close to the animal's feet. The lion now shook his mane, gave another angry roar; and by the glistening of his eyes, and the impatient switching of his tail, it was evident that he would soon become the attacking party.

"Load both your guns again," said Alexander, "and then let me have a shot, Major."

As soon as the Major's guns were loaded, Alexander took aim and fired. The shot broke the lion's fore-leg, which he raised up with a voice of thunder, and made a spring from the rock toward where our party stood.

"Steady now," cried the Major to Bremen, at the same time handing his spare rifle to Alexander.

The rush of the angry animal was heard through the bushes advancing nearer and nearer; and they all stood prepared for the encounter. At last out the animal sprang, his mane bristling on end, his tail straight out, and his eyeballs flashing rage and vengeance. He came down upon the hind-quarters of one of the horses, which immediately started off, overthrowing and dragging Omrah to some distance. One of the lion's legs being broken, had occasioned the animal to roll off on the side of the horse, and he now remained on the ground ready for a second spring, when he received a shot through the back from Bremen, who stood behind him. The lion, with another dreadful roar, attempted to spring upon the Major, who was ready with his rifle to receive him; but the shot from Bremen had passed through his spine and paralyzed his hind-quarters, and he made the attempt in vain, a second and a third time throwing his fore-quarters up in the air, and then falling down again, when a bullet from the Major passed through his brain. The noble beast sunk down, gnawing the ground and tearing it with the claws of the leg which had not been wounded, and then, in a few seconds, breathed his last.

"I am glad that is over, Alexander," said the Major; "it was almost too exciting to be pleasant."

"It was very awful for the time, I must acknowledge," replied Alexander. "What an enormous brute! I think I never saw such a magnificent skin.

"It is yours by the laws of war," said the Major.

"Nay," replied Alexander, "it was you that gave him his *coup de grace*"

"Yes, but if you had not broken his leg, he might have given some of us our *coup de grace*. No, no, the skin is yours. Now the horses are off, and we can not send for the Hottentots. They have got rid of Omrah, who is coming back with his shirt torn into tatters."

"The men will catch the horses and bring them here, depend upon it, sir," said Bremen, "and then they can take off the skin."

"Well, if I am to have the lion's skin, I must have that of the lioness also, Major; so we must finish our day's hunting with forcing her to join her mate."

"Very good, with all my heart."

"Better wait till the men come with the horses, sir," said Bremen; "three guns are too few to attack a lion – very great danger indeed."

"Bremen is right, Alexander; we must not run such a risk again. Depend upon it, if the animal's leg had not been broken, we should not have had so easy a conquest. Let us sit down quietly till the men come up."

In about half an hour, as Bremen had conjectured, the Hottentots, perceiving the horses loose, and suspecting that something had happened, went in chase of them, and as soon as they had succeeded in catching them, brought them in the direction to which they had seen our travelers ride. They were not a little astonished at so small a party having ventured to attack a lion, and gladly prepared for the attack of the lioness. Three of the dogs having accompanied them, it was decided that they should be put into the bushes where the lioness was lying when the Major fired at her, so as to discover where she now was; and leaving the lion for the present, they all set off for the first jungle.

The dogs could not find the lioness in the bushes, and it was evident that she had retreated to some other place; and

Swanevelt, who was an old lion-hunter, gave his opinion that she would be found in the direction near to where the lion was killed. They went therefore in that direction, and found that she was in the clump of mimosas to which the lion had first retreated. The previous arrangement of backing the horses toward where she lay was attempted, but the animals had been too much frightened in the morning by the lion's attack, to be persuaded. They reared and plunged in such a manner as to be with difficulty prevented from breaking loose; it was therefore necessary to abandon that plan, and trust to themselves and their numbers. The clump of trees was surrounded by the party, and the dogs encouraged to go in, which they did, every now and then rushing back from the paws of the lioness. The Hottentots now fired into the clump at random, and their volleys were answered by the loud roars of the animal, which would not, however, show herself, and half an hour was passed away in this manner.

At last she was perceived at one side of the jungle, by Swanevelt, who fired with

The Mission

effect, for the animal gave a loud roar, and then bounded out, not attempting to rush upon any person, but to make her escape from her assailants. A volley was fired at her, and one shot took effect, for she fell with her head to the ground, and tumbled right over; but immediately after she recovered herself, and made off for the bushes where she had been first discovered.

"She was hit hard that time, at all events," said the Major.

"Yes, sir," said Bremen, "that was her deathshot, I should think; but she is not dead yet, and may give us a great deal of trouble."

They followed her as fast as they could on foot, and the dogs were soon upon her again; the animal continued to roar, and always from the same spot; so that it was evident she was severely wounded. Alexander and the Major reserved their fire, and approached to where the dogs were baying, not twenty yards from the jungle. Another roar was given, and suddenly the body of the lioness rushed through the air, right in the direction where they stood; she passed, however, between them, and when she reached the ground, she fell on her side, quite dead. It was her last expiring effort, and she died in the attempt. Alexander and the Major, who were both ready to fire, lowered their rifles when they perceived that she was dead.

"Well," said the Major, "I will say that when I first saw her tail, I was more frightened than I was just now, when she made the spring; I was so taken by surprise."

"I don't doubt it. She is a very large animal, and will make a handsome companion to the lion. If we live and do well, and get home to England again, I will have her stuffed along with him, and put them in the same case."

"I trust you will, and that I shall come and see them," replied the Major.

"I am sure I do, from my heart, my good fellow. I am very much pleased at our having killed both these beasts, without Swinton being with us, as he would have been persuading us to leave them alone."

"And he would have done very right," replied the Major. "We are two naughty boys, and shall be well scolded when we go back."

"Which I vote we do now. I think we have done quite enough for to-day."

"Yes, indeed," replied the Major, mounting his horse; "enough to talk of all our lives. Now let us gallop home, and say nothing about having killed the lions until the Hottentots bring them to the caravan."

CHAPTER XXV

"Well, what sport have you had?" was Swinton's first question when he was joined by Alexander and the Major. Replied the latter – "Pretty well; we saw an antelope quite new to us, which we tried very hard to shoot, but were prevented by an unexpected meeting with a lioness." The Major then gave an account of his perceiving the tail of the lioness, and his rapid retreat.

"I am very glad to hear that you were so prudent, Major; it would have been a very rash thing to attack a lioness with only three guns. So the antelopes escaped?"

"Yes, but we have the elands, which you say are such good eating. Do we stay here any longer, or do we proceed up the river?"

"You must ask Wilmot to decide that point," said Swinton.

"It is just as you please," said Alexander; "but they say that the more you go to the northward, the more plentiful is the game."

"Yes, and we shall fall in with the giraffe," said the Major, "which is now the great object of my ambition. I have killed the rhinoceros and elephant, and now I must have the giraffe; they can kill the two first animals in India, but the other is only to be had in this country."

"And when you meet again your Indian friends, you wish to say that you have killed what they have not?"

"Certainly; what is the good of traveling so far, if one has not something to boast of when one returns? If I say I have hunted and killed the rhinoceros and elephant, they may reply to me, 'So have we;' but if I add the giraffe, that will silence them; don't you observe, Swinton, I then remain master of the field? But here come the Hottentots with our game; come, Swinton, leave your preparations for a little while, and see what our morning's sport has been."

Swinton put aside the skin of the sassaby that he was cleaning, and walked with them to where the men were assembled, and was not a little surprised when he saw the skins and jaws of the lion and lioness. He was still more so when the Major recounted how they had been shot.

"You certainly have run a great risk," said he, "and I am glad that you have been so successful. You are right in saying that I should have persuaded you not to attempt it; you are like two little boys who have taken advantage of the absence of their tutor to run into mischief. However, I am glad that it has been done, as I now hope your desire to kill a lion will not again lead you into unnecessary danger."

"No, indeed," replied Alexander; "having once accomplished the feat, and being fully aware of the great risk that is run, we shall be more prudent in future."

"That is all I ask of you," said Swinton, "for I should be unhappy if we did not all three return safe to the Cape. I never saw a finer lion's skin: I will arrange it for you, that it shall arrive at the Cape in good order."

As usual, the afternoon was by the

Hottentots devoted to eating as much as they could possibly contrive to get down their throats; the flesh of the eland was pronounced excellent by our travelers, and there was much more than they could possibly consume. The Hottentots were only allowed to bring a certain quantity into the camp, that they might not attract the wild beasts. They would have brought it all in, although they never could have eaten it. The cattle were driven up in the evening, the fires lighted, and the night passed quietly away.

At daylight they turned the cattle out to graze for a couple of hours, and then yoked and proceeded on their journey, keeping as near as they could to the banks of the river. They saw many hippopotami, snorting and rising for a moment above the water, but they passed by them without attempting to shoot at them, as they did not wish to disturb the other game. As they advanced, the variety of flowers which were in bloom attracted the notice of Alexander, who observed – "Does not this plain put you in mind of a Turkey carpet, Major; so gay with every variety of color?"

"Yes, and as scentless," replied the Major; "they are all very brilliant in appearance; but one modest English violet is, to my fancy, worth them all."

"I agree with you," replied Swinton; "but still you must acknowledge that this country is beautiful beyond description, – these grassy meads so spangled with numerous flowers, and so broken by the masses of grove and forest! Look at these aloes blooming in profusion, with their coral tufts – in England what would they pay for such an exhibition? – and the crimson and lilac hues of these poppies and amaryllis blended together: neither are you just in saying that there is no scent in this gay parterre. The creepers which twine up those stately trees are very sweetly scented; and how picturesque are the twinings of those vines upon the mimosas. I can not well imagine the garden of Eden to have been more beautiful."

"And in another respect there is a resemblance," said the Major, laughing; "the serpent is in it"

"Yes, I grant that," replied Swinton.

"Well, I can feel no real pleasure without security; if I am to be ever on the alert, and turning my eyes in every direction, that I may not tread upon a puff adder, or avoid the dart of the cobra capella, I can feel little pleasure in looking at the rich hues of those flowers which conceal them. As I said before, give me the violet and the rose of England, which I can pick and smell in security."

"I agree with you, Major," said Alexander; "but," continued he, laughing, "we must make allowance for Swinton, as a naturalist. A puff adder has a charm for him, because it adds one more to the numerous specimens to be obtained; and he looks upon these flowers as a botanist, rejoicing as he adds to his herbal, or gathers seeds and bulbs to load his wagon with. You might as well find fault with a husbandman for rejoicing in a rich harvest."

"Or with himself, for being so delighted at the number and the variety of the animals which fall to his rifle," replied Swinton, smiling. "There I have you, Major."

"I grant it," replied the Major; "but what is that in the river – the back of a hippopotamus?"

"No, it is the back of an elephant, I should rather think; but the reeds are so high, that it is difficult to ascertain. There may be a herd bathing in the river, nothing more likely."

"Let us stop the caravan; the creaking of these wheels would drive away any thing," replied the Major; "we will then ride forward and see what it is. It is not more than half a mile from us."

"Be it so," replied Swinton. "Omrah, get the rifles, and tell Bremen to come here. Now, Major, is it to be a regular hunt, or only a passing shot at them; for I now perceive through my glass that they are elephants?"

"Well, I think a passing shot will be best; for if we are to hunt, we must send a party on the opposite side of the river, and that will be a tedious affair."

"I think myself it will be better to proceed," said Swinton; "so now then, to scatter the enemy."

They soon arrived at that part of the river where they had at a distance discovered the elephants bathing; but as they approached, the high reeds prevented them from seeing the animals, although they could hear them plainly. At last, as they proceeded a little further up the river, they discovered a female with its young one by its side; the mother playing with its offspring, pouring water over it with its trunk, and now and then pressing it into the water, so as to compel it to swim. They watched the motions of the animals for some time, and the Major first broke silence by saying, "I really have not the heart to fire at the poor creature; its maternal kindness, and the playing of the little one, are too interesting. It would be cruel, now that we do not want meat, for an eland is to be killed every ten minutes."

"I am glad to hear you say so," replied Swinton. "Let us fire over them, and set them all in motion."

"Agreed," said the Major; "this is to start them," and he fired off his rifle in the air.

The noise that ensued was quite appalling; the shrieks and cries of the elephants, and the treading down and rushing through the reeds, the splashing and floundering in the mud, for a few seconds, was followed by the bounding out of the whole herd on the opposite bank of the river, tossing their trunks, raising up their ears, roaring wildly, and starting through the bushes into the forest from which they had descended. Two large males only were to be perceived among the whole herd, the rest were all females and their young ones, who scrambled away after the males, crowding together, but still occasionally looking behind after their young ones, till they had all disappeared in the forest, the cracking and crushing of the bushes in which were heard for many minutes afterward.

"That was a splendid scene," said Alexander.

"Yes, it was a living panorama, which one must come to Africa to behold."

"I do not think that I shall ever become a true elephant-hunter," said the Major.

"I feel a sort of repugnance to destroy so sagacious an animal, and a degree of remorse when one lies dead. At the same time, if once accustomed to the fearful crashing and noise attending their movements, I do not consider them very dangerous animals to pursue."

"Not if people are cool and collected. We have had several famous elephant-hunters among the Dutch farmers. I remember that one of them, after a return from a successful chase, made a bet that he would go up to a wild elephant and pluck eight hairs out of his tail. He did so and won his bet, for the elephant can not see behind him, and is not very quick in turning round. However, a short time afterward he made the same attempt, and being foolhardy from success, the animal was too quick for him, and he was crushed to death."

Bremen now came up to them, to say that there was a party of people to the eastward, and he thought that there was a wagon. On examination with their telescopes, they found that such was the case; and our travelers turned their horses' heads in the direction, to ascertain who they might be, leaving the caravan to proceed by the banks of the river. In about an hour, they came close to them, and Swinton immediately recognized them as Griquas, or mixed European and Hottentot races. Of course, they met in the most friendly manner, and the Griquas said that they had come to hunt the elephant, eland, and other animals; the former for their ivory, and the latter for their flesh. Their wagon, which was a very old one, was loaded with flesh, cut in long strips, and hanging to dry; and they had a great many hundred-weight of ivory, which they had already collected. As soon as our travelers had explained to them their own motions, the Griquas said that they would bring their wagon down in the evening and encamp with them. Our travelers then returned to the caravan.

As they promised, the Griquas joined them late in the afternoon. They were a party of sixteen; all stout fellows, and armed with the long guns used by the Dutch boors. They said that they had been two months from Griqua-town, and were thinking of returning very soon, as their wagon was loaded to the extent that it would bear. The Major stating that it was their intention to hunt the giraffe, the Griquas informed them that they would not find the animal to the southward of the Val River, and they would have to cross over into the territories of the king Moselekatsee, who ruled over the Bechuana country, to the northward of the river; and that it would be very dangerous to attempt so to do without his permission; indeed, that there would be danger in doing so, even with it.

"Do you know any thing of this person, Swinton?"

"Yes, I have heard of him, but I did not know that he had extended his conquests so low down as to the Val River."

"Who is he?"

"You have heard of Chaka, the king of the Zoolus, who conquered the whole country, as far as Port Natal to the eastward?"

"Yes," replied Alexander; "we have

heard of him."

"Well, Moselekatsee was a chief of two or three tribes, who, when hard pressed by his enemies, took refuge with Chaka, and became one of his principal warrior chiefs. After a time he quarreled with Chaka, about the distribution of some cattle they had taken, and aware that he had no mercy to expect from the tyrant, he revolted from him with a large force, and withdrew to the Bechuana country. There he conquered all the tribes, enrolled them in his own army, and gradually became as formidable as Chaka himself. In the arrangements of his army, he followed the same plans as Chaka, and has now become a most powerful monarch, and, they do say, is almost as great a tyrant and despot as Chaka himself was. I believe that the Griquas are right in saying there would be danger in passing through his dominions without his permission."

"But," said Alexander, "I suppose if we send a message to him and presents, there will be no difficulty?"

"Perhaps not, except that our caravan

may excite his cupidity, and he may be induced to delay us to obtain possession of its contents. However, we had better put this question to the Griquas, who probably can answer it better."

The Griquas, on being questioned, replied, that the best plan would be to send a message to the Matabili capital, where Moselekatsee resided, requesting permission to hunt in the country, and begging the monarch to send some of his principal men to receive the presents which they had to offer; – that it would not take long to receive an answer, as it would only be necessary to deliver the message to the first officer belonging to Moselekatsee, at the advanced post. That officer would immediately dispatch a native with the message, who would arrive much sooner than any one they could send themselves. Bremen and three other Hottentots offered to take the message, if our travelers wished it. This was agreed to, and that afternoon they mounted their horses, and crossed the river. By the advice of the Griquas, the camp was shifted about a mile further up the river, on account of the lions.

The weather now threatened a change; masses of clouds accumulated, but were again dispersed. The next day the weather was again threatening; thunder pealed in the distant mountains, and the forked lightning flew in every direction; but the rain, if any, was expended on the neighboring hills.

A strong wind soon blew up so as to try the strength of the canvas awning of their wagons, and they found it difficult to keep their fires in at night. They had encamped upon a wide plain covered with high grass, and abounding with elands and other varieties of antelopes: here they remained for five days, waiting the reply of the king of the Matabili, and went out every day to procure game. On the Sabbath-day, after they had, as usual, performed Divine service, they observed a heavy smoke to windward, which, as the wind was fresh, soon bore down upon them and inconvenienced them much.

Swanevelt stated that the high grass had been fired by some means or another, and as it threatened to come down upon the encampment, the

Hottentots and Griquas were very busy beating down the grass round about them. When they had so done, they went to windward some hundred yards and set fire to the grass in several places; the grass burned quickly, till it arrived at where it had been beaten down, and the fire was extinguished. That this was a necessary precaution was fully proved, for as the night closed in, the whole country for miles was on fire, and the wind bore the flames down rapidly toward them.

The sky was covered with clouds, and the darkness of the night made the flames appear still more vivid; the wind drove them along with a loud crackling noise, sweeping over the undulating ground, now rising and now disappearing in the hollows, the whole landscape lighted up for miles.

As our travelers watched the progress of the flames, and every now and then observed a terrified antelope spring from its lair, and appearing like a black figure in a phantasmagoria, suddenly the storm burst upon them and the rain poured down in torrents, accompanied with large hailstones and thunder and lightning. The wind was instantly lulled, and after the first burst of the storm a deathlike silence succeeded to the crackling of the flames. A deluge of rain descended, and in an instant every spark of the conflagration was extinguished, and the pitchy darkness of the night was unbroken by even a solitary star.

The next morning was bright and clear, and after breakfast, they perceived the Hottentots who had been sent on their message to Moselekatsee, on the opposite bank of the river, accompanied by three of the natives; they soon crossed the river and came to the encampment. The natives, who were Matabili, were tall, powerful men, well proportioned, and with regular features; their hair was shorn, and surmounted with an oval ring attached to the scalp, and the lobe of their left ears was perforated with such a large hole, that it contained a small gourd, which was used as a snuff-box. Their dress was a girdle of strips of catskins, and they each carried two javelins and a knobbed stick for throwing.

They were heartily welcomed by our travelers, who placed before them a large quantity of eland-steaks, and filled their boxes with snuff. As soon as they had finished eating, and drawn up a large quantity of snuff into their nostrils, they explained through the Griquas, who could speak their language, that they had come from the greatest of all monarchs in the world, Moselekatsee, who wished to know who the strangers were, what they wanted of him, and what presents they had brought.

Swinton, who was spokesman, returned for answer that they were hunters, and not traders; that they had come to see the wonders of the country belonging to so great a monarch, and that hearing that his majesty had animals in his country which were not to be found elsewhere, they wanted permission to kill some, to show upon their return to their own people what a wonderful country it was that belonged to so great a monarch; – that they had brought beads and copper wire, and knives, and boxes for making fire, and snuff and tobacco, all of which they wished to present to the great monarch; a part as

The Mission

soon as they had received his permission to enter his territory, and another part when they were about to leave it. A handsome present of the above articles was then produced, and the messengers of the king, having surveyed the articles with some astonishment, declared that their king would feel very glad when he saw all these things, and that he had desired them to tell our travelers that they might come into his dominions with safety, and kill all the animals that they pleased. That his majesty had commanded one of them to remain with the party, and that as soon as he had received his presents, he would send a chief to be answerable for their safety. The Matabili then packed up the articles presented, and two of them set off at full speed on their return to the king. The third, who remained, assured our travelers that they might cross the river and enter the Matabili country as soon as they pleased.

A debate now ensued as to whether they should go with their whole force or not. The Matabili had informed them that in three days' journey they would fall in with the giraffe, which they were in search of, and as there would be some risk in crossing the river, and they had every reason to expect that it would soon rise, the question was whether it would be prudent to take over even one of the wagons. The opinion of the Griquas was asked, and it was ultimately arranged that they should take over Alexander's wagon only, with fifteen pair of oxen, and that some of the Griquas should accompany them, with Swanevelt, Omrah, and Mahomed; — that Bremen and the Hottentots should remain where they were, with the other three wagons and the rest of the Griquas, until our travelers should return.

This arrangement was not at all disagreeable to the Hottentots, who did not much like the idea of entering the Matabili country, and were very happy in their present quarters, as they were plentifully provided with good meat. Alexander's wagon was therefore arranged so as to carry the bedding and articles they might require, all other things being removed to the other wagons. Their best oxen were selected, and eight of the fleetest of their horses, and on the following morning, having ascertained from the Matabili the best place to cross the river, our travelers set off, and in an hour were on the other side.

There was no change in the country during the first day's journey; the same variety and brilliancy of flowers were every where to be seen. The eland and the other antelopes were plentiful, and they were soon joined by parties of the natives, who requested them to shoot the animals for them, which they did in quantities even sufficient to satisfy them. Indeed if they found them troublesome, our travelers had only to bring down an eland, and the natives were immediately left behind, that they might devour the animal, which was done in an incredibly short space of time. The Matabili who had conducted them proved to be a chief, and if he gave any order, it was instantly obeyed; so that our travelers had no trouble with the natives except their begging and praying for snuff, which was incessant, both from the men and women. Neither did they fear any treachery from the Matabili king, as they were well armed, and the Griquas were brave men, and the superiority of their weapons made them a match for a large force. Every precaution, however, was taken when they halted at night, which they invariably did in the center of an open plain, to prevent any surprise; and large fires were lighted round the wagon.

They traveled on in this way for two days more, when in the evening they arrived at a large plain sprinkled with mimosa-trees, and abutting on the foot of a low range of hills. The Matabili told them that they would find the giraffes on these plains, and the Major, who was very anxious, kept his telescope to his eyes, looking round in every direction till nightfall, but did not succeed in descrying any of the objects of his search. They retired that night with anxious expectation for the following morning, when they anticipated that they should fall in with these remarkable animals. Their guns were examined and every precaution taken, and having lighted their fires and set the watch, they went to bed; and, after commending themselves to the care of Providence, were soon fast asleep.

CHAPTER XXVI

With the exception of three lions coming very near to the encampment and rousing up the Griquas, nothing occurred during the night. In the morning they yoked the oxen and had all the horses saddled ready for the chase; but they were disappointed for nearly the whole day; as, although they saw a variety of game, no giraffe appeared in sight. In the afternoon, as they passed by a clump of mimosas, they were charged by a rhinoceros, which nearly threw down Alexander's best horse; but a volley from the Griquas laid him prostrate. It was a very large animal, but not of the black or ferocious sort, being what is termed the white rhinoceros. Within the last two days they had also observed that the gnoo was not of the same sort as the one which they had seen so long, but a variety which Swinton told them was called the brindled gnoo; it was, however, in every other respect the same animal, as to its motions and peculiarities. Toward the evening the Matabili warrior who accompanied them pointed to a mimosa at a distance, and made signs to the Major that there was a giraffe.

"I can not see him – do you, Alexander?" said the Major; "he points to that mimosa with the dead stump on the other side of it, there. Yes, it is one, I see the stump, as I called it, move; it must be the neck of the animal. Let loose the dogs, Swanevelt," cried the Major, starting off at full speed, and followed by Alexander, and Omrah, with the spare horse. In a minute or two the giraffe was seen to get clear of the mimosa, and then set off in an awkward, shambling kind of gallop; but awkward as the gallop appeared, the animal soon left the Major behind. It sailed along with incredible velocity, its long, swan-like neck keeping time with its legs, and its black tail curled above its back.

"Push on, Alexander," cried the Major; "if ever there were seven-league boots, that animal has a pair of them on. He goes like the wind; but he can not keep it up long, depend upon it, and our horses are in capital condition."

Alexander and the Major were now neck

and neck, close to each other, at full speed, when of a sudden the Major's horse stumbled, and fell upon an ostrich, which was sitting on her nest; Alexander's horse also stumbled and followed after the Major; and there they were, horses and riders, all rolling together among the ostrich-eggs; while the ostrich gained her legs, and ran off as fast as the giraffe.

As soon as they had got on their legs again, and caught the bridles of their horses, they looked round, but could not distinguish the giraffe, which was out of sight among the mimosa-trees; while Omrah was very busy picking up their rifles, and laughing in a very disrespectful manner. The Major and Alexander soon joined in the laugh. No bones were broken, and the horses had received no injury. All they had to do was to return to the caravan looking very foolish.

"Your first essay in giraffe-hunting has been very successful," said Swinton, laughing, as they came up to him.

"Yes, we both threw very pretty

summersets, did we not?" said Alexander. "However, we have got some ostrich-eggs for supper, and that is better than nothing. It will soon be dark, so we had better encamp for the night, had we not?"

"I was about to propose it," said Swinton.

"Did you ever hunt the giraffe, Swinton?" inquired Alexander, as they were making their supper on roasted ostrich-eggs; each of them holding one between his knees, and dipping out with a large spoon.

"Never," replied Swinton; "I have often seen them in Namaqua-land, but never killed one. I remember, however, a circumstance connected with the giraffe, which would have been incredible to me, if I had not seen the remains of the lion. You are well aware how long and strong are the thorns of the mimosa (or kamel-tree, as the Dutch call it, from the giraffe browsing upon it), and how the boughs of these trees lie like an umbrella, close upon one another. A native chief informed me that he witnessed a lion attacking a giraffe. The lion always springs at the head or neck, and seizes the animal by that part, riding him, as it were. The giraffe sets off at full speed with its enemy, and is so powerful as often to get rid of him; for I have seen giraffes killed which had the marks of the lion's teeth and claws upon them. In this instance the lion made a spring, but the giraffe at that very moment turning sharp round, the lion missed his aim, and by the blow it received was tossed in the air, so that he fell upon the boughs of the mimosa on his back. The boughs were not only compact enough to bear his weight, but the thorns that pierced through his body were so strong as to hold the enormous animal where he lay. He could not disengage himself; and they pointed out to me the skeleton on the boughs of the tree, as a corroboration of the truth of the story."

"It does really approach to the marvelous," observed the Major; "but, as you say, seeing is believing. I trust that we shall be more fortunate to-morrow."

"I have gained a piece of information from Swanevelt," said Swinton, "which makes me very anxious that we should leave this as soon as possible; which is, that the Matabili king had no idea that we had Griquas in our company, and still less that we were to come into his country with only the Griquas as attendants. You are not perhaps aware that Moselekatsee is the deadly enemy of the Griquas, with whom he has had several severe conflicts, and that we are not very safe on that account?"

"Why did not the Griquas say so?" replied Alexander.

"Because they do not care for the Matabili, and I presume are glad to come into the country, that they may know something of it, in case of their making an attack upon it. Depend upon it, as soon as the king hears of it, we shall be looked upon as spies, and he may send a party to cut us off."

"Have you said any thing to the Griquas?"

"Yes, and they laughed, and said that they should not care if we went right up to the principal town, where Moselekatsee resides."

"Well, they are bold enough, and so far are good traveling companions; but we certainly did not come here to fight," observed the Major. "But does the Matabili with us know that they are Griquas?"

"He did not; he supposed that they were Cape people whom we had brought with us; but he has found it out by the Hottentots, I suppose. Swanevelt says, that the very first body of Matabili that we fell in with, he sent a runner off immediately, I presume to give the information. I think, therefore, that the sooner we can get away the better."

"Well, I agree with you, Swinton," replied Alexander.

"We will try for the giraffe to-morrow, and when the Major has had the satisfaction of killing one, we will retrace our steps, for should we be attacked, it will be impossible to defend ourselves long against numbers. So now to bed."

They rose early the next morning, and, leaving the wagon where it was, again proceeded on horseback in search of giraffes. They rode at a slow pace for four or five miles, before they could discover any. At last a herd of them were seen standing together browsing on the leaves of the mimosa. They made a long circuit to turn them, and drive them toward the camp, and in this they succeeded. The animals set off at their usual rapid pace, but did not keep it up long, as there were several not full grown among them, which could not get over the ground so fast as the large male of the preceding day. After a chase of three miles, they found that the animals' speed was rapidly decreasing, and they were coming up with them. When within a hundred yards, Alexander fired and wounded a female which was in the rear. The Major pushed on with the dogs after a large male, and it stopped at bay under a mimosa, kicking most furiously at the dogs. The Major leveled his rifle, and brought the animal down with his first shot. It rose again, however, and for a hundred yards went away at a fast pace; but it again fell, to rise no more. The female which Alexander had wounded received another shot, and was then also prostrated."

"I have killed a *giraffe*," said the Major, standing by the side of the one he had killed. "It has been a long way to travel, and there have been some dangers to encounter for the sake of performing this feat; but we have all our follies, and are eager in pursuit of just as great trifles through life; so that in this I am not perhaps more foolish than the rest of mankind. I have obtained my wishes – I have killed a giraffe; and now I don't care how soon we go back again."

"Nor do I," replied Alexander; "for I can say with you, when we arrive in England, I too have killed a giraffe; so you will not be able to boast over me. By Swinton's account if we stay here much longer, we shall have to kill Matabili, which I am not anxious to do; therefore, I now say with you, I don't care how soon we go back to the Cape."

As they were not more than two miles from the wagon, they rode back, and sent the Griquas to bring in the flesh of the animals; Swinton not caring for the skins, as he had already procured some in Namaqua-land, and the weight of them would be so very great for the wagon. On their return, they had some conversation with the Griquas, who candidly acknowledged that it was very likely that the Matabili king would attempt to cut them off, although they appeared not at all afraid of his making the attempt. They, however, readily consented to return the next morning. That night, a messenger arrived to the Matabili chief who was escorting them. What was the communication of course our travelers could not tell; but their suspicions were confirmed by the behavior of the man. When he found that, on the following morning, they yoked the oxen and retraced their steps, he begged them not to go, but to advance into the interior of the country, where they would find plenty of game; told them that the king would be very angry if they left so soon; and if he did not see them, his heart would be very sad. But our travelers had made up their mind, and traveled back during the whole of that day. The Matabili dispatched the messenger who had come to him, and who again set off at all speed; at night he urged our travelers not to go back, saying that the king would be very angry with him. But as the Griquas were now equally convinced that treachery was intended, they paid no attention to the Matabili chief, and continued their route, shooting elands by the way for their sustenance. Late in the evening of the third day they found themselves on the borders of the Val river. It was still two hours before dark, and as the Matabili pressed them to encamp where they were, they were satisfied that they had better not, and therefore they forded the river, and rejoined the caravan, under charge of Bremen, just as night closed in.

The Griquas said, that from the Matabili wishing them to remain on the other side of the river, they were persuaded that a force would arrive during that night or the following morning, and that it would be necessary to be on the look-out; although probably the enemy would not venture to attack them without further orders, now that they were no longer in Moselekatsee's dominions.

The Mission

Every preparation was therefore made: the Griquas and Hottentots were all supplied with ammunition, and mustered with their guns in their hands. The wagons were arranged, the fires lighted, and four men were posted as sentinels round the encampment. What added still more to their suspicions was, that, about an hour after dark, the Matabili chief was not to be found.

"My opinion is," said the Major, "that we ought to steal a march upon them. Our oxen are in excellent condition, and may travel till to-morrow evening without feeling it. Let us yoke and be off at once, now that it is dark. The moon will rise about two o'clock in the morning, but before that the wagons will be twelve or fifteen miles off. Alexander and I, with Bremen, will remain here with our horses and wait till the moon rises, to see if we can discover any thing: and we can easily join the wagons by daybreak. We will keep the fires up, to allow them to suppose that we are still encamped, that they may not pursue."

"And also to keep off the lions," observed Alexander, "which are not enemies to be despised."

"I think it is a very good plan; but why not have more men with you? We have plenty of horses, and so have the Griquas."

"Well then, let us talk to the Griquas."

The Griquas approved of the plan; and, having their own horses, six of them agreed to remain with Alexander and the Major, and Swanevelt and two more of the Hottentots were also mounted to remain; which made a force of twelve men, well mounted and well armed. The remainder of the caravan yoked the oxen to the wagons, and, under the direction of Swinton, set off in a southerly direction, across the desert, instead of going by the banks of the Val River, as before.

This had been arranged previously to any expected attack from the Matabili, as it would considerably shorten the distance on returning, although they knew that they would find much difficulty in procuring water for a few days. After the caravan had departed, it was found that Omrah had helped himself to a horse and a gun, and had remained in the camp; but as he was always useful, his so doing was passed over without notice. In half an hour the wagons were out of sight, and the noise of their wheels was no longer to be heard.

They fastened their horses in the center of the fires, and sat down by them till the moon rose, when they directed their eyes to the opposite bank of the river; but for some time nothing was discovered to confirm their suspicions. When the moon was about an hour high, they perceived a body of men coming, down toward the banks, and the moon shone upon their shields, which were white. As soon as they arrived at the bank of the river, they all sat down, without making any noise. Shortly afterward, another body with dark-colored shields, made their appearance, who came down and joined the first.

"We were not wrong in our suspicions, at all events," said the Major; "I should say that there are not less than a thousand men in these two parties which have already appeared. Now, what shall we do? Shall we remain here, or shall we be off, and join the wagons?"

"I really can hardly decide which would be the best," replied Alexander; "let us have a consultation with Bremen and the Griquas."

"If we were to go away now," said Bremen, "the fires would soon be out, and they might suspect something, and come over to reconnoiter. When they found that we were gone, they would perhaps follow us, and overtake the wagons; but if we remain here, and keep the fires up till daybreak, the wagons will have gained so much more distance."

The Griquas were of the same opinion; and it was decided that they would remain there till daybreak, and then set off.

"But," said Alexander, "shall we leave this before they can see us, or allow them to see us?"

The Griquas said, that it would be better that the enemy should see them, as then they would know that the fires had been kept up to deceive them, and that the wagons were probably a long way off.

This having been agreed upon, a careful watch was kept upon the enemy during the remainder of the night. Although the moon had discovered the approach of the Matabili to the party, the spot where the camp had been pitched was in the shade, so that from the opposite side of the river only the fires could be distinguished. A little before dawn, some one was heard approaching, and they were all prepared to fire, when they discovered that it was Omrah, who, unknown to them, had crawled down to the banks of the river to reconnoiter the enemy.

Omrah, who was out of breath with running, stated that some of the Matabili were crossing the river, and that six had landed on this side, before he came up to give the information. He pointed to a clump of trees, about three hundred yards off, and said that they had gone up in that direction, and were probably there by that time.

"Then we had better saddle and mount,"

said the Major, "and ride away gently to the wood on this side of the camp. We shall then be able to watch their motions without being seen."

This advice was good, and approved by all. They led out their horses without noise, and as soon as they had done so, they went back, and threw more fuel on the fires. They then retreated to the wood, which was about the same distance from the camp, on the other side, as the clump of trees where the Matabili were secreted.

They had hardly concealed themselves, before the Matabili in the clump, surprised at not seeing the awnings of the wagons, and suspecting that they had been deceived, came out from their ambuscade; first crawling on all-fours, and as they arrived at the camp, and found only fires burning, rising up one after another. After remaining about a minute in consultation, two of the party were sent back to the river to communicate this intelligence to the main body, while the others searched about in every direction. Alexander, with the Major and their party, remained

The Mission

where they were, as it was their intention to cross through the wood, until they came to the open ground, about a quarter of a mile to the southward, and then show themselves to the enemy, before they went to join the wagons.

In a few minutes it was daylight, and they now perceived that the whole body of the Matabili were crossing the river.

"They intend to pursue us, then," said Alexander.

Omrah now pointed to the side of the river, in the direction which the wagons had traveled when they came up by its banks, saying, "When go away – ride that way first – same track wagon go that way back – same way wagon come."

"The boy is right," said the Major; "when we start from the wood, we will keep by the riverside, in the track by which the wagons came; and when we are concealed from them by the hills or trees, we will then start off to the southward after the wagons."

"I see," replied Alexander; "they will

probably take the marks of the wagon-wheels coming here, for those of the wagons going away, and will follow them; presuming, as we go that way, that our wagons have gone also. But here they come up the banks; it is time for us to be off."

"Quite time," said the Major; "so now let us show ourselves, and then trust to our heels."

The Matabili force was now within four hundred yards of the camp. It was broad daylight; and, with their white and red shields and short spears in their hands, they presented a very formidable appearance.

There was no time to be lost, so the party rode out of the end of the wood nearest the river, and, as soon as they made their appearance, were received by a yell from the warriors, who dashed forward in the direction where they stood. The Major had directed that no one should fire, as he and Alexander did not wish that any blood should be shed unnecessarily. They therefore waved their hands, and turning their horses' heads galloped off by the banks of the river, keeping in the tracks made by the wagons when they came up.

As soon as they galloped a quarter of a mile, they pulled up, and turned their horses' heads to reconnoiter. They perceived that the Matabili force was pursuing them at the utmost speed: but as they had no horsemen, that speed was of course insufficient to overtake the well-mounted party in advance. As soon as they were near, our party again galloped off and left them behind. Thus they continued for four or five miles, the Matabili force pursuing them, or rather following the tracks of the wagons, when they observed a belt of trees before them about a mile off; this the Major considered as a good screen to enable them to alter their course without being perceived by the enemy. They therefore galloped forward, and as soon as they were hidden by the trees, turned off in a direction by which they made certain to fall in with the track which the wagons had made on their departure during the night.

They had ridden about two miles, still

concealed in the wood, when they had the satisfaction of perceiving the Matabili force still following at a rapid pace the tracks of the wagons on the riverside. Having watched them for half an hour, as they now considered that all was safe, they again continued their course, so as to fall in with the wagons.

"I think we are clear of them now," said the Major; "they have evidently fallen into the trap proposed by that clever little fellow, Omrah."

"He is a very intelligent boy," observed Alexander, "and, traveling in this country, worth his weight in gold."

"I wish Swinton would make him over to me," said the Major; "but, Alexander, do you observe what a change there is already in the country?"

"I do indeed," replied Alexander; "and all ahead of us it appears to be still more sterile and bare."

"Yes, when you leave the rivers, you leave vegetation of all kinds almost. There is no regular rainy season at all here, Swinton says; we may expect occasional torrents of rain during three months, but they are now very uncertain; the mountains attract the greater portion of the rain, and sometimes there will not be a shower on the plains for the whole year."

"How far shall we have to travel before we fall in with water again?" inquired Alexander.

"Swinton says there may be water in a river about sixty miles from where we started last night; if not, we shall have to proceed about thirty miles further, to the Gykoup or Vet River. After that we shall have to depend for many days upon the water we may find in the holes, which, as the season is now coming on, may probably be filled by the rain."

Alexander and his party rode for seven or eight miles before they fell in with the tracks of the caravan; they then pulled up their jaded horses, and proceeded at a more leisurely pace, so that it was not till late in the evening that they discovered the wagons at some distance, having passed the dry bed of Salt River ahead of them. During the whole day their horses had had neither food nor water, and the animals were much exhausted when they came up with the wagons. The oxen also were fatigued with so long a journey, having made nearly fifty miles since they started the evening before.

The country was now stony and sterile; a little vegetation was to be found here and there, but not sufficient to meet the wants of the animals, and water there was none. During the day but little game had been seen, – few zebras and ostriches only; all other varieties had disappeared. There was of course no wood to light the fires round the encampment: a sufficiency for cooking their victuals had been thrown into the wagons, and two sheep were killed to supply a supper for so numerous a party. But the absence of game also denoted the absence of lions, and they were not disturbed during the night. In the morning the Griquas parted company with them, on the plea that their oxen and horses were in too poor a condition to pass over the desert, and that they must make a direct course for the Val River and return by its banks.

Our travelers gave them a good supply of ammunition, the only thing that they wished for, and the Griquas, yoking their oxen to the crazy old wagon, set off in a westerly direction.

The route of the caravan was now directed more to the south-west, and they passed over an uninterrupted plain strewed with small land-tortoises, and covered with a profusion of the gayest flowers. About noon, after a sultry journey of nine hours, they fortunately arrived at a bog, in which they found a pool of most fetid water, which nothing but necessity could have compelled either them or the exhausted animals to drink. Near this pool in the desert they found several wild animals, and they obtained three gnoos for a supply of provision; the little wood that they had in the wagon for fuel was all used up in cooking their supper.

A heavy dew fell during the night, and in the morning, before the sun rose, they were enveloped in a thick fog. As the fog dispersed, they perceived herds of quaggas in all directions, but at a great distance. They again yoked the oxen and proceeded on their journey; the country was now covered with herbage and flowers of every hue, and looked like a garden.

"How strange that the ground should be covered with flowers where there is no rain or water to be found," observed Alexander.

"It is the heavy dews of the night which support them," said Swinton, "and perhaps the occasional rains which fall."

A line of trees to the southward told them that they were now approaching an unnamed river, and the tired oxen quickened their pace; but on their arrival they found that the bed of the river was dry, and not even a drop of water was to be found in the pools. The poor animals, which had been unyoked, snuffed and smelt at the wet, damp earth, and licked it with their tongues, but could obtain no relief. The water which they had had in the casks for their own drinking was now, all gone; and there were no hopes of obtaining any till they arrived at the Vet River, at least twenty-five to thirty miles distant. Two of the oxen lay down to rise no more, the countenances of the Hottentots were dejected and sullen, and our travelers felt that their situation was alarming.

While they were still searching and digging for water, the sky became overcast, thunder and lightning were seen and heard in the distance, and the clouds came rolling in volumes toward them. Hope was now in every face; they already anticipated the copious showers which were to succeed; their eyes ever fixed upon the coming storm; even the cattle appeared to be conscious that relief was at hand. All the day the clouds continued to gather, and the lightning to gleam. Night closed in, but the rain had not yet fallen; the wind rose up, and in less than an hour all the clouds had passed away, the stars shone out brightly, and they were left in a state of suffering and disappointment.

CHAPTER XXVII

As our travelers were sitting together, each occupied with his own melancholy thoughts, after the dispersion of the clouds and the anticipated relief, the Major said –

"It is useless our remaining here; we must all perish if we do not proceed, and it would be better for us to yoke and travel by night; the animals will bear the journey better, and the people will not be so inclined to brood over their misfortunes when on the march as when thus huddled together here, and communicating their lamentations to dishearten each other. It is now nine o'clock; let us yoke and push on as far as we can."

"I agree with you, Major," said Alexander; "what do you say, Swinton?"

"I am convinced that it will be the best plan, so let us rouse up the people at once. There is the roar of a lion at some distance, and we have no fires to scare them off."

"The creaking of the wagon-wheels will be better than nothing," replied the Major.

The Hottentots were roused, and the orders given to yoke: the poor fellows were all sound asleep; for a Hottentot, when he hungers or thirsts, seeks refuge from all his miseries in sleep. The oxen were yoked, and they proceeded; but hardly had they gone a mile, when the roar of three or four lions, close upon them, caused such alarm to the horses and the oxen which were not yoked that they started off in full gallop in a northerly direction.

Alexander, the Major, and Omrah, who were the best mounted, immediately set off in pursuit of them, desiring Swinton to proceed with the caravan, and they would drive on the cattle and join him. They galloped off as well as the horses could gallop, and perceived the stray horses and oxen still at full speed, as if they were chased by the lions. They followed in the direction, but it was now so dark that they were guided only by the clatter of their hoofs and their shoes in the distance; and after a chase of four or five miles they had lost all vestiges of them, and pulled up their panting steeds.

"We may as well go back again," said Alexander; "the animals must have made a circuit."

"I suppose so," said the Major; "but my horse trembles so, that I had better dismount for a little while, that he may recover himself; indeed, so had you too and Omrah, for the animals are completely worn out."

"The clouds are rising again," said Alexander; "I trust that we may not be disappointed a second time."

"Yes, and there is lightning again in the horizon – may the Almighty help us in our distress," exclaimed the Major.

The horses, exhausted from want of water, continued to pant so fearfully, that it was nearly half an hour before they ventured to mount, that they might return to the caravan. In the meantime the heavens had become wholly obscured by the clouds, and there was every prospect of a heavy shower; at last a few drops did fall.

"Thank God!" exclaimed Alexander, as he lifted his face up to the heavens, to feel the drops as they fell. "Now let us return."

They mounted their horses and set off, but the stars were no longer visible to guide them, and they proceeded on at a slow pace, uncertain whether they were right or wrong. This they cared little about; their thoughts were upon the coming rain, which they so anxiously awaited. For more than three hours they were tantalized by the lightning flashing and the thunder pealing, every moment expecting the flood-gate of the heavens to be opened; but, as before, they were doomed to disappointment. Before the morning dawned the clouds had again retreated; and when the sky was clear, they found by the stars that their horses' heads were turned to the northward and eastward.

They altered their course in silence, for they were worn out and despondent; they suffered dreadfully from thirst, and it was pitiable to see the tongues of the poor horses hanging out of their mouths. Day dawned, and there were no signs of the caravan. A thick vapor was rising from every quarter, and they hoped that when it cleared up they would be more fortunate; but no, there was the same monotonous landscape, the same carpet of flowers without perfume. The sun was now three hours high, and the heat was intense; their tongues clove to the roofs of their mouths, while still they went on over flowery meads; but neither forest nor pool, nor any trees which might denote the bed of the river, caught their earnest gaze.

"This is dreadful," said Alexander, at last, speaking with difficulty.

"We are lost, that is certain," said the Major; "but we must trust in God."

"Yes, we may now say, Lord help us, or we perish," replied Alexander.

At this moment, little Omrah, who had been behind, rode up to them, and offered them one of the Hottentots' pipes, which he had lighted saying, "Smoke, – not feel so bad." Alexander took it, and after a few whiffs found that it had the effect or producing a little saliva, and he handed it to the Major, who did the same, and felt immediate relief.

They continued to walk their horses in a southerly direction; but the heat was now so great, that it became almost insufferable, and at last the horses stood still. They dismounted and drove their horses slowly before them over the glowing plain; and now the mirage deluded and tantalized them in the strangest manner. At one time Alexander pointed with delight (for he could not speak) to what he imagined to be the wagons; they pushed on, and found that it was a solitary quagga, magnified thus by the mirage. Sometimes they thought that they saw lakes of water in the distance, and hastened on to them; and then they fancied they were close to rivers and islands, covered with luxuriant foliage, but still were doomed to disappointment; as all was the result of the highly-rarefied air, and the refraction of the sun's rays on the sultry plain. What would they have given for a bush even to afford them any shelter from the noonday sun, for the crowns of their heads appeared as if covered with live coal, and their minds began to wander. The poor horses moved at the slowest pace, and only when driven on by Omrah, who appeared to suffer much less than his masters. Every now and then he handed to them the pipe, but at last even that had no longer any relief. Speech had been for some hours totally lost. Gradually the sun sunk down to the horizon, and as his scorching rays became less intense they to a certain degree recovered their wandering senses.

At night they sat down by the side of the horses, and, worn out with fatigue and exhaustion, fell into a troubled sleep; a sleep which, if it relieved their worn-out frames, condemned them to the same tantalizing feelings as had been created by the mirage during the day. They dreamed that they were in the bowers of paradise, hearing heavenly music; passing from crystal stream to stream, slaking their thirst at each, and reclining on couches of verdant green. Every thing that was delightful appeared to them in their dreams; they were in the abodes of bliss, and thus did they remain for an hour or two, when they were wakened up by the roar of a lion, which reminded them that they were without food or water in the desert.

They awoke speechless with thirst, their eyes inflamed, and their whole bodies burning like a coal, and the awful roar of the lion still reverberated along the ground. They started on their legs, and found Omrah close to them, holding the bridles of the horses, which were attempting to escape. They were still confused, when they were fully restored to their waking senses by a second roar of the lion still nearer to them; and by the imperfect light of the stars they could now distinguish the beast at about one hundred yards' distance. Omrah put the bridles of their two horses in their hands, and motioned them to go on in the direction opposite to where the lion was. They did so without reflection, mechanically obeying the directions of the man-child, and not perceiving that Omrah did not follow them. They had advanced about one hundred yards with the terrified animals, when another loud roar was followed up by the shriek of the other horse, announcing that he had become a victim to the savage animal. They both started, and dropping the reins of their horses, hastened with their rifles to the help of Omrah, of whose absence they now for the first time were aware; but they were met half-way by the boy, who contrived to say with difficulty, "Lion want horse, not little Bushman." They waited a few seconds, but the cries of the poor animal, and the crushing and cracking of its bones, were too painful to hear; and they hastened on and rejoined the other horses, which appeared paralyzed with fear, and had remained stationary.

They again led their horses on for an hour, when they arrived at a small pile of rocks; there they again lay down, for they were quite exhausted and careless of life. Not even the roar of a lion would have aroused them now, or if it had roused them they would have waited for the animal to come and put an end to their misery. But another and a softer noise attracted the quick ear of Omrah, and he pushed Alexander, and put his finger up to induce him to listen.

The Mission

Having listened a little longer, Omrah made signs to Alexander and the Major to follow him. The noise which Omrah had heard was the croaking of a frog, which denoted water at hand, and the sniffing of the horses confirmed him in his supposition. Omrah led the way through the rocks, descending lower and lower; and ever and anon listening to the noise of the animal, till he perceived the stars of heaven above reflected in a small pool, which he pointed out to Alexander and the Major. Down they dropped to earth and drank, and as soon as their thirst was satisfied they rose, and pushed Omrah forward to make him drink also; and as the boy who had saved their lives was drinking, they kneeled down and prayed – not loud, for they had not yet recovered their speech; but if ever grateful prayers were offered up to the Almighty throne, they were by our two travelers, as they kneeled by the side of this small pool. They rose and hastened to their horses, and led them down to the water, when the poor animals filled themselves almost to bursting, walked away, and returned to drink more. They also repeated their draught several times, and then lay down, and would have fallen asleep by the side of the pool had not Omrah, who could now speak freely, said, "No, no; lion come here for water; up the rock again and sleep there – I bring horses." This good advice was followed, and when they had gained the summit of the rising ground they again lay down and slept till daylight.

When they awoke, they found themselves much refreshed, but they now felt – what they had not done during their extreme suffering from thirst – the craving pangs of hunger. Omrah was fast asleep, and the horses picking among the herbage, about two hundred yards off.

"We have much to thank God for," said Alexander to the Major.

"We have indeed, and, next to divine aid, we have to thank that poor boy. We have been as children in his hands, and we are indebted to him and his resources for our lives this night. I could not speak yesterday, nor could you; but his courage in remaining with the horse as an offering to the lion I shall not forget."

"He is a child of the desert," replied Alexander; "he has been brought up among lions, and where there is scarcity of water, and he has most wonderfully guided us in our path; but we are still in the desert, and have lost our companions. What must we do? Shall we attempt to regain the caravan, or push off to the westward, to fall in with the river again?"

"We will talk of this an hour hence," replied the Major; "let us now go down to the pool, and as soon as I have had a drink I will try if I can not kill something for a meal. My hunger is now almost as great as was my thirst."

"And mine too, so I will go with you; but we must be careful how we approach the water, as we may fall in with some animal to make a meal of."

"Or with a lion, ready to make a meal of us," replied the Major; "so in either instance we must approach it cautiously."

As they walked to the pool, they discovered the head of an antelope just above a rock. The Major fired, and the animal fell. The report of the rifle was answered by a roar; three lions bounded away from the rock, and went at a quick canter over the plain.

"Both our suppositions have proved correct," observed Alexander, as they walked up to where the antelope lay dead; "but how are we to cook the animal?"

"Any dry stuff will serve for a fire, if we can only get enough, and a very little cooking will serve us just now. Here comes Omrah. Let us carry the game up to where we slept last night, as soon as we have had a drink."

They went to the pool, and were surprised to behold the filthy puddle which had appeared to them so like nectar the night before. They were not sufficiently thirsty to overcome their disgust, and they turned away from it.

Omrah now began collecting dried grass, and herbs, and lichen from the rocks, and had soon a sufficiency to make a small fire; they struck a light, and cutting off steaks from the antelope, were in a short time very busy at the repast. When their hunger was appeased, they found that their thirst was renewed, and they went down to the pool, and shutting their eyes drank plentifully. Omrah cooked as much of the meat as the small fire would permit, that they might not want for the next twenty-four hours; and the horses being again led to the water to drink, they mounted, and proceeded to the southward, followed by Omrah on foot. Another day was passed in searching for the caravan without success. No water was to be found. The heat was dreadful; and at night they threw themselves down on the ground, careless of life; and had it not been sinful they would have prayed for death. The next morning they arose in a state of dreadful suffering; they could not speak, but they made signs, and resolved once more to attempt to join the caravan.

They proceeded during the whole of the forenoon in the direction by which they hoped to discover the tracks of the wagons. The heat was overpowering, and they felt all the agony of the day before. At last the horses could proceed no further; they both lay down, and our travelers had little hopes of their ever rising again. The scorching of the sun's rays was so dreadful, that they thrust their heads into some empty ant-hills to keep off the heat, and there they lay in as forlorn and hopeless a state as the horses. Speak they could not; their parched tongues rattled like boards against the roofs of their mouths; their lips were swollen and bloated, and their eyes inflamed and starting from the sockets. As Alexander afterward said to Swinton, he then recollected the thoughts which had risen in his mind on his departure from the English shore, and the surmise whether he might not leave his bones bleaching in the desert; and Alexander now believed that such was to be the case, and he prayed mentally and prepared for death. The Major was fully possessed of the same idea; but as they lay at some yards' distance, with their heads buried in the ant-hills, they could not communicate with each other even by signs. At last they fell into a state of stupor and lost all recollection. But an Almighty Providence watched over them, and during their state of insensibility the clouds again rose and covered the firmament, and this time they did not rise in mockery; for, before the day was closed, torrents descended from them and deluged the whole plain.

Omrah, who had held up better than his masters, crawled out of the ant-hill into which he had crept; and as soon as the rain descended, he contrived to pull the heads of the Major and Alexander, who still remained senseless, from out of the ant-hills, and to turn their blackened and swollen faces to the sky. As their clothes became saturated with the rain and the water poured into their mouths, they gradually revived, and at last were completely restored. The wind now rose and blew fresh, and before morning they were shivering with cold, and when they attempted to get up found their limbs were cramped.

Soon after daylight the rain ceased, and they were glad to bask in the then cheering rays of the sun, which had nearly destroyed them on the day before. The horses had recovered their legs and were feeding close to them; and the flesh of the antelope, which had been untasted, was now greedily devoured. Most devoutly did they return thanks for their preservation, and the hopes which were now held out to them of ultimately regaining the colony; for they had abandoned all hopes of reaching the caravan, as they considered the risk of crossing the desert too great. They made up their minds to push for the Val River as fast as they could, and proceed back by its banks.

They had two horses, and Omrah could ride behind one of them, when he was tired; they had guns and ammunition, and although they were fully aware of the dangers to which they would be exposed, they thought lightly of them after what they had suffered. They now mounted their horses, and proceeded at a slow pace toward the westward, for the poor animals were still very weak. At sunset they had traveled about ten miles, and looked out for a spot to pass the night. Wood to light fires they had none, but they hoped, if their horses were not taken away by the lions, to reach a branch of the river by the following evening. There was now no want of water, as they repeatedly passed by small pools, which, for a day or two at least, would not be evaporated by the heat of the sun. But they knew that by that time, if no more rain fell, they would have again to undergo the former terrible privations, and therefore resolved upon continuing their course toward the river as their safest plan, now that they had lost the caravan.

As they were seated on a rising ground which they had chosen for their night's rest, and occasionally firing off their rifles to drive away the lions which were heard prowling about; all of a sudden Omrah cried out, and pointed to the northward; our travelers turned and perceived a rocket ascending the firmament, and at last breaking out into a group of brilliant stars.

"It is the caravan," exclaimed the Major; "Swinton has remembered that I put some rockets into my wagon."

"We must have passed it," said Alexander, springing on his feet. "God be praised for all his mercies."

"Amen," replied the Major devoutly.

Omrah ran after the horses, which were feeding close to them, for their instinctive fear of the lions made them keep as close as possible to their masters. They were soon mounted, with Omrah behind the Major, and set off at all the speed that they could obtain from the animals. After an interval another rocket was seen, and by its light they discovered that they were not a mile from the wagons. The horses appeared to be sensible of this, and went off at a quicker pace; and in a few minutes they had rushed in among the cattle, and Alexander and the Major were received into the arms of Swinton, and surrounded by the Hottentots, who were loud in their congratulations at their return.

As soon as Alexander and the Major had made known their perils and sufferings to Swinton, the latter informed them that about three hours after they had left the caravan in pursuit of the cattle, the animals had returned, that of course, he had fully expected them to follow.

Finding that they did not arrive, he had decided upon remaining where he was, at all events, for another day; but that the cattle were by that time so exhausted, that it was with difficulty they were moved, and he could not proceed with them more than ten miles, when they lay down in their yokes. Thirteen had died, and the others must have shared their fate, if it had not been for the providential rain, which had restored them.

Swinton stated that he had been in a great state of alarm for them, and that he had almost satisfied himself that they had perished, although he had used every means that he could think of. When he fired the rockets off, he had scarcely a hope of thus bringing them back to the caravan.

"However," observed Swinton, "it shows that we should never despair, and never leave a chance untried, even in the most desperate circumstances. You are back again, and I thank the Almighty for it with all my heart and all my soul and all my strength, most fervently and most sincerely. I have been very, very miserable, I can assure you, my dear fellows. The idea of returning to the Cape without you was dreadful. Indeed, I never would have left the country until I had found you, or had some clew to your deaths."

"Our preservation has indeed been miraculous," replied the Major; "I never thought to have raised my head out of the ant-hill again."

"Nor I," replied Alexander; "and next to the Almighty, we certainly owe our lives to little Omrah. There is nothing that I would not do for that boy, if you will only give him over to my care."

"Or mine, Swinton," replied the Major.

"Depend upon it," replied Swinton, "I will do all for him that ought to be done; I owe him a debt of gratitude for preserving my friends, and will not forget to repay it."

"Well then, you must allow us to help him as well," replied the Major. "How

The Mission

far are we now from the Modder River?"

"About forty miles, I should think, and we had better push on as fast as we, can; for although the river will contain water, the pools in the desert between us and the river will soon be dried up. The cattle, however, are still very weak, and, as I have stated, we have lost all our relays. But you must long to have a good night's rest, so go to your wagons, and we will watch and keep off the wild beasts. We have been obliged to fire our guns all night long since your absence, and have burned one of the spare poles of the wagons to cook our victuals."

Every thing is comparative. When our travelers first took up their night's lodgings in the wagons they found their resting-places hard, after sleeping in comfortable beds at Cape Town; but now, after having passed their nights in the wild desert, their mattresses in the wagons were a luxury that was fully appreciated. Returning thanks to Heaven for their preservation, Alexander and the Major slept soundly till morning, notwithstanding that the latter was often half roused by the importunities of

Begum, who appeared delighted at the return of her master.

At daylight the oxen were yoked, and they proceeded on their journey. There was no want of game; indeed they were so plentiful, that they shot them from the caravan as they passed. At night they had made twenty-five miles, and before they had unyoked, a deluge of rain again fell, and they passed a very uncomfortable night, as it was very cold, and they could light no fires, from want of fuel. Any thing, however, was better than the want of water; and early in the morning they again yoked their oxen, and, after a hard day's toil, were rejoiced to perceive at a distance the trees which lined the banks of the Modder River. The sight was hailed with joy by the Hottentots, who shouted aloud; for they considered their dangers and difficulties to be over, now that they were approaching to the boundaries of the colony.

CHAPTER XXVIII

As the cattle required some repose, after the sufferings they had gone through, our travelers resolved to remain a few days on the banks of the Modder River. The pasturage was fine and the game abundant. Gnoos and springboks were to be seen in every direction, and quaggas, bonteboks, and several other varieties of antelopes, were in profusion over the now undulating country. Neither were our travelers sorry to have some repose for themselves, although every mile that they drew nearer to the Cape made them more anxious to return.

As usual, the caravan was halted on a rising ground, at some distance from the river, to avoid the wild beasts, which during the day were concealed, and during the night prowled on its banks, to spring upon the animals which came down for water. As there was now plenty of wood, the fires were again lighted at night, and the oxen driven in and tied up. During the day, the animals reveled on the luxurious pasture, and in a week had become quite sleek and in good condition.

Every day our travelers went out to hunt for a supply of provisions, and never returned without more than was sufficient. Swinton was anxious to possess one or two more specimens of the oryx, or gemsbok. This antelope, we have before observed, from having very straight horns, which at a distance appear as one, has given rise to the fabulous animal the unicorn, which is now one of the supporters of the royal arms. It is a very formidable animal; being the one that our travelers found with its horns pierced through the lion which had attacked it. The horses being now fresh and in good heart, Alexander and the Major went in pursuit of this animal very often, but without success, as the chase was continually interrupted by the herds of ostriches and other game which fell in their way.

One morning, having discovered with the telescope that three of these gemsbok were some miles distant on a rising ground, they set off, accompanied by a portion of the Hottentots on foot, who were desired to go round, so as to drive the animals toward the camp. Bremen and Big Adam were of the party, and they had made a circuit of three or four miles, so as to get on the other side of the game, which now darted down from the high ground, and, descending on the plain, stopped for a while looking at their pursuers, while the horsemen advanced toward them in the opposite direction. A shot from Alexander at last brought one of these splendid animals to the ground, while the others fled off to a distance, so as to give no hopes of again coming up with them; and the party on foot, as well as the horsemen, now proceeded to the spot where the gemsbok lay dead.

As Swinton wanted the animal for a specimen, it was placed on the back of the horse which Omrah rode as usual, and one of the Hottentots went off with it to the camp, which was not more than three miles distant. They were debating whether they should make an attempt to get near to the other gemsbok, which were still in sight at a distance, or try for some other game, when they perceived three lions not far from them

The Mission

on a rising ground; and suddenly the horses, from which they had dismounted to give them time to recover their wind, broke loose from the Hottentots who held the bridles, and galloped away toward the camp. The cause of the panic was now evident, for a very large male lion had detached himself from the other two, and was advancing slowly toward the party.

As soon as they perceived the approach of the lion, which they had not at first, they all seized their guns; but being wholly unprepared for such a sudden attack, there was a great deal of confusion; the Major crying out, "Let no one fire till I tell him," only produced more alarm among the Hottentots, all of whom, except Bremen, appeared to be at their wits' ends. When within fifty yards, the lion made one or two bounds, and in a moment was among them all, before they could bring their guns to their shoulders; the retreat was general in every direction, and not a shot was fired.

All, however, did not escape; Big Adam had started back, and coming with all his force against Omrah, who was standing behind him, had fallen over the boy, and they were both flat on their backs, when the lion made his spring. The lion was standing up, looking proudly at his flying enemies, when Big Adam, who was close to him, attempted to rise and gain his feet; but perceiving this, the animal, with a blow of its fore-paw, laid him prostrate again, set its foot upon his breast, and in this attitude again looked proudly round him, as if confident of his superiority.

Omrah, who had sense enough to lie still, had yet his eyes sufficiently opened to see what was going on; and as the lion appeared to be looking at the scattered party, in a direction away from him, Omrah made one or two turns over, so as to get further off, hoping that he might escape unperceived. The lion, however, heard the rustling, and turning round growled at him, and Omrah remained still again. As Big Adam's feet were turned toward Omrah, the lion now took up his position, deliberately lying down at full length upon Big Adam's body, with his hind-quarters upon the Hottentot's face, so that he not only secured his prisoner, but watched

Omrah, who lay about three yards from him.

In the mean time the anxiety of the other party may be imagined; they considered that Big Adam and Omrah must be sacrificed. It was proposed to fire with good aim, so as, if possible, to bring the animal's attention and indignation upon themselves; but Swinton cried out not to fire on any account. "The animal is not hungry or even angry," said Swinton. "If let alone, he will probably walk away without doing them injury. At all events, our firing will be the signal for their destruction."

The advice of Swinton was considered good, especially as it was backed by that of Bremen, who also said that the lion was not hungry, and that, by the way in which he, moved his tail, he was evidently more inclined to play than any thing else.

But in the mean time the pressure of the lion, whose weight was enormous, was not only more than Big Adam could bear, but the hind-quarters of the animal being over his face prevented him from breathing; and at last he was compelled to struggle to get his head clear. The consequence of his struggling was a severe bite on the leg, inflicted on poor Adam; not, however, in a furious manner; for the lion merely caught at him as a cat would at a mouse, to prevent its escape, or because it was not quite dead. However, Big Adam had so far disengaged his head that he could now breathe; and as the party kept crying out to him to lie still, he continued so to do, although nearly suffocated with the enormous weight of the animal.

Omrah, who had remained still during all this time, perceiving that the lion was licking the blood which flowed from the wound in Big Adam's leg, thought that he might as well try another roll over, and being on his back, he turned over on his face away from the lion. Thereupon the lion rose from off Big Adam, walked up to Omrah, and, to the horror of our travelers, took up the boy by his waistcloth, and, carrying him like a small bundle in his mouth, went back to Big Adam, and laying Omrah close down to the Hottentot's head, again took up his position on his body; now, however, with his paws upon the Hottentot's breast, so that he might keep Omrah in view before him. Little Omrah had sense enough not to move during the time that the lion carried him, or after he was laid down.

The change in the position of the lion occasioned our travelers and the party to walk round, so as to be able to watch the countenance of the animal, as every thing depended upon the temper he might be in. The Major and Alexander became very impatient, and were for advancing to the attack, but Swinton persuaded them not to do so until the last moment.

The lion now put its fore-paw upon the Hottentot's mouth, and again stopped his breath; this occasioned another struggle on the part of Big Adam, which was followed by the animal seizing him by the arm and biting him severely; but in so doing the lion removed its paw, and the man could breathe again. The taste of blood appeared pleasant to the lion, for it continued biting the arm, descending from the shoulder to the hand, and as the blood flowed from the wounds on its paws, the lion licked it off. Again and again it licked its paw clean, and then, with its glaring eyes fixed intently upon the Hottentot's face, it smelt him first on one side and then on the other, and appeared only to be waiting for a return of appetite to commence a deliberate meal upon the poor fellow's body.

In the mean time our travelers were standing about seventy yards distant, waiting for the signal to attack, when Bremen observed to Swinton –

"He won't wait much longer, sir; the blood has given him an appetite. We must now drive him away, or they will both be killed."

"I think so too," replied Swinton; "let us first try if we can disturb him without making him angry; that will be the best way. We must go back out of springing distance, and then all shout together, and keep hallooing at him."

This advice was followed; they retreated a hundred yards, and then all shouted at once, and after that the Hottentots hallooed and bawled to the lion. This had the effect intended: the lion rose from the bodies and advanced toward the party, who stood still hallooing at him, but not attempting to irritate him by presenting their guns. The lion looked steadfastly at them for some time, and then turned away. After retreating a few steps, it turned back to face them; the whole party continued on the same spot, neither advancing so as to irritate him, nor retreating so as to let the animal suppose that they were afraid of him. When the lion had continued for a few minutes this course of retreating and advancing, he turned right round, and went away at a hand canter, and our travelers immediately hastened to the spot where Big Adam and Omrah were still lying.

Omrah, who was not at all hurt, instantly jumped on his legs, and, if he had been afraid, appeared to have quite recovered his courage, as he cut all manner of capers, and laughed immoderately; but Big Adam was greatly exhausted and could not move, as much from the immense pressure of the lion's enormous body, as from the blood that he had lost by the wounds which he had received. On examination, the bite in his leg was found to be much the most serious, as the bone was injured; the wounds on his arm were all flesh-wounds, and although very painful, were not dangerous. He was at present unable to speak, and was carried by his comrades to the camp. Our travelers followed the Hottentots, as they all had enough of hunting for that day. As soon as they arrived, Big Adam's wounds were dressed by Swinton, and the poor fellow was accommodated with a bed, made up for him in the baggage-wagon. They remained two days more on the banks of the Modder River, and then they forded it and continued their journey.

On the second day they perceived some small human figures on the summit of a hill at some distance, which the Hottentots declared to be Bushmen, of which people there were numerous hordes in this part of the country. An attempt was made to open a communication with them, but in vain, as when any of the party advanced on horseback toward them, the Bushmen made a precipitate retreat. As they were now in the neighborhood of these plunderers, every care was taken of the cattle, which were tied up before dark to prevent their being stolen.

On the following day they very unexpectedly fell in with a party of nine of the Bushmen, who were very busy devouring a quagga, which they had killed. They replied to questions put to them with much fear and trembling, and, having been presented with some tobacco, they made a precipitate retreat. On that night the fires of the Bushmen were to be seen on several of the surrounding hills. They continued their course on the following day, when they fell in with about twenty women of the race we have just mentioned, who approached the caravan without fear, requesting tobacco and food; the former was given to them in small quantities, and a shot from the Major's rifle soon procured them the latter. They were now without water again, and had no chance of procuring any, except from the pools, until they arrived at the Nu Gariep, or Black River, which they had crossed when they came out from the Caffre Land.

Having traveled till dark, they halted under a hill, and were soon afterward joined by a party of Bushwomen, who continued with them in spite of all their attempts to get rid of them. They were very small in person, well made, and the young were rather pretty in their features, but their ornaments were enough to disgust any one but a Hottentot; for they were smeared with grease and red ocher, and were adorned with the entrails of animals as necklaces. The Hottentots, however, appeared to think this very delightful, and were pleased with their company, and as the women showed them a pool of water, where the oxen could drink, it was not considered advisable to drive them away. But Swinton observed, that it would be necessary to keep a very sharp lookout, as the women were invariably sent by the Bushmen as spies, that they might watch the opportunity for stealing cattle.

They now resumed their former plan; starting at a very early hour, and traveling till afternoon, when the cattle were allowed several hours to feed, and were then tied up for the night to the wagons. Indeed the lions were now not so numerous as they had been, and they had more to fear from the Bushmen and the hyenas, which were very plentiful.

The next day fully proved the truth of this, for the oxen, having been unyoked as usual to feed, about two o'clock in the afternoon, had been led to a hollow of luxuriant pasture by the cattle-keepers, where they could not be seen from the caravan, although they were not half a mile off. Toward dusk, when it was time to drive them in and tie them up to the wagons, it was found that the cattle-keepers, who had been in company with the Bushwomen, had neglected their charge, and they were not to be found.

The keepers came running in, stating that a lion had scared the cattle, and that the animals had galloped off to a great distance. But Omrah, who had gone to where the cattle had been feeding, returned to the camp and told Swinton that it was not lions but

Bushmen who had stolen them; and, bringing the horses ready saddled to the Major and Alexander, said, that if they did not follow them immediately, the cattle would be all killed. It was also observed that the Bushwomen had all disappeared.

Swinton, who was well aware of the customs of the Bushmen, immediately proposed that they should mount as many as they could, and go in chase, as there was not an hour to be lost. In half an hour a party, consisting of our three travelers, Bremen, Omrah, and three of the most trusty of the Hottentots, who were all that they could mount, set off in the direction which they knew must have been taken, so as to conceal the cattle from the sight of those in the caravan; and it being a fine moonlight night, the keen eyes of Omrah tracked them for more than five miles, where they were at fault, as the traces of their hoofs were no longer to be seen.

"What shall we do now?" said the Major.

"We must trust to Omrah," replied Swinton, "he knows the habits of his people well, and they will not deceive him."

Omrah, who had been very busy kneeling on the ground, and striking a light every now and then with a flint and steel, to ascertain the track more distinctly, now came up and made them comprehend that the Bushmen had turned back upon the very track they had gone upon, and that they must return and find where they diverged from it again.

This created considerable delay, as they had to walk the horses back for more than a mile, when they again found the footing of the cattle diverging from the track to the southward and eastward, in the direction of some hills.

They now made all the haste that they could, and proceeded so rapidly on the track, that in about an hour they perceived the whole herd of oxen driven up the side of a hill by a party of Bushmen. They put spurs to their horses and galloped as fast as they could in pursuit, and soon came up with them; when a discharge of rifles left three

Bushmen on the ground and put all the rest to flight. The cattle, which were much frightened, were with some difficulty turned and driven back toward the encampment. In the mean time the disappointed Bushmen had turned upon those near, and were letting fly their arrows from the bushes where they were concealed and continued thus to assail them until the party arrived at the open plain. One of the Hottentots was wounded by an arrow in the neck; but that was the only accident which occurred to any of the party, and this was not known to our travelers until after their arrival at the encampment, when it was almost daybreak; and then, tired with the fatigues of the night, all were glad to obtain a few hours' rest.

When they rose the next morning, Swanevelt informed them that nine of the oxen were so wounded with the poisoned arrows of the Bushmen, that they could not live; and also, that Piets the Hottentot had been badly wounded in the neck with one of the arrows. Swinton immediately ordered the man to be brought to him, as he was well aware of the fatal effects of a wound from a

Bushman's arrow.

It appeared that Piets had pulled the arrow out of his neck, but that some pieces of the barb had remained in the wound, and that these his companions had been extracting with their knives, and the wound was very much inflamed in consequence. Swinton immediately cut out as much of the affected part as he could, applied ammonia to the wound, and gave him laudanum to mitigate the pain, which was very acute; but the poor fellow lay groaning during the whole of the day.

They now examined the wounded oxen, which were already so swollen with the poison that there were no hopes of saving them, and they were immediately put out of their pain. Several others were found slightly hurt, but not so as to lose all hopes of their recovery; but this unfortunate circumstance prevented them from continuing their journey for two days; as the whole of the oxen had been much harassed and cut by the Bushmen, although not wounded by poisoned arrows. During this delay, the poor Hottentot became hourly worse; his head and throat were much swollen, and he said that he felt the poison working within him.

After many hours of suffering, during which swellings appeared in various parts of his body, the poor fellow breathed his last; and the next day being Sunday, they remained as usual, and the body of the unfortunate man was consigned to a grave. This event threw a cloud over the whole caravan, and whenever any of the Bushwomen made their appearance at a distance, and made signs that they wished to come into the camp, an angry bullet was sent instantly over their heads, which made them take to their heels.

On the Monday morning they again started with their reduced trains, for now they had barely sufficient cattle to drag the wagons. Fortunately they were but a few miles from the Nu Gariep, and they arrived at its banks before evening. The next day they crossed it with difficulty, putting all the oxen to two of the wagons and then returning for the others.

They were now once more in the colony, and their dangers and difficulties were now to be considered over. It was not, however, till a week afterward that they succeeded in crossing the Sweenberg and arriving at Graff Reynet. At this beautiful spot they remained for a few days, to make arrangements and to procure horses, that they might proceed to Cape Town as fast as possible, leaving Bremen in charge of the wagons, which he was to bring down to them as soon as he could. We shall pass over the remainder of their journey on horseback, as there was nothing remarkable to be related. Suffice it to say, that on the 11th of January, 1830, they arrived safe and sound at Cape Town, and were warmly congratulated by Mr. Fairburn and their many friends, after all the dangers and difficulties which they had encountered.

CHAPTER XXIX

Alexander Wilmot again took possession of the apartments in Mr. Fairburn's house, and was not sorry once more to find himself surrounded by all the comforts and luxuries of civilization. He could scarcely believe where he was when he woke up the first morning, and found that he had slept the whole night without being disturbed by the roar of a lion or the cries of the hyena and jackal: and after the habit to which he had been so long accustomed, of eating his meals in the open air with his plate on his knees, he could hardly reconcile himself for a few days to a well laid-out table. The evenings were passed in narrating their adventures to Mr. Fairburn, who was truly glad of the result of the mission to Port Natal, as it would be so satisfactory to old Sir Charles.

Alexander was now most anxious to return to England, and resolved to take his passage in the first ship which sailed after the arrival of the wagon with his effects. In the mean time his mornings were chiefly passed with Swinton and the Major, the latter of whom intended to go to England by the same vessel as Alexander. In three weeks after their return to the Cape, the four wagons arrived, and excited much curiosity, as they were filled with every variety of the animal kingdom which was indigenous to the country. Swinton's treasures were soon unloaded and conveyed to his house, and our naturalist was as happy as an enthusiastic person could be in the occupation that they gave him. Alexander only selected a few things, among which were the skins of the lion and lioness. As for the Major, he had had all his pleasure in the destruction of the animals.

Bremen reported that all the Hottentots had behaved very well, and that Big Adam had nearly recovered, and was able to limp about a little, although it would be a long while before he would regain the perfect use of his leg. Alexander now sent for them all, and paid them their wages, with an extra sum as a gratuity for their good conduct. To Bremen and Swanevelt, who had invariably conducted themselves faithfully, and who had been the leading

The Mission

and most trustworthy men, he gave to each a wagon and span of ten oxen as a present by which they might in future obtain their livelihood, and the poor fellows considered themselves as rich as the king of England. The other wagons and cattle of every description were left with Swinton to be disposed of.

The Major pressed Swinton very hard to part with little Omrah, but Swinton would not consent. The Major therefore presented Omrah with one of his best rifles, and accouterments to correspond, as a mark of his attachment; and Alexander desired that all the money which was realized by the sale of the remaining wagons and other articles, as well as the cattle and horses, should be put by for Omrah's benefit. As a keepsake, Alexander gave the lad his telescope, with which he knew that would be highly pleased.

We may here as well observe, that, a few months after Alexander and the Major left the Cape, Omrah, who had been placed at a school by Swinton, was admitted into the church, and baptized by the name of Alexander Henderson

Omrah; Alexander and the Major being his sponsors by proxies. He turned out a very clever scholar, and remains with Swinton at this moment. He has more than once accompanied him into the interior, and has done much in reclaiming his countrymen, the bushmen, from their savage way of life, and has been of great service to the missionaries as interpreter of the Word to his heathen brethren.

About a fortnight after the return of the wagons to Cape Town, a free trader cast anchor in Table Bay to take in water, and Alexander and the Major secured a passage in her to England. Alexander parted with great regret from Mr. Fairburn and Swinton, with whom he promised to correspond, and they sailed with a fair wind for St. Helena, where they remained for a few days, and took that opportunity of visiting the tomb of Napoleon, the former emperor of the French. A seven weeks' passage brought them into the Channel-and they once more beheld the white cliffs of England.

Alexander's impatience to see his uncle, from whom he had found a letter waiting for him on his return to the Cape, stating that he was in tolerable health, induced him to leave the ship in a pilot-boat, and land at Falmouth. Taking leave for a time of the Major, who preferred going on to Portsmouth, Alexander traveled with all possible speed, and on the second day arrived at his uncle's.

"Is my uncle quite well!" said Alexander, as he leaped out of the chaise, to the old butler who was at the door.

"No sir, not quite well: he has been in bed for this last week, but there is nothing serious the matter, I believe."

Alexander hastened up stairs and was once more in the arms of Sir Charles Wilmot, who embraced him warmly, and then, exhausted with the emotion, sank back on his pillow.

"Leave me for a little while, my dear boy, till I recover myself a little," said Sir Charles. "I have no complaint, but I am very weak and feeble. I will send for you very soon."

Alexander, who was himself much affected, was not sorry to withdraw for a while, and sent the housekeeper, who attended his aged relative, into the room. In about an hour a message arrived requesting that he would return to his uncle.

"And now, my dear, kind boy, tell me every thing. I am indeed overjoyed to see you back again; I have not had one line from you since you left the Cape, and I really think that the worry and anxiety that I have felt have been the cause of my taking to my bed. Now you are back I shall be quite well again. Now tell me all, and I will not interrupt you."

Alexander sat down on the bed, and entered into a full detail of the results of his expedition to Port Natal; reading over all the memoranda which they had collected, and satisfactorily proving that the descendants of the Europeans then existing could not by any possibility be from those who had been lost in the *Grosvenor* East Indiaman.

Sir Charles Wilmot listened in silence to all Alexander had to say, and then, joining his hands above the bed-clothes, exclaimed, "Gracious Lord, I thank Thee that this weight has been removed from my mind." He then for some minutes prayed in silence, and when he had finished, he requested Alexander to leave him till the evening.

The physician having called shortly after Alexander left his uncle, Alexander requested his opinion as to Sir Charles's state of health. The former replied – "He has but one complaint, my dear sir, which all the remedies in the world are not very likely to remove: it is the natural decay of nature, arising from old age, I do not consider that he is in any immediate danger of dissolution. I think it very likely that he may never rise from his bed again; but, at the same time, he may remain bedridden for months. He sinks very gradually, for he has had naturally a very strong constitution, I believe the anxiety of his mind, arising from your absence, and the blame he laid on himself for having allowed you to undertake your expedition, have worn him more than any thing else; but now that you have returned, I have no doubt, after the first excitement is over, that he will rally. Still man is born to die,

Mr. Wilmot, and your uncle has already lived beyond the three-score years and ten allotted to the average age of man. Depend upon it, every thing shall be done which can protract a life so dear to you."

Alexander thanked the physician, and the latter then went up stairs to Sir Charles. On his return, he informed Alexander that Sir Charles's pulse was stronger, but something must be allowed for the excitement which he had undergone.

When Alexander saw his uncle in the evening, the latter again thanked him for having undertaken the expedition, and having brought back such satisfactory accounts.

"I am much your debtor, my dear boy," said he; "and if it is any satisfaction to you (which I am sure it must be from your kind heart) to know that you have smoothed the death-bed of one who loves you, you have your reward. I feel quite strong now; and if it will not be too much trouble, I should like you to give me a narrative of the whole expedition;

not all at once, but a little now and then. You shall begin now, and mind you enter into every little detail, – every thing will interest me."

Alexander commenced his narrative, as his uncle requested, stating to him how they were fitted out; the names of all the people; describing Swinton and the Major, and giving a much closer narrative of what passed than we have done in these pages. After an hour or so, during which Alexander had not got so far in his narrative as to have quitted the Cape for Algoa Bay, he left off, that he might not weary his uncle, and wished him good-night.

For many weeks did the narrative, and the conversation produced by it, serve to amuse and interest the old gentleman, who still remained in his bed. But long before it was finished, Major Henderson had arrived at the hall, and had been introduced to Sir Charles, who was much pleased with him, and requested him to remain as long as he found it agreeable. The Major, at Alexander's request, had the lion and lioness set up in Leadbeater's best style, and the case had now arrived at the hall, and was brought up into Sir Charles's room, that he might have some idea of the animals with which they had had to contend; and there it remained, for the old gentleman would not allow it to be taken away.

"I must send out a present to that little Omrah," said Sir Charles, one morning, as he was conversing with the Major; "what shall it be?"

"Well, sir, I hardly know; but I think the best present for him would be a watch."

"Then, Major, order one of the best gold watches that can be made, when you go to town, and send it out to him; and, Major, – I am sorry to give you that trouble, but I am an old bedridden man, and that must be my excuse, – take the keys from the dressing-table, and open the small drawer of that cabinet, and you will find two morocco cases in it, which I will thank you to bring to me."

The Major did so, and Sir Charles, raising himself on his pillow, opened the cases, which contained each a massive ring, in which was set a diamond of great value.

"These two rings were presented me by Eastern princes, Major, at the time that I was resident in their country. There is little difference in their value, but you would find it difficult to match the stones, even in England. I will shut the cases up again, and now that I have shut them up in my hands, take one out for me. Thank you, Major; that one is a present from me to our friend Swinton, and you must send it out to him with the watch for the Bush-boy. The other, Major, I hope you will not refuse to accept as a testimony of my gratitude to you, for having accompanied my dear boy on his expedition."

Sir Charles put the other case into the Major's hands.

"I certainly will not refuse any thing as a remembrance from you, Sir Charles," replied the Major; "I accept your splendid present with many thanks, and so will Swinton, I am certain; but he will be more pleased with the kind attention than he will be with its great value; and I

The Mission

trust you will believe me when I add that such is also my own feeling."

"I only hope you may have both as much pleasure in receiving as I have in giving them," replied Sir Charles; "so put them in your pocket and say no more about them. There is Alexander coming up, I know his tread; I hope you do not mean to desert him now that the shooting season is coming on; he will be very lonely, poor fellow, without you."

"I have good news, my dear uncle," said Alexander, as he entered; "Swinton is coming home; I have a letter from him, and he will be here, he trusts, a fortnight after his letter."

"I shall be most happy to shake hands with him," said Sir Charles. "Pray write for him to come down immediately he arrives."

Three weeks after this announcement Swinton made his appearance, and we hardly need say was most warmly welcomed. Omrah he would not bring with him, as he wished him to continue his education; but the Major declared that he had left the boy because he was afraid of his being taken from him. Our travelers were thus all reunited, and they agreed among themselves that it was quite as comfortable at the hall as it was at the Bechuana country; and that if the sporting was not quite so exciting, at all events it was not quite so dangerous.

Swinton and the Major remained with Alexander till the opening of the next year, and then they both left at the same time, and sailed in the same ship; the Major to rejoin his regiment in India, Swinton to his favorite locality in Africa, to obtain some more specimens in natural history.

As the physician had declared, Sir Charles never rose from his bed again; but he sunk so gradually that it was almost imperceptible, and it was not until the summer of that year that he slept with his fathers, dying without pain, and in perfect possession of his senses.

Alexander now came into possession of the estates and title, and certainly he entered upon them without any reproach as to his conduct toward his uncle, who died blessing him. And now my tale is ended, and I wish my young readers farewell.

THE END.

Printed in the United Kingdom by
Lightning Source UK Ltd., Milton Keynes
137084UK00001B/6/P